POCKET NATURE

NIGHT SKY

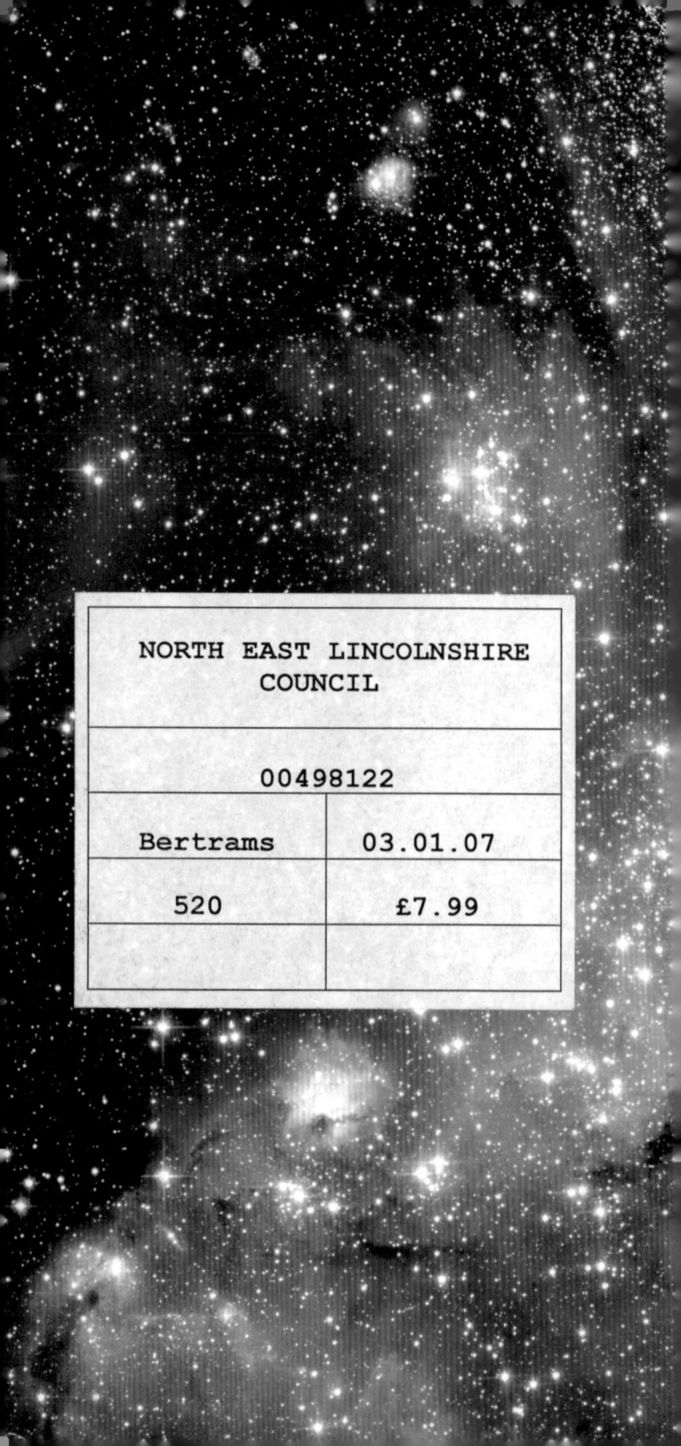

POCKET NATURE

NIGHT SKY

KEVIN TILDSLEY
PHILIP EALES

DORLING KINDERSLEY

LONDON, NEW YORK, MUNICH,
MELBOURNE, AND DELHI

DK LONDON
Senior Art Editor Ina Stradins
Senior Editor Angeles Gavira Guerrero
DTP Designer John Goldsmid
Production Controller
Rita Sinha
Managing Art Editor Phil Ormerod
Publishing Manager Liz Wheeler
Art Director Bryn Walls
Publishing Director Jonathan Metcalf

DK DELHI
Designers Shefali Upadhyay, Romi
Chakraborty, Arunesh Talapatra
DTP Designers Balwant Singh,
Sunil Sharma, Pushpak Tyagi
Editors Dipali Singh, Rohan Sinha,
Aekta Jerath, Glenda Fernandes
Manager Aparna Sharma

First published in Great Britain in 2005 by
Dorling Kindersley Limited
80 Strand, London WC2R 0RL

A Penguin Company

Copyright © 2005
Dorling Kindersley Limited

ISBN-13: 978-1-40530-758-1
ISBN-10: 1-4053-0758-7

Reproduced by Colourscan, Singapore
Printed and bound in China
by Sheck Wah Tong Printing Press Ltd.

see our complete catalogue at
www.dk.com

CONTENTS

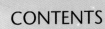

How this book works

This guide covers all the main features visible in the night sky. At the beginning of the book is a concise introduction to astronomy, including explanations of what stars, galaxies, and nebulae are, as well as practical advice on equipment and how to navigate around the sky. The next two sections are dedicated to the Moon and the planets. A catalogue section profiling the 88 constellations comes next, followed by a month-by-month companion to the sky. Sample pages are explained below; fuller explanations to the charts are given at the opening of each section.

△ THE MOON
The Earth's only satellite is described in this section. Detailed maps showing selected surface features of interest are divided into four quadrants for clarity and easy reference.

△ PLANETS
This section contains illustrated profiles of each of the eight planets visible from the Earth: Mercury, Venus, Mars, Jupiter, Saturn, Uranus, Neptune, and Pluto.

△ PLANET ENTRY
Each planet entry consists of a main image of the planet, a diagram showing it in cross-section, and additional images to show surface features, moons, and phases. A data panel provides essential statistical information.

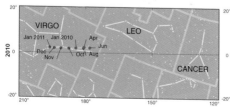

◁ PLANET TRACKING MAPS
These maps trace the movement of each planet in the night sky from the year 2006 to 2010, to help locate it at a particular time.

▷ CONSTELLATIONS

All 88 constellations are covered in this section in half-, full-, or double-page entries. Each constellation is illustrated by a detailed chart, showing the position and names of its stars and deep-sky objects; all stars above the approximate threshold of naked-eye visibility are plotted. A data box lists and describes the main features, some of which are the subject of supporting images in the entry. A scale device, a visibility map, and a locator complete each entry. See page 57 for more details.

PLANET LOCATOR STRIP This shows the relative positions of the planets; the one profiled is picked out in red.

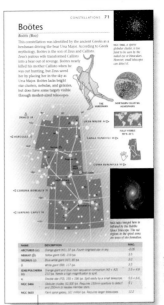

CONSTELLATIONS 71

Boötes
Boötis (Boo)

This constellation was identified by the ancient Greeks as a herdsman driving the bear Ursa Major. According to Greek mythology, Boötes is the son of Zeus and Callisto. Zeus's jealousy wife transformed Callisto into a bear out of revenge. Boötes nearly killed his mother Callisto when he was out hunting, but Zeus saved her by placing her in the sky as Ursa Major. Boötes lacks bright star clusters, nebulae, and galaxies, but does have some targets visible through modest-sized telescopes.

NGC 5466, a globular cluster, is too faint to be seen by the naked eye or binoculars. However, small telescopes can detect it.

THE HERDSMAN

NORTHERN CELESTIAL HEMISPHERES

FULLY VISIBLE 90°N–35°S

NGC 5665 is imaged here in infrared by the Hubble Space Telescope. The red regions in the spiral arms are areas of star formation.

NAME	DESCRIPTION	MAG.
ARCTURUS (α)	Orange giant (K2). 37 lya. Fourth brightest star in sky.	–0.06
NEKKAT (β)	Yellow giant (G8). 219 lya	3.5
SEGINUS (γ)	Blue-white giant (A7). 85 lya	3.0
δ	White giant (B8). 117 lya.	3.5
IZAR/PULCHERIMA (ε)	Orange giant and blue-white companion stars—a double (K0 + A2). 210 lya. Needs a high magnification to split.	2.5 & 4.9
κ	Double star (F0). 155 + 196 lya. Split easily by a small telescope.	5.6 & 6.6.
μ	Triple star (F0). 121 lya. Requires 150mm aperture to detect and 250mm to resolve member stars.	9.1
NGC 5466	Globular cluster. 50,000 lya. Requires 150mm aperture to detect.	9.1
NGC 5653	Faint spiral galaxy. 161 million lya. Requires larger telescopes.	12.2

PLANETS 51

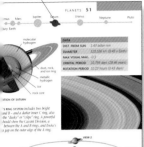

molecular hydrogen

dust, rock, and ice ring

metallic hydrogen

rock core

...TION OF SATURN

DATA	
DIST. FROM SUN	1.43 billion km
DIAMETER	120,536 km (9.48 × Earth)
MAX VISUAL MAG.	–0.3
ORBITAL PERIOD	10,759 days (29.46 years)
ROTATION PERIOD	10.23 hours (0.43 days)

DATA BOX
The data box lists the main stars and deep-sky objects in the constellation, providing a brief description of each.

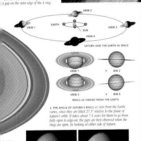

'S RING SYSTEM includes two bright ...and B – and a darker inner C ring, also ...the "dusky" or "crêpe" ring. A powerful ...enoull show the Cassini Division, a ...between the A and B rings, and Encke's ...a gap on the outer edge of the A ring.

VIEW 2

VIEW 1   VIEW 3

EARTH

SUN

VIEW 4

SATURN AND THE EARTH IN SPACE

VIEW 1   VIEW 2

VIEW 3   VIEW 4

RINGS AS VIEWED FROM THE EARTH

▲ THE ANGLE OF SATURN'S RINGS as seen from the Earth varies, since they are tilted 27.3° relative to the plane of Saturn's orbit. It takes about 7.5 years for them to go from fully open to edge-on; the gaps are best observed when the rings are open, by looking at either side of Saturn.

...'S HAZE ...was pierced by ...sini probe's ...d cameras in ...ear right).

▽ MONTH BY MONTH

This section contains detailed charts of the night sky through the months of the year. Each month has two double spreads; the first covers the northern hemisphere, looking north (on the left hand page) and looking south (on the right hand page), the second covers the southern hemisphere with the same division into north and south.

PHOTOGRAPHS
These include images taken by space probes as well as views of the night sky from the Earth by astronomers.

166 MONTH BY MONTH

January NORTHERN LATITUDES
Northern latitudes looking North

Ursa Major, shaped like a saucepan standing on its handle, is easily identifiable. A straight line through the two stars at the "pan" end of Ursa Major, Dubhe (α) and Merak (β), points to Polaris, the Alpha (α) star of Ursa Minor. The W-shape of Cassiopeia is at the left of Ursa Major, while the bright star of Capella lies overhead. This is the mouth of the Quadrantid meteor show. The meteors radiate from a point in Boötes, near Ursa Major's handle.

JANUARY NORTHERN LATITUDES

HORIZON LINES
Where the viewing horizon lies in relation to the celestial sphere depends on the latitude of the location you are watching from. Colour-coding helps you pick the right line, see page 165 for more details.

LATITUDES
A selection of cities located in the northern and southern hemispheres represents a range of latitudes.

HOW TO USE THE SKY CHARTS
To view the sky to the south, hold the right-hand edge of the book (with the "Looking South" label) nearest to you. The cross near the chart centre represents the zenith (the point directly overhead). The area of the chart beyond the zenith represents the sky to the north. To view this, turn the book around.

The Universe

The Universe contains all that exists, including all matter, time, and space. The theory is that the Universe originated from the explosion (known as the Big Bang), of a singularity or single point up to 20,000 million years ago. The Universe has been expanding ever since, extending to about 10,000 million light years in all directions around the Earth, as far as the largest telescopes can see. All matter in the Universe is held together in structures of varying size by gravity.

The Milky Way

Most visible matter in the Universe is contained within galaxies. A galaxy is a huge structure consisting of stars, gas, and dust. Our galaxy, the Milky Way, contains over 100,000 million stars, including the Sun, and is about 100,000 light years in diameter. The Sun is located about two-thirds of the way out from the galaxy's centre, in a spiral arm called the Orion Arm. The Milky Way rotates, and the Sun orbits its centre, which contains a supermassive, invisible object, most likely a black hole. All the stars we see from the Earth are in our galaxy. Its shape and the Earth's position within it means that when we look up into the sky, the more distant stars appear to form a hazy white band, which gave rise to the galaxy's name. Stars that are relatively near to us in our galaxy appear in the sky as familiar stars and constellations – in astronomical terms, these stars are our neighbours.

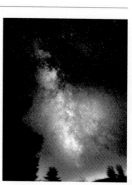

A FAINT BAND OF LIGHT *consisting of the background light of millions of stars, is all we see of the Milky Way from the Earth.*

THE MILKY WAY *is a spiral galaxy, as depicted by this computer-generated image. No space probe has gone far enough to get an external view of it and the brightness of the nucleus is shielded from us by the intervening gas and dust.*

Clusters of Galaxies

Galaxies are usually members of clusters and superclusters. The Milky Way is a member of the Local Group, a small cluster of about 30 galaxies, the largest member of which is the Andromeda Galaxy. Some galaxy clusters, such as the Virgo Cluster, can be huge and often contain thousands of galaxies, ranging from dwarf to giant sizes. Chains of galaxy clusters are themselves linked into superclusters, which are, in turn, arranged in sheets, filaments, chains, and walls that form the network of the Universe.

THE VIRGO CLUSTER *is a dense collection of 2,000 or more galaxies at the heart of the larger supercluster to which the Local Group also belongs.*

Galaxies

A galaxy is a huge system of stars and dust, containing a few million to thousands of millions of stars. Galaxies vary in size, ranging from dwarf galaxies a few thousand light years in diameter, up to giants hundreds of thousands of light years across. Galaxies are classified according to their shape: spiral, elliptical, irregular, and lenticular.

Spiral galaxies

This type of galaxy consists of two main structures: a flat, rotating disc of stars, gas, and dust, and a central bulge or nucleus. Some may have a bar of stars across the nucleus. The different orbital speeds of the stars around a spiral galaxy's centre makes them pile up, causing the formation of spiral arms.

M81 is an example of a type of spiral galaxy with a prominent nucleus and weak spiral arms.

NGC 2997 *is a type of spiral galaxy that has a small nucleus and dominant spiral arms.*

M109 *is a typical barred spiral galaxy, with a central bar across its large nucleus, and weak arms.*

NGC 1300 *is a type of barred spiral galaxy with a small nucleus and strong spiral arms.*

Elliptical galaxies

Named for their shape, elliptical galaxies are classified according to the degree of ellipticity or elongation. Some are virtually spherical and others are very elongated in shape. Ellipticals tend to contain old stars.

M32, *an elliptical galaxy in the Andromeda constellation, is a satellite of the Andromeda Galaxy (M31) and appears as a star-like object.*

Irregular galaxies

These galaxies do not fit into the classification scheme for ellipticals and spirals. They shown signs of distortion caused by the gravitational forces of nearby galaxies, and have often been the victims of galactic collisions.

THE LARGE MAGELLANIC CLOUD *in the constellation of Dorado is an irregular galaxy that shows no dominant nucleus or spiral arms.*

Lenticular galaxies

These galaxies are not as common as ellipticals and spirals. They are old spiral galaxies, but show no signs of any spiral structure. Telescopically, they look similar to elliptical galaxies.

A LENTICULAR GALAXY *is lens-shaped, as seen in this image, with a roughly spherical nucleus of old red and yellow stars; it has no spiral arms and little sign of star-forming activity.*

Nebulae

Actually clouds of gas and dust, nebulae reveal themselves in various ways: by emitting light, by reflecting light from a nearby star, or by blocking starlight from stars behind them. Nebulae are associated with regions of star formation and star clusters. Although the source material for new stars, they can also be created by stars themselves.

Emission nebulae

An emission nebula is a cloud of gas at high temperature. A nearby star emits ultraviolet light that energizes the atoms in the nebula. As the atoms fall back into a lower energy state, they emit light at a particular wavelength or colour. The colour of the light emitted depends on the chemistry of the cloud.

THE TARANTULA NEBULA *is to be found in an irregular galaxy outside our own, called the Large Magellanic Cloud. It is one of the brightest known emission nebulae.*

THE ORION NEBULA *is an emission nebula visible to the naked eye, and illuminated by hot, bright young stars.*

Reflection nebulae

This nebula type is a cloud of gas and dust that does not shine with its own light. Its atoms are not energized, but merely reflect light from a nearby star.

THE PLEIADES *open cluster in Taurus consists of stars surrounded by reflection nebulosity. Here, a nebula is passing through the star cluster.*

Dark nebulae

Dark nebulae are clouds of dust that block the light from stars behind them, and do not shine either with their own light or reflected light.

THE HORSEHEAD NEBULA *(Barnard 33), a dark, cold, distinctively shaped cloud of dust in Orion, blocks light from the stars behind it.*

Planetary nebulae

Deriving its name from its telescopic appearance as a hazy disc, similar to a planet, this type of nebula is created by the ejection of a star's outer atmosphere when the star is dying.

THE RING NEBULA *(M57) is a planetary nebula in Lyra, formed by a star shedding its atmosphere.*

Supernova remnants

Some stars end their lives with a huge explosion, called a supernova, and the star sheds its atmosphere. When the supernova dies down, the ejected atmosphere shines as a supernova remnant (SNR).

THE CRAB NEBULA *(M1) in Taurus is a supernova remnant caused by the explosion of a star.*

What is a Star?

A star is a large ball of gas that is heated from within its core by thermonuclear reactions. The huge amount of energy created within the star's core travels through its internal layers, and leaves its surface as heat and light. The vast distances to the stars mean that, although many stars are more luminous than the Sun, they appear only as points of light in the night sky.

Star Formation

Stars are formed from huge clouds of gas and dust called nebulae. The clouds collapse under the pull of their own gravity, first forming a protostar. The density and temperature of the gas at the protostar's centre become so high that thermonuclear reactions begin, and a star is born. The star, at this stage, is known as a main sequence star, generating its own heat and light. The way a star develops and eventually ends its life, depends on the mass of the star.

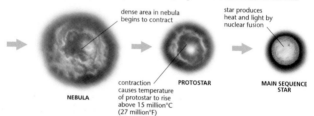

dense area in nebula begins to contract

star produces heat and light by nuclear fusion

contraction causes temperature of protostar to rise above 15 million°C (27 million°F)

PROTOSTAR

MAIN SEQUENCE STAR

NEBULA

Massive Stars

A massive star, a main sequence star with a mass of ten times more than the Sun, uses up its fuel, sometimes within a million years, and expands to become a red giant or supergiant star. The star's core then collapses and the outer layers of its atmosphere are ejected violently in a supernova explosion. The core of low mass becomes a tiny neutron star while a large core becomes a black hole.

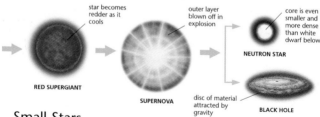

star becomes redder as it cools

outer layer blown off in explosion

core is even smaller and more dense than white dwarf below

NEUTRON STAR

RED SUPERGIANT

SUPERNOVA

disc of material attracted by gravity

BLACK HOLE

Small Stars

Smaller stars also expand to form a red giant, and shed their outer layers, but in a quieter manner. There is no supernova explosion; rather, the outer layers form a shell around the star, known as a planetary nebula. The stellar core at the nebula's centre shines as a hot white dwarf, taking thousands of millions of years to slowly cool down, until it becomes a black dwarf that stops emitting light.

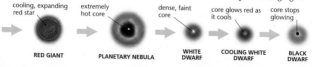

cooling, expanding red star

extremely hot core

dense, faint core

core glows red as it cools

core stops glowing

RED GIANT

PLANETARY NEBULA

WHITE DWARF

COOLING WHITE DWARF

BLACK DWARF

Types of Star

For thousands of years, stars were regarded as single objects, perhaps because our own Sun seems solitary and in the night sky, stars appear as single points of light. However, most stars do not live out their lives in isolation, but are members of multiple star systems, or belong to large star clusters, either open or globular.

Double and Multiple Stars

Stars linked by gravity and orbiting each other around a common centre of mass, are called double or binary (a pair) and multiple (more than two) stars, while optical doubles are stars that appear double merely as a line-of-sight effect. Double and multiple stars appear as a single source of light, but binoculars and telescopes can "split" (divide) the star so that its component stars are visible.

THE DOUBLE DOUBLE
Epsilon (ε) of Lyra, a multiple star, appears as a binary to the naked eye.

A BINARY STAR *consists of two stars in mutual orbit around a common centre of mass.*

MULTIPLE STAR *with four stars, bound by gravity, orbiting a centre of mass.*

Variable Stars

Stars that change their brightness over time are called variable stars. About 20 per cent are eclipsing binaries (when the change is due to eclipses between a star and a companion); others are pulsating variables (when there are physical changes, mostly due to pulsations of the star's size), such as the Cepheid variables. The diagram below depicts Algol, an eclipsing binary in Perseus.

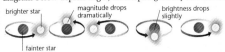

brighter star

magnitude drops dramatically

brightness drops slightly

fainter star

ALGOL'S *two stars eclipse each other to give a regular variation in brightness.*

Open Clusters

An open cluster is a group of dozens or hundreds of young stars bound by the force of gravity. Formed from clouds of interstellar gas and dust, open clusters are found within the spiral arms of our galaxy. They often remain embedded in dust clouds, and their light illuminates the surrounding material, which shines as a reflection or emission nebula.

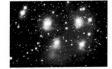

PLEIADES *in Taurus, is a large open cluster, with dozens of stars visible through binoculars.*

Globular Cluster

A globular cluster is group of ancient stars held together by gravity and containing between ten thousand and a million stars, all within a volume often less than 200 light years across. Over 150 globulars are now known; they are found within a halo surrounding the Milky Way, but have their own orbits around the galaxy.

M3I IN HERCULES, *the brightest globular cluster in the northern sky, lies at a distance of about 25,000 light years from the Earth.*

The Celestial Sphere

In ancient times, the sky was regarded as a rotating, solid sphere around the Earth, to the insides of which stars were attached. Nowadays, we know it is neither solid nor rotating; the stars lie at different distances from the Earth and their apparent movement from east to west is caused by the Earth's rotation from west to east. However, the concept of the celestial sphere is still useful when explaining the apparent movement of stars and recording their positions.

Celestial Lines

The important lines on the celestial sphere are similar to those on the Earth's globe. The celestial equator is a circle on the sphere directly above the Earth's equator, while the celestial poles, around which the sphere appears to turn each day, lie above the Earth's poles. Another line, the ecliptic, represents the Sun's path around the celestial sphere in the course of a year.

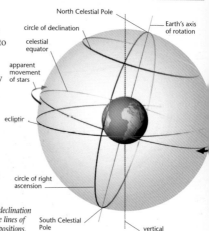

North Celestial Pole
Earth's axis of rotation
circle of declination
celestial equator
apparent movement of stars
ecliptic
circle of right ascension
South Celestial Pole
vertical

THE CELESTIAL SPHERE'S *circles of declination and right ascension work much like lines of latitude and longitude to pinpoint positions.*

Latitude

An observer's view of the celestial sphere depends on the latitude. From either pole, only half the sphere can be seen. Through the night, the stars will appear to travel parallel to the horizon, but will neither rise nor set (they are circumpolar). At the Earth's equator, however, the two poles of the sphere will lie on the horizon, and the stars will appear to rise straight up from the horizon; the whole celestial sphere can be seen over the year. From mid-latitudes, some objects are circumpolar while others rise and set; as the seasons progress, the whole of a celestial hemisphere can be seen.

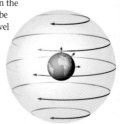

THE APPARENT MOTION *of stars makes them appear to move differently, according to the observer's position.*

SEEN FROM THE NORTH POLE, *all celestial objects move without rising or setting.*

SEEN FROM MID-LATITUDES, *some objects rise and set; others are circumpolar.*

SEEN FROM THE EQUATOR, *all celestial objects rise and set as the Earth rotates.*

Coordinates

The celestial sphere has its own coordinate system, similar to latitude and longitude on the Earth. Celestial latitude is known as declination (dec.), and runs from 90° South, through the celestial equator, to 90° North. Northern values are given a + sign, and southern values a – sign. Celestial longitude is known as right ascension (RA), and runs anti-clockwise along the celestial equator. Declination is measured in degrees, while RA is measured in hours, minutes, and seconds.

90° North

star's position

one hour of right ascension equals 15° of rotation

12ʰ

celestial equator

45° angle of declination

0°

right ascension of 1 hour

A STAR'S POSITION *is measured here at a declination of +45° and a right ascension of one hour, or 15°.*

The Changing Sky

As the Earth rotates, the stars appear to travel across the sky. However, they do not change their declination or right ascension positions, as the coordinate system is fixed to the celestial sphere and rotates along with it. The celestial sphere rotates once in the time it takes the Earth to complete one rotation, which takes 23 hours and 56 minutes. The terrestrial day is four minutes longer. This means that a star will rise four minutes earlier each night.

LONG-EXPOSURE *photography captures the movement of the stars at night, showing up star trails. This photograph shows how the stars around the North Celestial Pole rotate.*

The Ecliptic and the Zodiac

The ecliptic is the plane of the Earth's orbit around the Sun. Viewed from the Earth, it also represents the apparent motion of the Sun against the background stars. However, it is not the Sun that is moving, but the Earth. As the Sun makes its annual journey around the ecliptic, it passes in front of Ophiuchus and 12 constellations, which form a group known as the zodiac.

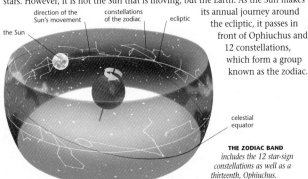

direction of the Sun's movement

constellations of the zodiac

ecliptic

the Sun

celestial equator

THE ZODIAC BAND *includes the 12 star-sign constellations as well as a thirteenth, Ophiuchus.*

Constellations

The celestial sphere is divided into 88 areas, called constellations. The origins of some can be traced to ancient times – in 150CE, the Greek astronomer Ptolemy listed 48 while others are more recent introductions. The boundaries of the 88 constellations recognized today, were defined by the International Astronomical Union in 1930.

Mapping the Sky

Although we commonly refer to the patterns that stars make as constellations, technically a constellation is the area that has been defined around one of these patterns. All stars within the area belong to that constellation, even if they do not make up the pattern. As well as a defined area, each constellation has a Latin (genitive) name, which usually forms part of a star's name. Orion's genitive name, for example is Orionis.

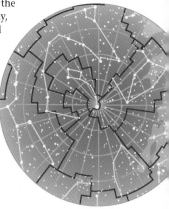

CONSTELLATION BORDERS in the Northern Polar sky are clearly marked in dark blue on this overhead view of the celestial sphere.

Star Patterns

The stars within a constellation are not related to each other. They are at varying distances from us and usually light years from each other; it is our line of sight that makes them appear related and our brains instinctively make patterns out of them. For thousands of years, civilizations have traced mythological figures in the sky and many constellations have multiple legends associated with them. Orion was seen as a hunter by ancient Greeks and Romans, but the ancient Egyptians saw it as Osiris, the god of light. Some constellations clearly resemble their names – Scorpius with its curved body and claws resembles a scorpion; others bear no resemblance at all to their names.

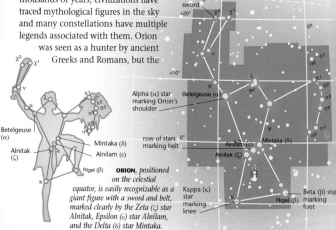

ORION, positioned on the celestial equator, is easily recognizable as a giant figure with a sword and belt, marked clearly by the Zeta (ζ) star Alnitak, Epsilon (ε) star Alnilam, and the Delta (δ) star Mintaka.

Chi (χ) star marking sword

Alpha (α) star marking Orion's shoulder

row of stars marking belt

Kappa (κ) star marking knee

Beta (β) star marking foot

Betelgeuse (α)

Alnitak (ζ)

Alnilam (ε)

Mintaka (δ)

Rigel (β)

Star Names

Several naming schemes, such as the Bayer scheme and the Messier (M), New General (NGC), and Flamsteed catalogue number systems, are used to name stars and deep-sky objects. Well-known bright stars also have common names, derived from Latin, Greek, or Arabic.

Naming Schemes

In the Bayer letter scheme, a constellation's brightest stars are given Greek letters, alphabetically in order of brightness, with Alpha (α) being the brightest, combined with the genitive name of the constellation, so the brightest star in Canis Major is Alpha Canis Majoris. Most naked-eye stars are assigned numbers, such as 51 Pegasi, known as Flamsteed numbers. Variable stars are assigned letters, starting from R. The Messier catalogue gives numbers to deep-sky objects; the Pleiades for example, is M45. The New General Catalogue gives objects an NGC number, such as NGC 224, the Andromeda Galaxy, while two supplemental Index Catalogues label objects with IC numbers.

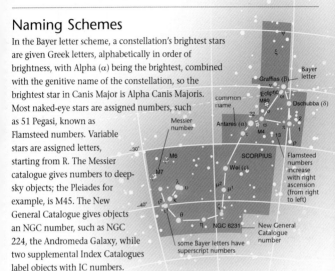

Bayer letter

Graffias (β)

common name

Dschubba (δ)

Messier number

Antares (α)

Flamsteed numbers increase with right ascension (from right to left)

SCORPIUS

Wei (ε)

New General Catalogue number

some Bayer letters have superscript numbers

NGC 6231

Magnitude

The apparent magnitude is a measure of how bright a star appears in the night sky. It depends on the actual brightness of the star, its distance from the Earth, and the amount of starlight absorbed as the light travels towards the Earth. In a clear sky, the naked eye can see stars down to magnitude 6.5.

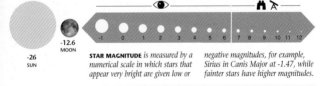

-26 SUN

-12.6 MOON

STAR MAGNITUDE *is measured by a numerical scale in which stars that appear very bright are given low or negative magnitudes, for example, Sirius in Canis Major at -1.47, while fainter stars have higher magnitudes.*

Spectral Type

Starlight can be split into a spectrum, which relates to the colour, chemical composition, and temperature of a star. Astronomers classify stars into seven spectral types: from O, the hottest to M, the coolest.

SPECTRAL TYPE	COLOUR	TEMP. (K)	EXAMPLE
O	*Blue-white*	25,000–40,000	*Zeta Puppis*
B	*Blue-white*	11,000–25,000	*Rigel*
A	*White*	7,500–11,000	*Vega, Sirius*
F	*Yellow-white*	6,000–7,500	*Polaris*
G	*Yellow*	5,000–6,000	*Capella*
K	*Orange*	3,500–5,000	*Aldebaran*
M	*Red*	3,000–3,500	*Betelgeuse*

The Solar System

The Sun is orbited by nine planets, most with their own moons, and a host of minor bodies – the asteroids and comets. These bodies are held in orbit by the gravitational pull of the Sun, which contains 99.9% of the mass of the Solar System. The planets can be grouped by their position and composition into the small, rocky inner planets and the large, gaseous outer planets. Tiny, icy Pluto is an unusual body on the edge of the observable Solar System. Many more icy bodies, including most comets, lie beyond.

Orbits

The planets move around the Sun in roughly circular orbits, anti-clockwise when viewed from above the Sun's north pole, all in approximately the same plane (the ecliptic). Some orbits are more elliptical (eccentric) than others, so the distance of the planet from the Sun varies. Pluto's orbit is the most extreme, with an eccentricity of 0.24 (a perfect circle has an eccentricity of 0.00) and its distance from the Sun varies from 4,400 to 7,500 million km. The Earth's orbit has an eccentricity of 0.01, varying from 147 to 152 million km, and its mean radius is 149,597,970 km. This distance is used to define the astronomical unit (AU), a convenient measure of distance within the Solar System.

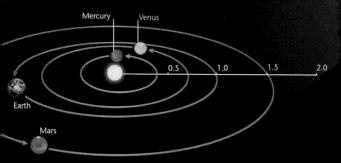

The Inner Planets

Mercury, Venus, and Mars share many characteristics with the Earth, the third planet from the Sun. They have solid surfaces made of rock and are of broadly similar size. For this reason, these three planets are called the "terrestrial" planets. While the Earth has a relatively large natural satellite, the Moon, which dominates the night sky, the two tiny moons of Mars are too small for the amateur astronomer to observe. Mercury and Venus have no natural satellites.

THE NINE PLANETS *are shown in scale in this image, with Jupiter the largest and Pluto the smallest.*

Asteroids

A belt of asteroids (also known as "minor planets") lies between Mars and Jupiter, caught between the gravitational pulls of the Sun and Jupiter. Asteroids are irregularly shaped lumps of rock, left over from the formation of the planets. The largest is Ceres, with a diameter of 940 km, and the brightest is Vesta, which can reach magnitude 5, making it visible with binoculars.

MAIN BELT ASTEROIDS *were visited by the Galileo probe in the 1990s. Ida (left) is 55 km long and orbited by its own small satellite, Dactyl. Gaspra (right) is younger than Ida.*

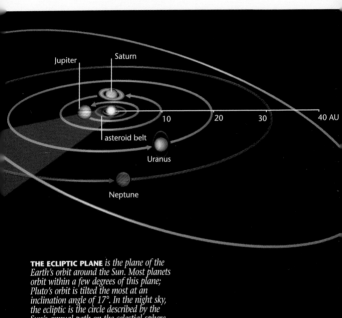

THE ECLIPTIC PLANE *is the plane of the Earth's orbit around the Sun. Most planets orbit within a few degrees of this plane; Pluto's orbit is tilted the most at an inclination angle of 17°. In the night sky, the ecliptic is the circle described by the Sun's annual path on the celestial sphere.*

The Outer Planets

Jupiter, Saturn, Uranus, and Neptune are gas giants, with deep atmospheres, composed mainly of hydrogen and helium, and no solid surface. They all have large families of moons and ring systems – Saturn's rings are the most spectacular, while those of Jupiter, Uranus, and Neptune are much less substantial. Pluto is the most distant planet, although there is some debate about its status due to its unusual orbit and small size. A larger body orbiting beyond Pluto, tentatively called Xena, is being considered as a possible tenth planet.

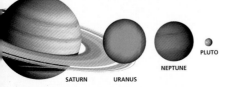

SATURN   URANUS   NEPTUNE   PLUTO

Comets

Like asteroids, comets are some of the oldest bodies in the Solar System after the Sun. They are thought to be assemblies of dirt and rock held together by ice and frozen gases.

Development

Billions of comets are thought to lie beyond the orbits of Neptune and Pluto, but a few have eccentric orbits which sometimes bring them closer to the Sun. The increased exposure to solar radiation heats up these icy bodies, causing the release of dust and gas from the nucleus, the comet's only solid part and usually less than 10 km across. The gas and dust forms a large, bright cloud up to 100,000 km across, called the coma (Latin for hair). Some comets develop spectacular tails blown out over tens of millions of kilometres

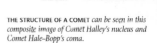

bright area of gas and dust (coma)

fountains of gas and dust

solid nucleus

THE STRUCTURE OF A COMET *can be seen in this composite image of Comet Halley's nucleus and Comet Hale–Bopp's coma.*

THE NUCLEUS OF COMET TEMPEL 1, *shortly after the Deep Impact probe triggered eruptions from the surface in April 2005.*

by the solar wind, so that they dominate the night sky. After a comet swings around the Sun and recedes, its tail and other features shrink back and it returns to its dormant stage. Comets colliding with the early Earth are thought to be the source of most of our planet's water and organic material.

Occurrence

About a thousand comets have been observed in the inner Solar System. Some are periodic comets, returning within 200 years, the brightest of which is Halley's Comet. Others are long-period comets, such as Hale–Bopp and Hyakutake, which may not return for thousands of years. A few, such as Tempel 1, spend all their time in the inner Solar System.

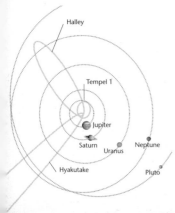

Halley

Tempel 1

Jupiter

Saturn

Uranus

Neptune

Hyakutake

Pluto

COMET HALE–BOPP *was a spectacular sight in 1997 and was easily visible to the naked eye. It showed a yellow-white dust tail and a distinct blue plasma tail of glowing charged particles.*

Meteors

Dust left behind by comets is the origin of most meteors or "shooting stars". They appear as bright streaks in the night sky as dust grains burn up in the atmosphere. Although there is a continuous low rate of sporadic or random meteors, the rate peaks at certain times of the year.

Meteor Showers

Meteor showers occur at the same time each year as the Earth's orbit passes through the trail of dust left along a comet's orbit. Bright streaks lasting less than a second are caused by fine dust burning up as it hits the atmosphere at an altitude of 70–100 km. Meteors in a shower appear to diverge from a common point (the radiant) and they are named after the constellation containing that point. Some of the strongest showers are the Geminids, seen in Gemini in December, and the Perseids, which are seen in Perseus in August. The hourly rate of sporadic meteors is about 5–10, but a heavy shower can give thousands per hour.

A METEOR SHOWER occurs when the Earth crosses the path of a comet. Heavier showers (storms) occur in the years of the comet's reappearance.

SHOWER	PEAK DATE	CONSTELLATION	HOURLY RATE
QUADRANTIDS	4 January	Boötes	100
LYRIDS	22 April	Lyra	10
ETA AQUARIDS	5 May	Aquarius	35
DELTA AQUARIDS	28 July; 6 Aug.	Aquarius	25; 10
PERSEIDS	12 August	Perseus	80
ORIONIDS	21 October	Orion	25
TAURIDS	3 November	Taurus	10
LEONIDS	17 November	Leo	10
GEMINIDS	13 December	Gemini	100
URSIDS	22 December	Ursa Major	10

Meteorites

EUCRITE METEORITE

Large rocks falling to the Earth from space may form spectacular fireballs as they break up, and the fragments that reach the ground are called meteorites. About ten hit the surface every day, mostly in the ocean. Smaller ones are slowed down by the atmosphere to land intact, but larger ones can form craters on impact.

METEORITE FROM MARS

Aurora

The aurora, or northern and southern lights, are caused by the solar wind interacting with the Earth's magnetic field. As electrically charged particles enter the Earth's atmosphere, they collide with oxygen atoms, which release energy in the form of light.

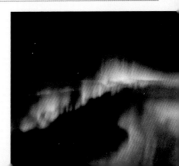

GREEN-PHASE AURORA *as viewed from the International Space Station. The colours (red or green) are related to the energy released.*

Equipment

Binoculars and telescopes make objects appear brighter and larger because they collect more light than the human eye, making it possible to see even very faint objects. They also magnify objects, so that small details are visible. Beginners will find binoculars easier to use, but more serious observation requires a telescope. Cameras can be used to take close-up and long-exposure pictures of the night sky.

Magnification and Apertures

The amount of detail that can be seen in the night sky depends on the aperture (diameter) of the lens used and on its magnification. The lens in the human eye is only about 8mm across once it has adapted to seeing in the dark. Binocular lenses, however, are from 50mm to 80mm across, up to 10 times better at observing detail and up to 100 times better at detecting faint objects. Greater apertures in telescopes increase the collection of light, enabling fainter objects to be seen. A moderate telescope will have a mirror of between 100mm and 150mm, while a large telescope will start at 250mm. Magnification is closely related to the field of view, which means the size of a circular area of sky as seen through a telescope or a pair of binoculars– the lower the magnification, the wider the field of view.

CLOSE-UP VIEW OF THE MOON, *through binoculars; seen upright and appears large.*

TELESCOPIC VIEW *of the Moon, using high magnification power to see details of surface features.*

Binoculars

For simple observation of astronomical objects, a pair of binoculars is a useful investment. The view provided by binoculars is upright, unlike an image seen through a telescope, which is inverted. Binoculars have a low magnification and a wide field of view, making them ideal for observation of

KEEP BINOCULARS STEADY *by sitting and placing the elbows on the knees to support the weight of the binoculars.*

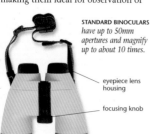

STANDARD BINOCULARS *have up to 50mm apertures and magnify up to about 10 times.*

eyepiece lens housing

focusing knob

objective lens housing

comets, large open clusters, such as the Pleiades, and for sweeping constellations, such as Cygnus, that contain rich star fields. The typical field of view of medium-sized binoculars is 7x or 10x, which is adequate for a beginner. A higher magnification can make an image look larger (but fainter) and magnifications greater than 10 times make it more difficult to keep binoculars steady.

Telescopes

A telescope is far superior in gathering light and observing fine detail than binoculars. However, a telescope provides an inverted image, and because it operates at a higher magnification, any unsteadiness in its mounting soon becomes apparent. When choosing telescopes, the important criteria are the aperture and quality of the main lens, and the sturdiness of its mount. Telescopes are of two basic types: refractors and reflectors. A refractor has a main lens, known as the objective, which gathers

objective lens housing

finder scope (for aiming at objects)

altazimuth mount

THIS REFRACTING TELESCOPE *is on a mount that allows it to tilt up and down and side to side.*

eyepiece

light and focuses it towards an eyepiece placed at the opposite end of the tube. Large diameter refractors provide very crisp and clear images. A reflector does not use an objective lens at the front of the tube, but instead has a concave mirror at the bottom of the tube, which collects and focuses the light back up to a small flat mirror, known as a diagonal, which then directs the light to an eyepiece.

secondary mirror housing

finder scope

eyepiece

objective lens

equatorial mount

THIS NEWTONIAN TELESCOPE *is on an equatorial mount, one axis of which is aligned with the celestial pole, the other at right angles to it; to follow an object across the sky only one axis is moved.*

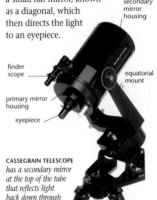

finder scope

primary mirror housing

eyepiece

equatorial mount

CASSEGRAIN TELESCOPE *has a secondary mirror at the top of the tube that reflects light back down through a hole in the primary mirror.*

Photography

The easiest photography is achieved by pointing a camera at the sky and exposing the film – long exposures will show star trails due to the Earth's rotation. The best results come from using the camera in place of the telescope's eyepiece, thereby using the power of the telescope's optics. The telescope, if placed on a motor-driven equatorial mount, allows long-exposure photography without blurring. The latest imaging innovation is the charge-coupled device (CCD), a light-sensitive chip, which allows faint objects to be captured with shorter exposures.

A CCD *attached to the eyepiece can capture an image much quicker than conventional photography and download it to a computer.*

Viewing Planets

Jupiter

When viewing the night sky, the planets can be differentiated from stars in two ways: they are not point sources of light, so they do not flicker or "twinkle" like stars, and they move relative to the "fixed" background of stars. Most planets are brighter than stars, with Venus and Jupiter being the brightest objects in the sky after the Sun and the Moon. Planet movements become apparent over the weeks as they move through the constellations of the zodiac, the region of the sky on either side of the Sun's path.

Elongation

The angle of separation between the Sun and a planet as viewed from the Earth is called the elongation. Mercury and Venus are never far from the Sun; they are both best viewed just before sunrise or just after sunset. When a planet rises before the Sun in the morning, it is further west in the sky, so it has a western (or morning elongation). When it sets after the Sun in the evening, it is further east in the sky, so it has an eastern (or evening elongation).

conjunction of superior planet

superior conjunction of inferior planet

maximum eastern (evening) elongation

Sun

inferior conjunction of inferior planet

opposition of superior planet (planet appears large)

Earth

A PLANET'S POSITION with respect to the Sun affects its visibility. Mercury and Venus ("inferior" planets) orbit closer to the Sun than does the Earth. Mars and the other planets ("superior" planets) orbit further out..

Conjunction and Opposition

A conjunction is when two bodies line up with each other along a line of sight from the Earth. When a planet lies in the same direction as the Sun (its elongation is then 0°), it is said to be "at conjunction". For an inferior planet, the planet may lie between the Earth and the Sun (an inferior conjunction), or lie on the far side of the Sun (a superior conjunction). When a planet lies in the exact opposite direction to the Sun it is "at opposition"; only possible for a superior planet. Opposition is the time when the Earth and a superior planet are closest, so the planet appears at its largest and brightest. It is also visible throughout the night.

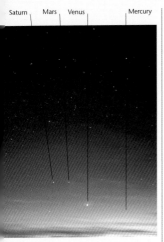

Saturn | Mars | Venus | Mercury

PLANETARY ALIGNMENT *seen in April 2002, when all five naked-eye planets were visible after sunset in the same part of the sky. The lower planets appear close, but are separated by tens or hundreds of millions of kilometres in space.*

Phases

Like the Moon, the planets Mercury and Venus show "phases" caused by changes in the relative direction of solar illumination when there is a wide variation in the angle between the Earth, the planet, and the Sun. Venus exhibits half-phase at maximum elongation; its disc then becomes a thin crescent, disappearing altogether at inferior conjunction, before growing again to full phase at superior conjunction. Venus appears dimmer when it is almost full since it is at its most distant; in fact, its maximum brilliance occurs as a crescent near its greatest elongations. Mercury behaves in the same manner, but is more difficult to observe because

gibbous phase

Venus

Sun

eastern elongation (evening sky)

western elongation (morning sky)

Earth

crescent phase

PHASES OF VENUS *occur as the planet orbits the Sun and can be observed with high-powered binoculars; it appears largest in its crescent phase when closest to the Earth and smallest when full.*

maximum western (morning) elongation

it is smaller and closer to the Sun. The superior planets also experience illumination changes but are too distant to show clear phases when viewed from the Earth.

Retrograde Motion

Planets generally move from west to east relative to the stars, but periodically move from east to west for a short time. This is known as retrograde motion and occurs when the Earth, moving more quickly on a smaller orbit, "catches up" with an outer planet around the time of opposition. The planet appears to slow down, stop, and reverse direction, resuming its normal motion across the sky when the Earth has "overtaken" it.

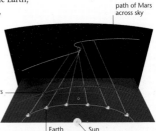

path of Mars across sky

Mars

Earth | Sun

A BACKWARD LOOP *or zigzag is produced by the retrograde motion of Mars and the other superior planets about the time of opposition.*

Viewing Stars

At first glance, the night sky can seem confusing. However, once a few bright stars and key constellations have been found, imaginary lines can be drawn outwards from them to find other patterns, which in turn can be used as guides to yet more stars. With these reference points to start with and an understanding of how to measure distances simply, it soon becomes easier to navigate across the sky.

DOUBLE CLUSTER (NGC 869+884) *in Perseus is best viewed through binoculars or a small telescope.*

Scale in the Sky

A hand held at arm's length is a convenient aid to determine how large a celestial object will appear in the sky. The index finger will cover the Sun or Moon, which are about half a degree wide. The back of the hand, again at arm's length, covers a width in the sky of about 10 degrees. If the fingers are splayed, the night sky width becomes about 16 degrees. In this book, an open hand symbol is used to indicate the overall size of each constellation.

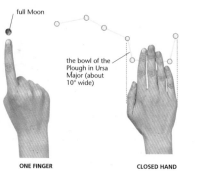

full Moon

the bowl of the Plough in Ursa Major (about 10° wide)

the Great Square of Pegasus

ONE FINGER   **CLOSED HAND**   **OPEN HAND**

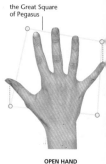

NORTHERN SIGNPOSTS *include the Plough in Ursa Major, a pointer to the bright stars Polaris, Vega, Regulus, Arcturus, and Spica.*

Northern Skies

Perhaps the easiest constellation to start with is Ursa Major, with its key pattern of the Plough, especially the bowl of the Plough. A line through the two stars at the end of the bowl point to Polaris, the Pole Star, about which the northern sky appears to rotate. On the other side of the celestial pole is the easily recognizable W- or M-shape of the constellation Cassiopeia. If the curve of the tail of the Plough is followed, it will reach the bright star Arcturus, lying in Boötes. The curve can be extended further until it reaches Spica, the brightest star in the constellation of Virgo.

Mid-latitude Skies

During the northern winter (southern summer) the most prominent constellation is Orion. The three bright blue-white stars of Orion's belt form a line that points eastwards towards the brightest star in the sky – Sirius, in Canis Major. Betelgeuse in Orion is easily identified by its red colour, and a line from Rigel, another bright star, through Betelgeuse will lead to Castor and Pollux, in Gemini. West of Orion, the distinctive V-shape of the horns of Taurus can be found, containing the orange star Aldebaran. Nearby, and further west, is the bright open cluster M45, the Pleiades.

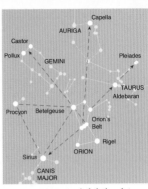

MID-LATITUDE SIGNPOSTS *include the red star Betelgeuse, which together with Procyon and Sirius, forms a huge triangle in the sky.*

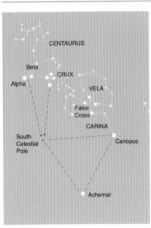

SOUTHERN SIGNPOSTS *are the two brightest stars of Centaurus and the cross-shape of Crux, the Southern Cross.*

Southern Skies

Crux, the smallest constellation in the sky but one of the most distinctive, is a good place to start. Not to be confused with the False Cross in Carina, which lies closer to the bright star Canopus, Crux lies at its highest in the sky during the evenings of April and May, near the Alpha (α) and Beta (β) stars of Centaurus. The long axis of Crux points southwards to the South Celestial Pole, about which all the southern constellations appear to rotate as the night progresses. The Pole can also be found using a line at right angles to the line connecting the Alpha (α) and Beta (β)stars of Centaurus. Canopus in Carina and Achernar in Eridanus form a triangle with the South Celestial Pole.

Skywatching

It is important to prepare for an evening of stargazing. Allow at least ten minutes for your eyes to become fully adapted to the dark before beginning observation as it takes that much time for the pupils to adjust to darkness. Always wear warm clothing. Keep a notebook to record observations, especially the date and the time. Avoid artificial light, such as street lights. In order to refer to a book or chart during observation, use a dim torch covered with red transparent plastic as

this will not interfere with your night vision. Very faint objects can often be best observed by using averted vision, that is, looking to one side of the object rather than directly at it.

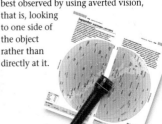

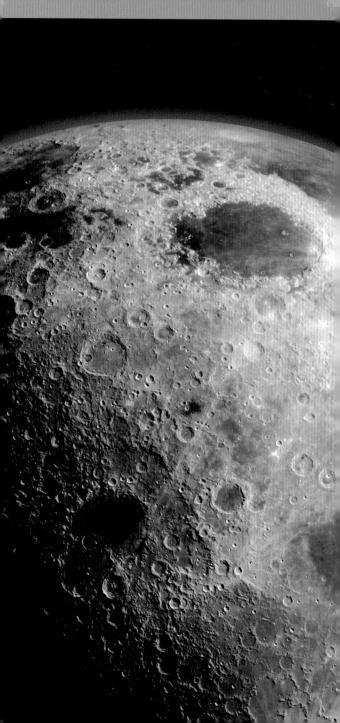

The Moon

The Moon is our nearest neighbour and when it is visible, it dominates the night sky. It is the Earth's only natural satellite, orbiting at a distance of 384,400 km. It is close enough to make its presence felt, being responsible for the ocean tides, which are due to its gravitational pull. The periodic changes in the Moon's appearance are the basis of the months in our calendar. Its surface markings are familiar to the naked eye and it makes an excellent target for binocular observations.

MPACT CRATER

METEOR IMPRINT

APOLLO 17
LUNAR ROVER

ASTRONAUT'S
FOOTPRINT

The Moon

The Moon has a diameter of 3,476 km, making it quite a large satellite, a little over one-quarter the size of its parent, the Earth, and larger than the planet Pluto. With the naked eye, we can see that the Moon has distinct dark and bright areas. Early observers called the dark areas seas (*maria* in Latin). In fact, they have never contained any water, but exist due to the flooding of low-lying areas by dark basaltic lava from the Moon's interior. These floods were probably triggered by asteroid impacts that created deep basins and fractured the crust. The bright areas are highlands (*terrae*) and are more heavily cratered than the maria.

SIZE RELATIVE TO EARTH

Sea of Tranquillity

Apollo 11 landing site

Mare Imbrium

Copernicus

Oceanus Procellarum

Tycho

heavily cratered highlands

◄ **THE FAR SIDE** *of the Moon is mainly highland. The lunar crust is thicker, so no large basins have formed and there were fewer lava eruptions.*

▼ **THE APOLLO MISSIONS** *(1969–72) returned with rock samples; these showed that the Moon's chemical composition is similar to the Earth's crust, suggesting that the Moon was blasted out from the young Earth by a large impact.*

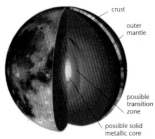

COMPOSITION OF THE MOON

▼ **PHASES OF THE MOON** *arise because differing amounts of the Moon's sunlit side can be seen as it orbits the Earth. As the Moon rotates, light from the Sun illuminates different parts of its disc. At full Moon, the near side is fully lit by the Sun, while at new Moon it is fully in shadow. The lunar month, from full to new Moon, lasts 29.5 days – a little longer than the Moon's rotational period, since the Moon and the Earth are also travelling around the Sun. After new Moon, the illuminated area grows, or waxes, from a crescent to the "gibbous" phase and then to full phase. The illuminated area then shrinks, or wanes, back to a crescent. A new Moon may be faintly illuminated by light reflected from the Earth ("earthshine").*

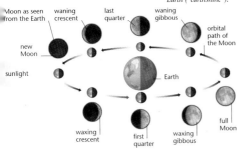

CRESCENT

FIRST QUARTER

WAXING GIBBOUS

FULL

WANING GIBBOUS

SECOND QUARTER

CRESCENT

NEW MOON

▼ **LUNAR ECLIPSES** *occur when the Earth's shadow falls across the Moon. Since the Earth and its shadow are much bigger than the Moon, lunar eclipses last quite a long time: up to four hours compared with a maximum 7.5 minutes for a total solar eclipse.*

During a lunar eclipse, the shadowed part of the Moon can appear quite red. This is due to sunlight refracting (bending) through the Earth's atmosphere. Blue light is scattered in the atmosphere along the way, leaving predominantly red light.

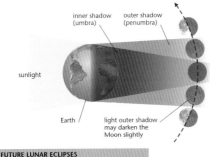

FUTURE LUNAR ECLIPSES	
2007	3 March / 23h22m (Universal Time)
2007	28 August / 10h38m (UT)
2008	21 February / 03h27 (UT)
2008	16 August / 21h11m (UT)
2009	9 February / 14h39m (UT)
2010	21 December / 08h18m (UT)

Northwest Quadrant

The northwest quadrant of the Moon is dominated by large impact basins flooded by lava – Oceanus Procellarum and Mare Imbrium. Oceanus Procellarum contains the large crater Kepler, and Aristarchus, one of the Moon's brightest areas. Mare Imbrium is surrounded by mountain ranges on three sides, with the craters Eratosthenes and Copernicus lying to the south.

ARISTARCHUS, *a young crater, about 300 million years old, is surrounded by a bright area of debris thrown out by the meteoric impact that formed it.*

PLATO, A LAVA-FLOODED CRATER ▶ *in the highlands north of Imbrium, has a dark floor that was formed when molten rock filled a depression left by a meteorite impact.*

▲ **ERATOSTHENES** *is a large crater in Mare Imbrium. Both mare and highland terrains are covered by craters of various sizes, due to the impact of meteorites. With no atmosphere to burn up incoming dust and rock, the Moon receives a higher rate of impacts than the Earth and their imprints last a long time.*

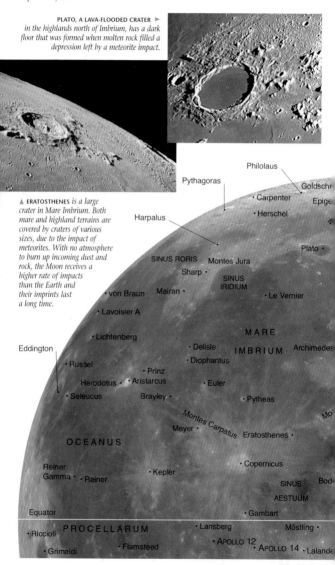

Philolaus
Pythagoras
Goldschr
· Carpenter   Epige
· Herschel
Harpalus
Plato ·
SINUS RORIS   Montes Jura
Sharp ·   SINUS
IRIDIUM
· von Braun   Mairan ·   · Le Vernier
· Lavoisier A
· Lichtenberg   M A R E
Eddington   · Delisle   I M B R I U M   Archimedes
· Russel   · Diophantus
· Prinz
Herodotus · · Aristarcus   · Euler
· Seleucus   Brayley ·   · Pytheas
Montes Carpatus   Mo
Meyer ·   Eratosthenes ·
O C E A N U S
· Copernicus
Reiner
Gamma · · Reiner   · Kepler   SINUS   Bod
AESTUUM
Equator   · Gambart
P R O C E L L A R U M   · Lansberg   Möstling ·
· Riccioli
· Grimaldi   · Flamsteed   · APOLLO 12   APOLLO 14 · Lalande

Northeast Quadrant

Mare Serenitatis and Mare Tranquillitatis are the large impact basins that dominate this quadrant. The 1969 landing site of Apollo 11 is on the Equator in Mare Tranquillitatis (the Sea of Tranquillity). To the east lies the smaller Mare Crisium, with Mare Frigoris to the north. Mare Marginus and Mare Humboltianum lie right on the eastern limb. Serenitatis is traversed by a bright ray from the distant crater Tycho, lying in the southwest quadrant.

IMPACT CRATERS, *large and small, pepper the highlands in the northeast; as many craters are destroyed by new impacts as are created.*

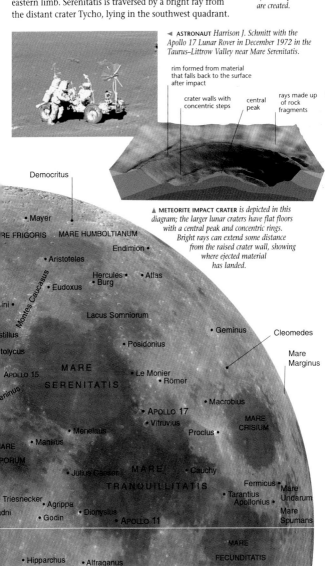

◀ **ASTRONAUT** *Harrison J. Schmitt with the Apollo 17 Lunar Rover in December 1972 in the Taurus–Littrow Valley near Mare Serenitatis.*

rim formed from material that falls back to the surface after impact

crater walls with concentric steps

central peak

rays made up of rock fragments

▲ **METEORITE IMPACT CRATER** *is depicted in this diagram; the larger lunar craters have flat floors with a central peak and concentric rings. Bright rays can extend some distance from the raised crater wall, showing where ejected material has landed.*

Democritus

• Mayer

RE FRIGORIS   MARE HUMBOLTIANUM

• Aristoteles   Endimion •

Montes Caucasus   Hercules •   • Atlas
                    • Burg
• Eudoxus

ini   Lacus Somniorum

stillus   • Geminus   Cleomedes
                    • Posidonius
tolycus   Mare
        MARE   Marginus
APOLLO 15   • Le Monier
        SERENITATIS   • Römer
eninus
                              • Macrobius
                • APOLLO 17   MARE
                  • Vitruvius   CRISIUM
ARE   • Menelaus   Proclus •
PORUM • Manilius
                              MARE   • Cauchy
        • Julius Caesar   TRANQUILLITATIS   Fermicus •   Mare
• Triesnecker • Agrippa   • Tarantius   Undarum
adni   • Godin   • Dionysius   Apollonius •   Mare
                        • APOLLO 11   Spumans

                                          MARE
• Hipparchus   • Alfraganus   FECUNDITATIS

Southwest Quadrant

Extending south from Oceanus Procellarum are Mare Cognitum, Mare Humorum, and Mare Nubium. Heavily cratered highlands lie to the south and west. The mountain ranges around Mare Orientale, the Moon's youngest impact basin, can sometimes be seen on the western limb. Tycho is the most prominent crater, with extensive bright rays highlighted around full Moon.

▲ TYCHO *in close-up from the Clementine space probe (sent in the mid-1990s), showing its central peak and raised rim.*

▼ CRESCENT MOON *with the terminator crossing Humorum and its large crater Gassendi.*

▲ LONG SHADOWS *help to highlight mountains, valleys, and craters near the terminator (the edge of the shadowed area); best times for observation are around first and last quarters.*

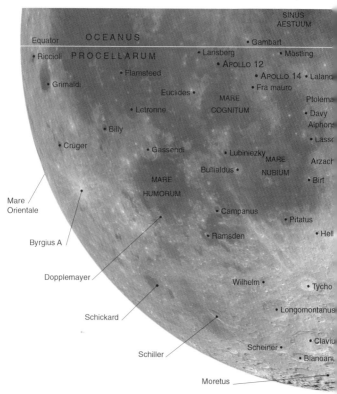

Equator
OCEANUS
PROCELLARUM
SINUS AESTUUM
• Gambart
• Riccioli
• Lansberg
• Möstling
• Grimaldi
• Flamsteed
APOLLO 12
APOLLO 14 • Laland
Euclides •
• Fra mauro
MARE COGNITUM
Ptolema
• Letronne
• Davy
Alphons
• Billy
• Lasse
• Crüger
• Gassendi
• Lubiniezky
MARE NUBIUM
Arzach
Bullialdus •
MARE HUMORUM
• Birt
Mare Orientale
• Campanus
• Pitatus
Byrgius A
• Ramsden
• Hell
Dopplemayer
Wilhelm •
• Tycho
Schickard
• Longomontanus
Schiller
Scheiner •
• Claviu
• Blanoan
Moretus

Southeast Quadrant

Mare Nectaris extends south from Tranquillitatis, which is also linked to Mare Fecunditatis to the east. On the eastern limb under favourable "libration", Mare Smythii may be seen at the Equator and Mare Australe in the south. Most of this quadrant is highland terrain. Numerous craters have central peaks, including Langrenus and Stevinus. Vallis Rheita is a 450-km chain of craters lying radial to the Nectaris Basin between Stevinus and Jansen. Rupes Altai, thought to be a fault created by the Nectaris basin-forming impact, is a 480 km-long scarp, concentric with Nectaris and lying to the southwest.

▲ **THE APOLLO ASTRONAUTS** *found that the surface of the Moon was covered with a layer of fine dust or "regolith", the result of repeated bombardment by meteorites.*

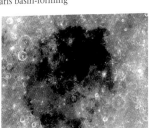

▶ **MARE SMYTHII** *lies right on the Moon's eastern limb. It is seen in its entirety here from an orbiting spacecraft. It is only visible from the Earth at certain times of the month, when it is tilted towards us due to the Moon's slightly eccentric orbit. This monthly rocking back and forth is called "libration". There is also a north-south libration due to the tilt of the Moon's axis.*

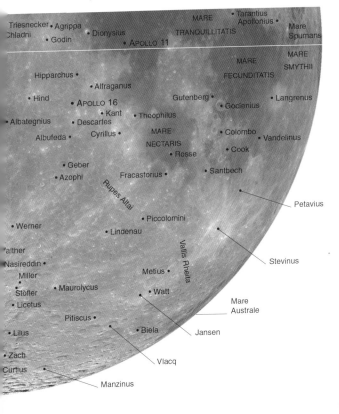

Triesnecker • Agrippa
Chladni • Godin • Dionysius
• APOLLO 11
MARE • Tarantius
Apollonius •
MARE TRANQUILLITATIS
Mare Spumans

MARE SMYTHII

Hipparchus •
• Alfraganus
MARE FECUNDITATIS

• Hind • APOLLO 16
Gutenberg •
• Gocienius
• Langrenus

• Albategnius • Descartes
• Kant • Theophilus
Cyrillus • MARE NECTARIS
• Colombo
• Vandelinus

Albufeda •
• Rosse
• Cook

• Geber
Fracastorius •
• Santbech

• Azophi
Rupes Altai

Petavius

• Werner
• Piccolomini
• Lindenau

Walther
Vallis Rheita

Nasireddin •
Miller
Metius •
Stevinus

• Stöfler • Maurolycus
• Watt

• Licetus
Mare Australe

Pitiscus •

• Lilus
• Biela
Jansen

• Zach
Vlacq

Curtius •

Manzinus

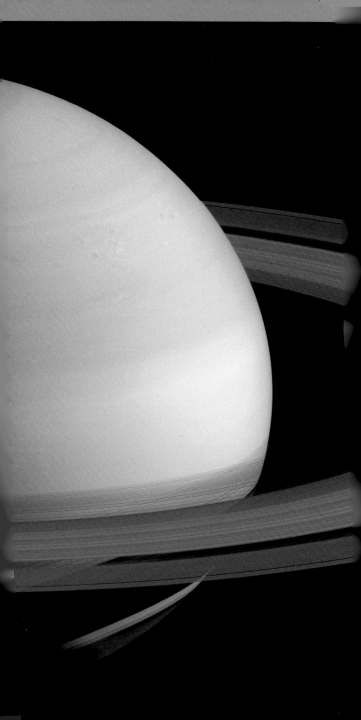

Planets

Five planets – Mercury, Venus, Mars, Jupiter, and Saturn – were
known to the ancient world without optical aids, while Uranus
and Neptune were found with large telescopes in the eighteenth
century; these can be examined today with amateur equipment.
Pluto, discovered in the twentieth century, is hard to distinguish
from stars, except by its motion. The planets provide rewarding
viewing, with Mars' surface features, Jupiter's moons, and
Saturn's rings within reach of a moderately large telescope.

MARS   NEPTUNE   IO   TITAN

Mercury

Fast-moving and one of the most difficult planets to
observe, Mercury was aptly named by the Romans after
the fleet-footed messenger of the gods. It is only visible
shortly after sunset or before sunrise, appearing as
a pinkish star-like object of first magnitude. It can be seen
with the unaided eye about a dozen times a year and
telescopic observation may reveal its phase. Mercury is
a small planet, a little larger than the Moon, with barely
any atmosphere and a surface covered with impact craters,
such as Beethoven, 643 km across, which is the largest
crater in the Solar System. Radar observations have found
a highly reflective region near Mercury's north pole, which
is possibly water ice hidden from the Sun by permanent
shadows at the bottom of craters.

**SIZE RELATIVE TO
EARTH**

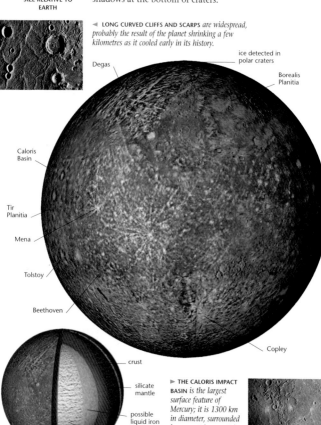

◄ **LONG CURVED CLIFFS AND SCARPS** *are widespread,
probably the result of the planet shrinking a few
kilometres as it cooled early in its history.*

Degas

ice detected in
polar craters

Borealis
Planitia

Caloris
Basin

Tir
Planitia

Mena

Tolstoy

Beethoven

Copley

crust

silicate
mantle

possible
liquid iron
outer core

solid
iron core

COMPOSITION OF MERCURY

► **THE CALORIS IMPACT
BASIN** *is the largest
surface feature of
Mercury; it is 1300 km
in diameter, surrounded
by concentric mountain
rings 3 km high, and
partly flooded by lava.
It is pitted with impact
craters of varying sizes.*

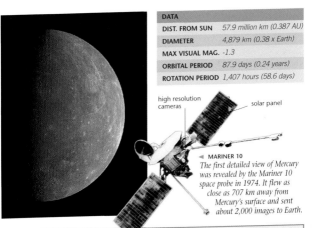

Sun Venus Mars Jupiter Saturn Uranus Neptune Pluto
Mercury Earth

DATA	
DIST. FROM SUN	*57.9 million km (0.387 AU)*
DIAMETER	*4,879 km (0.38 x Earth)*
MAX VISUAL MAG.	*-1.3*
ORBITAL PERIOD	*87.9 days (0.24 years)*
ROTATION PERIOD	*1,407 hours (58.6 days)*

high resolution cameras
solar panel

◄ MARINER 10
The first detailed view of Mercury was revealed by the Mariner 10 space probe in 1974. It flew as close as 707 km away from Mercury's surface and sent about 2,000 images to Earth.

TRACKING MERCURY

Never far from the Sun, Mercury reaches a maximum elongation of 28 degrees. There are several elongations a year, but only a few of them are good viewing times. Shown here is Mercury's position above the western horizon, just after sunset, on the dates of favourable evening elongations.

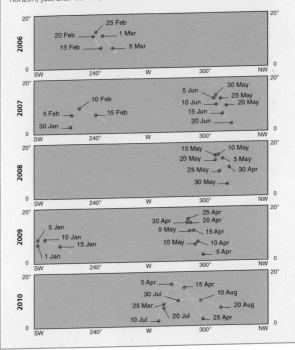

Venus

VENUS *near a crescent Moon just after sunset as viewed with the naked eye; its thick cloud layer makes it highly reflective.*

Named after the Roman goddess of love and beauty, the planet Venus is bright enough to be seen with the naked eye in daylight and, on some nights, can even cast a shadow. At its closest, the planet is the nearest body to the Earth after the Moon. Uniquely, Venus has a retrograde rotation – from east to west, opposite to that of the Earth and the other planets. The carbon dioxide-rich atmosphere has produced a runaway "greenhouse effect", with a baking hot surface (464°) hidden by a thick cloud layer.

SIZE RELATIVE TO EARTH

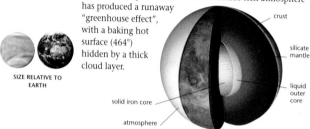

crust

silicate mantle

liquid outer core

solid iron core

atmosphere

COMPOSITION OF VENUS

Ananke Tessera

Niobe Planitia

Atalanta Planitia

Atla Regio

Thetis Regio

Aphrodite Terra

Sapas Mons

Dali Chasma

Artemis Chasma

◀ **DARKER PATCHES** *can sometimes be discerned in the atmosphere of Venus (far left), but variations are better revealed at ultraviolet wavelengths (near left). Radar instruments are required to penetrate the clouds and map the features of the planet's surface – a task achieved in great detail by the Magellan orbiter in the 1990s.*

DATA	
DIST. FROM SUN	*108.2 million km (0.72 AU)*
DIAMETER	*12,104 km (0.95 x Earth)*
MAX VISUAL MAG.	*-4.4*
ORBITAL PERIOD	*225 days (0.615 years)*
ROTATION PERIOD	*5,833 hours (243 days)*

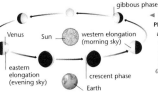

▲ **THE PHASES OF VENUS** *were first observed by Galileo in 1610. He noticed that it was smallest at full phase (above right) and much larger and brighter when it was a thin crescent (above left).*

◄ **VENUS' CYCLE OF PHASES** *is completed as the planet circles the Sun, showing more, then less, of its sunlit face to an observer on the Earth.*

TRACKING VENUS

Venus can reach a maximum angular distance of 47 degrees from the Sun. It is best observed shortly after sunset or before sunrise, when its contrast with the sky is not too great. Its position above the western horizon just after sunset is shown here for dates including the maximum evening elongations.

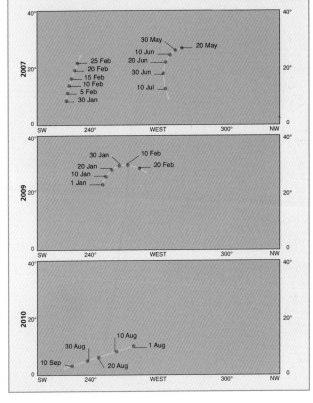

Mars

Blood-red in colour, Mars is named after the Roman god of war and was also associated with war by the Assyrians, Greeks, and Vikings. The red colour is due to "rust", caused by oxidation of the surface rocks by the atmosphere. Its most prominent features are the white polar caps and large, dark, low-lying plains. Water ice clouds occur in the atmosphere and the surface is often obscured by dust storms. It is too cold and the atmospheric pressure too low for liquid water to exist on the surface today, but evidence suggests that water existed in the past and orbiting spacecraft have detected underground water ice. More robotic probes are scheduled and some may continue the search for evidence of life on Mars.

SIZE RELATIVE TO EARTH

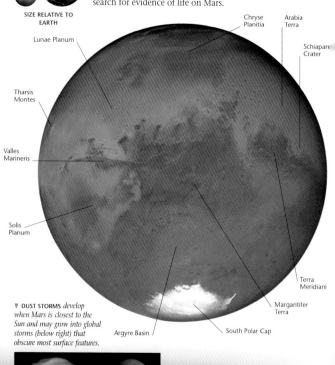

Chryse Planitia

Arabia Terra

Schiapare Crater

Lunae Planum

Tharsis Montes

Valles Marineris

Solis Planum

Terra Meridiani

Margaritifer Terra

Argyre Basin

South Polar Cap

▼ **DUST STORMS** *develop when Mars is closest to the Sun and may grow into global storms (below right) that obscure most surface features.*

Sun Mercury Venus Earth Mars Jupiter Saturn Uranus Neptune Pluto

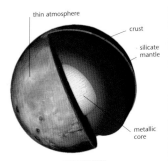

thin atmosphere

crust

silicate mantle

metallic core

COMPOSITION OF MARS

DATA	
DIST. FROM SUN	228 million km (1.52 AU)
DIAMETER	6,780 km (0.53 x Earth)
MAX VISUAL MAG.	-2.9
ORBITAL PERIOD	687 days (1.88 years)
ROTATION PERIOD	24.62 hours (1.02 days)

▲ **THE MOONS OF MARS,** Phobos (right) and Deimos (left) are small, irregular moons that are possibly captured asteroids. Their names, meaning "fear" and "dread", continue Mars' warlike association. Both are too faint to see without a large telescope.

▼ **OPPOSITIONS OF MARS** occur every 26 months when Mars is closest to the Earth and it is positioned in the exact opposite direction to the Sun. The distance to Mars from the Earth at opposition varies due to Mars' elliptical orbit.

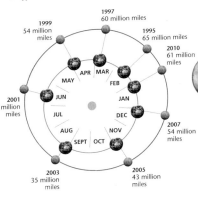

1999 54 million miles

1997 60 million miles

1995 65 million miles

2010 61 million miles

APR MAR MAY FEB JUN JAN JUL DEC AUG NOV SEPT OCT

2001 million miles

2003 35 million miles

2005 43 million miles

2007 54 million miles

1995

2003

▲ **THE SIZE OF MARS** in the sky varies from one opposition to the next, as seen in these same-scale images taken by the Hubble Space Telescope during 1995 and 2003. The 2003 opposition (above right) was the closest for 59,000 years.

◀ **SEASONAL VARIATIONS** are displayed by Mars due to its axial tilt of 25°, similar to that of the Earth. The polar ice caps expand and contract considerably through the Martian year.

▼ **THE SURFACE OF MARS** can be seen in this close-up view transmitted in 2005 from the summit of the Columbia Hills in Gusev Crater by NASA's Mars Exploration Rover, Spirit.

TRACKING MARS

Moving from west to east through the constellations of the zodiac, Mars can cover up to 240 degrees in one year. These maps, centred on the plane of the ecliptic, show where to find it month-by-month. The planet is best viewed near opposition (p.24), when it is closest to the Earth, which occurs roughly every 2.2 years. Its highly elliptical orbit means that its distance from us at opposition

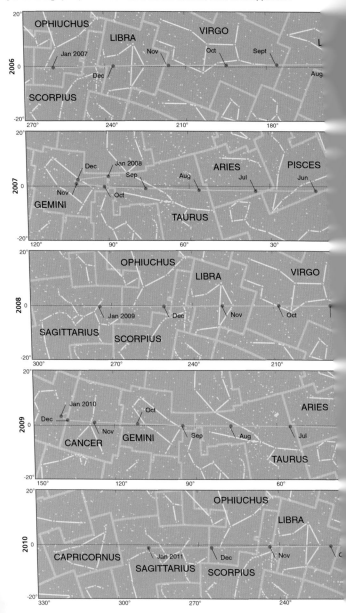

varies. At the closest oppositions, every 15 or 17 years, it appears as the largest and brightest planet apart from Venus. Dates of opposition to look out for are 24 December 2007, when it will be in Gemini, and 29 January 2010, in Cancer. At these times, the planet's eastwards motion is reversed and it appears to travel in a loop. This backward movement (see retrograde motion, p.25), is exhibited by all the outer planets but is most obvious in the motion of Mars.

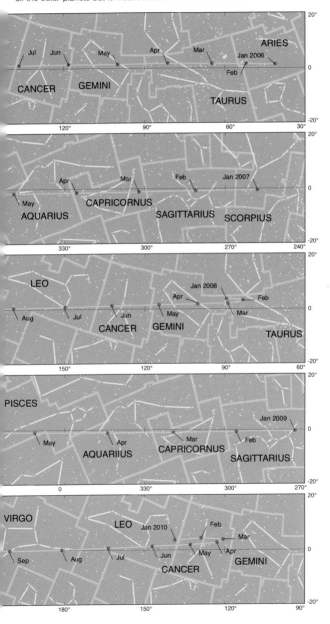

Jupiter

JUPITER THROUGH A
telescope is seen as
a rounded disc with
cloud bands parallel
to its equator.

The largest and most massive planet in the Solar System,
Jupiter is named after the king of the Roman gods. It is the
brightest planet apart from Venus and large enough for
binoculars to reveal it as a disc, not merely a point of light.
Its dynamic weather patterns and family of large moons
make it an interesting object of observation. A gas giant, it
consists mainly of hydrogen, with ammonia and methane
in its upper atmosphere. Its rapid rotation, with a period
just under ten hours, causes a polar flattening of six per
cent that can be observed with a small telescope.
Latitudinal bands of cloud can be seen in bright "zones"
and dark "belts", with transient wisps and spots between.
A telescope with an aperture of 75mm or more shows some
of the larger features within the clouds.

SIZE RELATIVE TO
EARTH

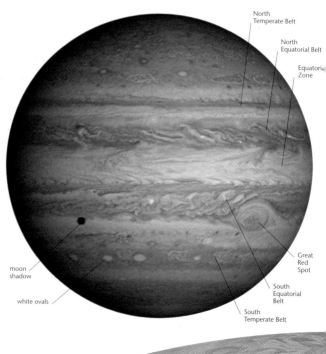

North
Temperate Belt

North
Equatorial Belt

Equatorial
Zone

Great
Red
Spot

South
Equatorial
Belt

South
Temperate Belt

moon
shadow

white ovals

Sun
Mercury Venus Earth Mars Jupiter Saturn Uranus Neptune Pluto

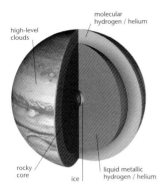

high-level clouds

molecular hydrogen / helium

rocky core

ice

liquid metallic hydrogen / helium

COMPOSITION OF JUPITER

DATA	
DIST. FROM SUN	*778 million km (5.20 AU)*
DIAMETER	*142,984 km (11.2 x Earth)*
MAX VISUAL MAG.	*-2.9*
ORBITAL PERIOD	*4,332 days (11.86 years)*
ROTATION PERIOD	*9.92 hours (0.41 days)*

▶ COMET CATCHER
Jupiter was struck repeatedly in 1994 by fragments from the Shoemaker–Levy comet, which was caught in Jupiter's powerful gravitational field. Dark scars of the impacts were still visible months later.

▶ JUPITER'S *ring system consists of dust-sized charged particles from the planet's four moons. Not visible from the Earth, Jupiter's rings were discovered during the Voyager fly-bys in 1979.*

thin, faint ring

red spot's colour perhaps due to red sulphur, phosphorus or carbon compounds

◀ THE GREAT RED
SPOT, *observed since about 1631, is an enormous, long-lived storm, three times the size of the Earth, rotating anti-clockwise once every six days. It was twice as large a hundred years ago, and has been getting paler in recent years.*

▼ JUPITER'S SURFACE *consists of swirling banded clouds. The brighter clouds are higher up and thought to be ammonia crystals. Below them lie orange ammonium sulphide clouds.*

▲ IO (mag. 5.5) is the most volcanically active body in the Solar System.

▲ EUROPA (mag. 5.7) has an icy crust, with a possible liquid water ocean deep underneath.

▲ GANYMEDE (mag. 5.1), the largest moon of any planet, has complex features.

▲ CALLISTO (mag. 6.3) has the darkest surface of the four.

◄ THE GALILEAN MOONS are part of Jupiter's large family of more than 60 moons. They were discovered by the Italian astronomer Galileo Galilei in 1610 and were the first solar system objects discovered with a telescope. Galileo's telescope had a magnification of only about 20x, which means that the Galilean moons can be viewed with some modern-day binoculars, appearing like faint stars or small points of light. Io, Europa, and Callisto were named after nymphs with whom Jupiter fell in love, and Ganymede was named after his cupbearer. While many of Jupiter's moons are irregular bodies that may be captured asteroids, the four Galilean moons are spherical bodies that were formed at the same time as Jupiter. They were the first moons to be discovered after the Earth's Moon.

DAY 1

I G E   C

DAY 2

E I   G   C

▲ DAY-TO-DAY OBSERVATION of Jupiter and its Galilean moons with a small telescope shows them to be moving rapidly. The moons' positions are shown (above) over two nights. They change position as they orbit Jupiter and may sometimes be obscured. Their orbital periods vary from 1.7 days for Io to 16 days for Callisto.

◄ THE SHADOWS OF Jupiter's moons are sometimes easier to spot than the moons themselves, as in this Hubble image of Io in transit across the face of the planet.

▼ AN ACTIVE VOLCANO ON IO sends a plume of material high over the horizon in this Voyager space probe image.

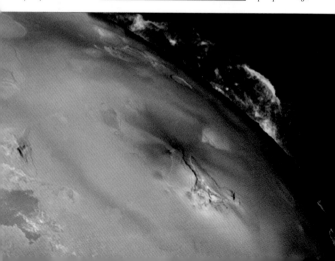

TRACKING JUPITER

From 2006 to 2010 Jupiter makes its way from Libra to Pisces. Each year, it performs a loop as it nears opposition, when it is brightest. Opposition dates: 4 May 2006, 5 June 2007, 9 July 2008, 14 Aug. 2009, 21 Sept. 2010.

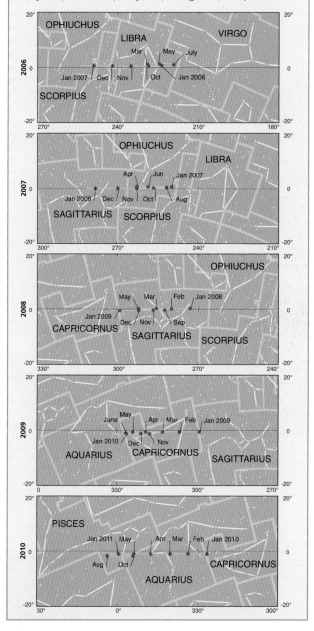

Saturn

TELESCOPIC VIEW *of Saturn showing its prominent rings, which are a mixture of dust, rock, and ice.*

The Romans associated the most distant and slow-moving of the five planets they knew with the lethargic god Saturn, the father of Jupiter. Like the planet Jupiter, Saturn is a gas giant with a turbulent atmosphere, but its latitudinal bands are far less distinct and, occasionally, a short-lived bright spot may appear as a storm grows and dissipates. Saturn is a spectacular sight due to its extensive system of rings, the three main rings consisting of thousands of closely packed ringlets. Six of Saturn's 30 moons are visible with amateur telescopes, including Titan, Saturn's largest moon, which is obscured by a thick photochemical haze. The moons are best viewed when Saturn's rings are edge-on. Without the rings' glare, Saturn's polar flattening of 11 per cent is also easier to see.

SIZE RELATIVE TO EARTH

bands of clouds

Encke's Division

Cassini Division

A ring

B ring

C ring

D ring

▼ **THE HUYGENS LANDER** *found river-like features and shorelines on Titan, possibly formed by flowing liquid ethane or methane.*

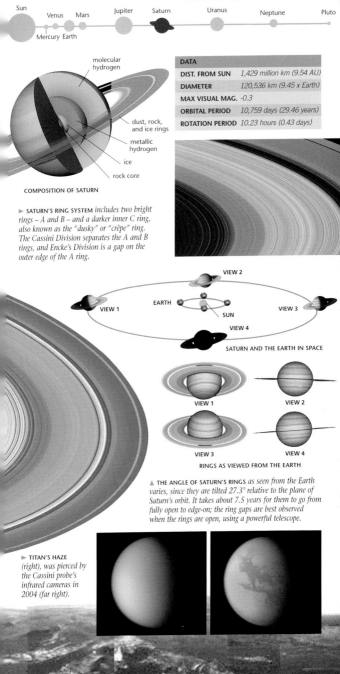

Sun · Mercury · Venus · Earth · Mars · Jupiter · Saturn · Uranus · Neptune · Pluto

molecular
hydrogen

dust, rock,
and ice rings

metallic
hydrogen

ice

rock core

COMPOSITION OF SATURN

DATA	
DIST. FROM SUN	1,429 million km (9.54 AU)
DIAMETER	120,536 km (9.45 x Earth)
MAX VISUAL MAG.	-0.3
ORBITAL PERIOD	10,759 days (29.46 years)
ROTATION PERIOD	10.23 hours (0.43 days)

▶ **SATURN'S RING SYSTEM** *includes two bright rings – A and B – and a darker inner C ring, also known as the "dusky" or "crêpe" ring. The Cassini Division separates the A and B rings, and Encke's Division is a gap on the outer edge of the A ring.*

VIEW 2

VIEW 1 · EARTH · SUN · VIEW 3

VIEW 4

SATURN AND THE EARTH IN SPACE

VIEW 1

VIEW 2

VIEW 3

VIEW 4

RINGS AS VIEWED FROM THE EARTH

▲ **THE ANGLE OF SATURN'S RINGS** *as seen from the Earth varies, since they are tilted 27.3° relative to the plane of Saturn's orbit. It takes about 7.5 years for them to go from fully open to edge-on; the ring gaps are best observed when the rings are open, using a powerful telescope.*

▶ **TITAN'S HAZE** *(right), was pierced by the Cassini probe's infrared cameras in 2004 (far right).*

TRACKING SATURN

Saturn moves through Cancer, Leo, and Virgo from 2006 to 2010. It is brightest near opposition (see p.24) on: 13 Jan. 2006, 10 Feb. 2007, 24 Feb. 2008, 8 Mar. 2009, 22 Mar. 2010.

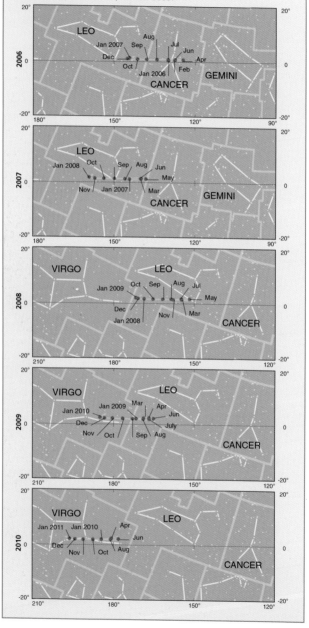

Uranus

Discovered by Sir William Herschel in 1781, Uranus is named after the father of the Roman god Saturn. Mainly composed of hydrogen and helium, Uranus also has methane in its upper atmosphere which absorbs red light, leaving a blue-green colour. It can only just be seen with the unaided eye. Uranus is tilted almost perpendicular to its orbit, probably due to a collision with an Earth-sized body during its formation.

FOUR MOONS of Uranus' known 27 can be seen in this large telescopic view.

hydrogen-helium atmosphere

ice mantle

SIZE RELATIVE TO EARTH

faint rings of rock and ice

equatorial storms

rocky core

COMPOSITION OF URANUS

south pole

▼ THE RINGS OF URANUS *are shown in this infrared view from the Hubble Space Telescope.*

bright haze around sunlit pole

TRACKING URANUS
Uranus moves into Pisces in 2010. Opposition: 5 Sep. 2006, 9 Sep. 2007, 13 Sep. 2008, 17 Sep. 2009, 21 Sep. 2010.

PISCES

2011   2006

0   0

AQUARIUS

360°   330°

▼ TITANIA AND OBERON, *the two largest Uranian moons, can be seen with an eight inch reflector, whilst Miranda (below right), the fifth largest, is not visible to amateur equipment.*

DATA	
DIST. FROM SUN	2,870 million km (19.2 AU)
DIAMETER	51,118 km (4.01 x Earth)
MAX VISUAL MAG.	+5.65
ORBITAL PERIOD	30,684 days (84.01 years)
ROTATION PERIOD	17.23 hours (0.72 days)

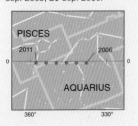

Sun

Venus   Mars   Jupiter   Saturn   Uranus   Neptune   Pluto

Mercury Earth

Neptune

A TELESCOPIC IMAGE *of Neptune, the outermost gas giant, appearing as a featureless disc.*

SIZE RELATIVE TO EARTH

Discovered in 1846 by the astronomer Johann Gottfried Galle, acting on a predicted position provided by Urbain Jean Joseph Le Verrier, Neptune is named after the Roman god of the sea. It appears like a 7.6-magnitude bluish star, near the resolving limit of most amateur telescopes and seems bluer than Uranus because it has more methane in its atmosphere. Its atmosphere is very dynamic, with the highest recorded wind speed in the Solar System at 2,400 km per hour.

molecular hydrogen atmosphere

ice-rock mantle

rocky core

methane ice clouds

COMPOSITION OF NEPTUNE

Great Dark Spot visible in 1989

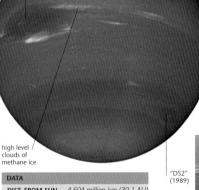

high level clouds of methane ice

▼ **HIGH WHITE STREAKS** *of methane ice clouds sometimes accompany dark spots or appear alone. The dark spots seen by Voyager in 1989 were gone when Hubble viewed the planet in 1994.*

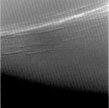

"DS2" (1989)

DATA	
DIST. FROM SUN	4,504 million km (30.1 AU)
DIAMETER	49,572 km (3.89 x Earth)
MAX VISUAL MAG.	+7.66
ORBITAL PERIOD	60,118 days (164.79 years)
ROTATION PERIOD	16.11 hours (0.67 days)

▼ **TRITON** *(mag. 13.5) is Neptune's only large moon, with a 2,705- km diameter.*

TRACKING NEPTUNE
Neptune remains in Capricornus in 2006–2010. It comes into opposition (p.24) on: 11 Aug. 2006, 13 Aug. 2007, 15 Aug. 2008, 17 Aug. 2009, 20 Aug. 2010.

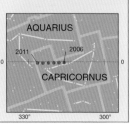

AQUARIUS

2011   2006

CAPRICORNUS

330°   300°

Sun   Mercury Venus Earth Mars   Jupiter   Saturn   Uranus   Neptune   Pluto

Pluto

Lurking at the edge of the Solar System is Pluto, named after the Roman god of darkness. It was discovered in 1930 by the American astronomer Clyde Tombaugh. Pluto has a higher orbital inclination and eccentricity than any other planet, and is, at times, closer to the Sun than Neptune. Pluto is the smallest planet; seven moons are larger, including our own. With a surface of nitrogen and methane ice, it has more in common with a comet than a terrestrial planet.

EVEN THE BEST *telescope view of Pluto, from the Hubble Space Telescope, shows little detail.*

SIZE RELATIVE TO EARTH

methane rich ice crust

water ice

rocky core

bright polar caps

surface markings due to ice and frost

water and organic ice mantle

COMPOSITION OF PLUTO

▼ CHARON *(mag. 16.8) is bluer than Pluto, with more water ice on its surface.*

transient atmosphere of nitrogen and methane

possible ice volcanoes

TRACKING PLUTO

To locate Pluto, its motion has to be tracked against the stars over several nights using digital images or photographs, since it appears only as a point of light even with a large telescope. It strays from the ecliptic due to its tilted orbit. It moves into Sagittarius during 2006.

OPHIUCHUS
2006
2011
0
SAGITTARIUS
SCORPIUS
270°

▼ CHARON *was discovered in 1978. It is shown, together with Pluto, in this image from Hubble. The pair will be examined by a space probe in 2015.*

DATA	
DIST. FROM SUN	5,913 million km (39.5 AU)
DIAMETER	2,320 km (0.182 x Earth)
MAX VISUAL MAG.	+13.6
ORBITAL PERIOD	90,777 days (248.6 years)
ROTATION PERIOD	153.3 hours (6.39 days)

Sun
Mercury Earth
Venus Mars
Jupiter
Saturn
Uranus
Neptune
Pluto

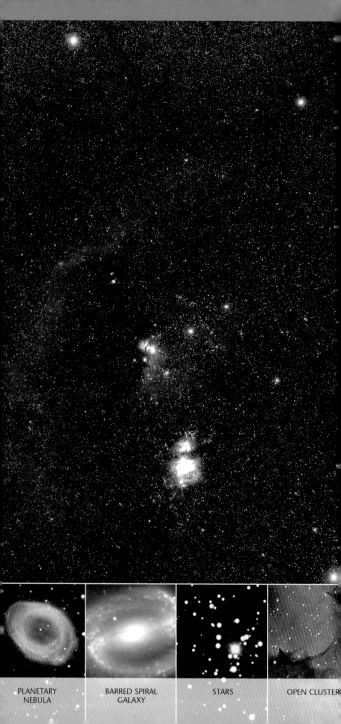

PLANETARY
NEBULA

BARRED SPIRAL
GALAXY

STARS

OPEN CLUSTER

Constellations

This section of the book profiles all 88 constellations. The order in which these appear follows a spiral pattern around the celestial sphere starting at the north and ending at the south. Cross-reference markers lead you to adjoining constellations so you can navigate around the sky and the book easily.

constellation name

genitive and standard abbreviated name

introductory description of constellation

constellation chart

markers at the edges of the charts give the name and page reference of adjoining constellations

line of right ascension

line of declination

linking lines form constellation pattern

star name

stars

star names are in alphabetical order according to the Greek alphabet (see p.215 for key); deep-sky objects are in numerical order according to their catalogue numbers.

figure represented by constellation

celestial globe showing location of constellation

map of Earth showing areas where constellation is visible

constellation size as compared to handspan (see p.26)

deep-sky object

additional images of stars or objects

data boxes list and provide key information on stars and deep-sky objects; these may be listed together or in separate boxes

spectral type (see p.17)

distance in light years from Earth

magnitude (see p.17)

type of object

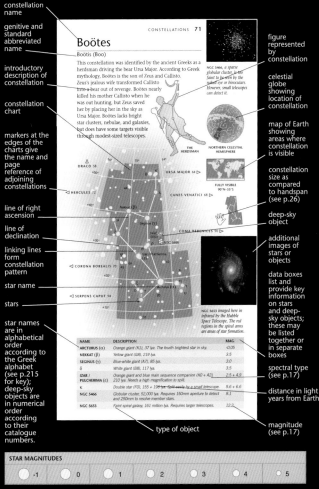

CONSTELLATIONS **71**

Boötes

Boötis (Boo)

This constellation was identified by the ancient Greeks as a herdsman driving the bear Ursa Major. According to Greek mythology, Boötes is the son of Zeus and Callisto. Zeus's jealous wife transformed Callisto into a bear out of revenge. Boötes nearly killed his mother Callisto when he was out hunting, but Zeus saved her by placing her in the sky as Ursa Major. Boötes lacks bright star clusters, nebulae, and galaxies, but does some targets visible through modest-sized telescopes.

NGC 5466, a sparse globular cluster, is too faint to be seen by the naked eye or binoculars. However, small telescopes can detect it.

THE HERDSMAN

NORTHERN CELESTIAL HEMISPHERE

FULLY VISIBLE 90°N–35°S

NGC 5653 imaged here in infrared by the Hubble Space Telescope. The red regions in the spiral arms are areas of star formation.

NAME	DESCRIPTION	MAG.
ARCTURUS (α)	Orange giant (K1), 37 lya. The fourth brightest star in sky.	-0.05
NEKKAT (β)	Yellow giant (G8), 219 lya.	3.5
SEGINUS (γ)	Blue-white giant (A7), 85 lya.	3.0
δ	White giant (B8), 117 lya.	3.5
IZAR / PULCHERIMA (ε)	Orange giant and blue main sequence companion (K0 + A2), 210 lya. Needs a high magnification to split.	2.5 + 4.9
κ	Double star (F0), 155 + 196 lya. Split easily by a small telescope.	5.6 + 6.6
NGC 5466	Globular cluster, 52,000 lya. Requires 150mm aperture to detect and 250mm to resolve member stars.	9.1
NGC 5653	Faint spiral galaxy, 161 million lya. Requires larger telescopes.	12.3

STAR MAGNITUDES

-1   0   1   2   3   4   5

STAR MAGNITUDE KEY indicates the brightness of an object in the sky. In this numerical scale, bright stars are given low or negative numbers, such as -1 and 0 .

Faint stars are given higher or positive numbers, such as 4 and 5. A star of magnitude 1 is about 100 times brighter than a star of magnitude 6.

Draco

Draconis (Dra)

NGC 3147, a faint galaxy, shows multiple, branched spiral arms around a small nucleus, with the fainter arm on the outside.

According to Greek mythology, Draco the dragon guarded the golden apples belonging to the Hesperides, the daughters of Atlas. Draco was killed by Hercules, and in the night sky, the constellation of Hercules stands on Draco's head. Draco also represents the dragon that guarded the Golden Fleece, and was killed by Jason and the Argonauts. The constellation is the eighth largest in the sky. However, it is devoid of bright objects of interest to amateur astronomers. It contains no nebulae, nor open or globular clusters, but does contain some faint galaxies and one interesting planetary nebula. Furthermore, Draco's stars are faint and insignificant.

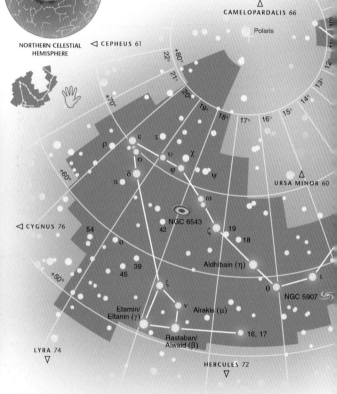

NORTHERN CELESTIAL HEMISPHERE

◁ CEPHEUS 61

△ CAMELOPARDALIS 66

Polaris

△ URSA MINOR 60

◁ CYGNUS 76

NGC 6543

Aldhibain (η)

NGC 5907

Etamin/Eltanin (γ)

Alrakis (μ)

Rastaban/Alwaid (β)

16, 17

LYRA 74 ▽

HERCULES 72 ▽

OBJECT NAME	DESCRIPTION	MAG.
NGC 3147	Spiral galaxy, 120 million lya. Very faint; requires large telescope.	11.4
NGC 4125	Elliptical galaxy, 80 million lya. Requires large telescope.	9.8
NGC 4236	Barred spiral galaxy, 10 million lya. Requires moderate telescope.	9.7
NGC 5907	Spiral galaxy, 40 million lya. Very faint; requires large telescope.	11.3
CAT'S EYE NEBULA (NGC 6543)	Planetary nebula, 3,500 lya. Binoculars show disc; larger instruments show a 9.5-mag. central star.	8.8

STAR NAME	DESCRIPTION	MAG.
THUBAN (α)	*Blue-white giant (A0), 305 lya. Considered the Pole Star around 3800$_{BCE}$.*	*3.7*
RASTABAN/ALWAID (β)	*Yellow giant (G2), 360 lya.*	*2.8*
ETAMIN/ELTANIN (γ)	*Orange giant (K5), 150 lya. The brightest star in Draco.*	*2.2*
ALDHIBAIN (η)	*Close double (G8) for large telescopes, 75 lya.*	*2.2*
ALRAKIS (μ)	*Double (F6 + F6), 88 lya. High magnification splits stars.*	*5.6 + 5.7*
ν	*Two white stars (A5 + A5), binocular double, 100 lya.*	*4.9 + 4.9*
o	*Orange giant (K0), 320 lya. Has a faint companion.*	*4.6 + 7.8*
ψ	*Yellow-white star with yellow companion (F5 + G0), 72 lya.*	*4.6 + 6.1*
16 AND 17	*Two blue-white stars (A0 + A0), 400 lya.*	*5.1 + 5.5*
39	*Binocular double (A1 + F5), 188 lya. Small telescope reveals third star (F8).*	*5.0 + 7.4 + 8.0*

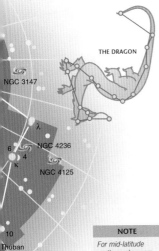

THE DRAGON

NGC 3147

λ

NGC 4236

6 4
κ

NGC 4125

10

Thuban (α)

URSA MAJOR 64 ▷

BOÖTES 71 ▷

FULLY VISIBLE 90°N–4°S

NOTE

For mid-latitude northern observers, the Draconids meteor shower can be seen, with a maximum on 9 October. The Draconids are very slow meteors and are associated with the comet Giacobini–Zinner.

CAT'S EYE NEBULA (NGC 6543), *a planetary nebula, gets its name from its appearance in the Hubble Space Telescope images.*

NGC 4236 *is a galaxy that requires 100mm of aperture or more for viewing and is, therefore, not visible with binoculars.*

NGC 5907, *an edge-on spiral galaxy, is a difficult target for the amateur astronomer and is only visible with a powerful telescope.*

Ursa Minor

Ursae Minoris (UMi)

Known as a constellation since 600BCE, when it is believed to have been introduced by Thales, the Greek astronomer, Ursa Minor is most famed for containing the Alpha (α) star Polaris, also called the Pole Star. Polaris occupies a point in the sky very close to the North Celestial Pole. The axis of the Earth's rotation points to the Pole, but due to the Earth's slow wobble on its axis (precession), this direction is slowly changing. As Polaris is so close to the Pole, the star is known to all northern hemisphere observers.

POLARIS, the Pole Star, is a variable star and lies in the "tail" of "The Lesser Bear".

NORTHERN CELESTIAL HEMISPHERE

FULLY VISIBLE
90°N–0°

NOTE

The Little Dipper is a pattern formed by the main stars of Ursa Minor, the brightest of which are Beta (β) and Gamma (γ), known as the Guardians of the Pole.

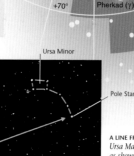

THE LESSER BEAR

Polaris (α)

North Celestial Pole

δ

+80°

ε

◁ DRACO 58

17ʰ   16ʰ   15ʰ   14°

η   ζ   4

5

Kochab (β)

+70°

Pherkad (γ)

DRACO 58 ▷

Ursa Major   Ursa Minor

Pole Star

A LINE FROM Beta (β) through Alpha (α) in Ursa Major points to Polaris in Ursa Minor, as shown in this diagram; a line from Polaris to the horizon identifies the north.

STAR NAME	DESCRIPTION	MAG.
POLARIS / POLE STAR (α)	Variable yellow supergiant (F8), variations not detectable by amateurs, 431 lya. Main sequence companion visible with small telescope (F3).	1.9–2.1 + 8.2
KOCHAB (β)	Orange giant (K4), 126 lya.	2.1
PHERKAD (γ AND 11)	White giant and orange giant forming a line-of-sight double (A3 + K4), 480 + 390 lya.	3.0 + 5.0
δ	White main sequence star (A1), 183 lya.	4.3
ε	Yellow giant eclipsing binary (G5), 347 lya.	4.2
ζ	White main sequence star (A3), 376 lya.	4.3
η	White main sequence star (F5), 97 lya.	5.0

Cepheus

Cephei (Cep)

According to Greek mythology, Cepheus was a king of the ancient kingdom of Ethiopia, the husband of Cassiopeia, and father to Andromeda. This insignificant constellation is best known for its Delta (δ) star, a pulsating variable that varies over a period of 5.366341 days. It is the prototype of a class of variable stars known as Cepheid variables.

NGC 6946 is not visible to the naked eye; this spiral galaxy requires moderate telescopes to resolve its structure.

NORTHERN CELESTIAL HEMISPHERE

FULLY VISIBLE
90°N–1°S

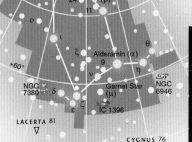

CAMELOPARDALIS 66
URSA MINOR 60 ▷
Polaris
Errai (γ)
CEPHEUS
DRACO 58 ▷
Alfirk (β)
24
11
ο
ι
ξ
Alderamin (α)
9
ν
θ
η
NGC 7380
δ
Garnet Star (μ)
NGC 6946
ε
ζ
IC 1396
LACERTA 81 ▽
CYGNUS 76 ▽

IC 1396 is seen here through a moderate telescope; the bright red star on top is the Garnet, the Mu (μ) star.

NGC 7380 is an open cluster of about 40 stars embedded in faint nebulosity. It is easily detectable with binoculars.

NAME	DESCRIPTION	MAG.
ALDERAMIN (α)	*White sub-giant (A7), 49 lya.*	*2.5*
ALFIRK (β)	*Blue giant and blue-white star (B2 + A3), 590 lya.*	*3.2 + 7.9*
ERRAI / ALRAI (γ)	*Orange sub-giant (K1), 45 lya.*	*3.2*
δ	*Yellow supergiant and pulsating variable (F5), 982 lya. Companion visible with binoculars.*	*3.5–4.4 + 6.3*
GARNET STAR (μ)	*Red supergiant and largest star known (M2), 2,800 lya.*	*3.4–5.1*
ξ	*Blue-white and yellow stars (A3 + F7), 102 lya.*	*4.4 + 6.5*
NGC 6946	*Face-on spiral galaxy, 15 million lya. Needs 150mm or better.*	*8.9*
NGC 7380	*Bright open cluster, 7,000 lya.*	*7.2*
IC 1396	*Nebula and cluster, 2,400 lya. Cluster requires low magnification.*	*3.5*

Cassiopeia

Cassiopeiae (Cas)

M52 *is an open cluster that contains more than a hundred stars, although a telescope is needed to see its individual stars.*

According to Greek mythology, Cassiopeia was the queen of the ancient kingdom of Ethiopia, wife to King Cepheus and mother to Andromeda. This northern constellation, shaped as a large M or W, is easily recognized in the night sky. It is found on the opposite side of the Pole Star from Ursa Major and lies against a rich part of the Milky Way, between Perseus and Cepheus and north of Andromeda.

Cassiopeia contains a variety of clusters and nebulae that can be observed by the amateur astronomer. The constellation, however, lacks galaxies.

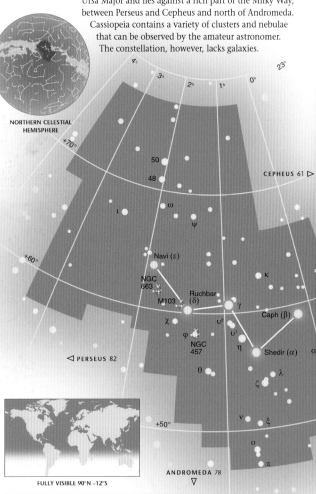

NORTHERN CELESTIAL HEMISPHERE

CEPHEUS 61 ▷

Navi (ε)

NGC 663

M103

Ruchbar (δ)

Caph (β)

χ

φ

NGC 457

Shedir (α)

◁ PERSEUS 82

θ

+50°

ANDROMEDA 78

FULLY VISIBLE 90°N –12°S

OBJECT NAME	DESCRIPTION	MAG.
M52	Open cluster, 5,000 lya. Hazy patch in binoculars, 75mm aperture resolves stars.	7.3
M103	Open cluster of about 80 stars, 8,100 lya. Binocular object.	7.5
NGC 457	Open cluster, 10,000 lya. Stars resolved easily with binoculars.	6.4
NGC 663	Loose open cluster of about 80 stars, 8,200 lya.	7.1

STAR NAME	DESCRIPTION	MAG.
SHEDIR (α)	Orange giant (K0), 229 lya.	2.2
CAPH (β)	White main sequence star (F2), 54 lya.	2.3
γ	Blue-white unpredictable variable star (B0), 613 lya.	1.6–3.0
RUCHBAR (δ)	Blue-white star (A5), 99 lya. An eclipsing binary but change too small for amateur observation.	2.7
NAVI (ε)	Blue-white giant (B3), 442 lya.	3.3

CASSIOPEIA

NGC 663 is a fairly bright but scattered open cluster covering an area about half the size of a full Moon. It is easily visible with binoculars.

M103 is a small, elongated open cluster that is easily visible through binoculars. Its main feature is a chain of three stars.

NOTE

The constellation of Cassiopeia is useful for locating the positions of other northern constellations: if a line is drawn from Cassiopeia through Ursa Minor, it will lead to Ursa Major. Continuing with the line will lead to the bright star Arcturus in the constellation Boötes.

152

LACERTA 81 ▷

NGC 457, an open cluster containing about 80 stars, is visible through binoculars. Its appearance has been compared to an owl, with its two brightest stars as the owl's eyes.

Ursa Major

Ursae Majoris (UMa)

M81 *is one of the brightest spiral galaxies in the sky and is easily visible with binoculars or a small telescope.*

The third largest constellation and one of the best known, Ursa Major has been regarded by many ancient civilizations as a bear (which is why it is named the "Great Bear"), while for European civilizations it has represented a wagon. The seven brightest stars form a pattern known as the Big Dipper or the Plough. Most of the bright stars are members of the Ursa Major Moving Cluster, an open cluster so close to the Earth (about 70 light years away) that the stars appear scattered in the sky. When looking towards Ursa Major, the observer is gazing at a field of galaxies that presents several rewarding targets for amateur astronomers.

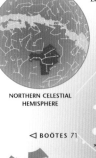

NORTHERN CELESTIAL
HEMISPHERE

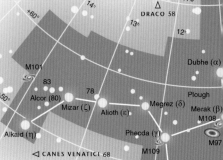

◁ BOÖTES 71

M101
83
Alcor (80)
78
Mizar (ζ)
Alioth (ε)
Megrez (δ)
Alkaid (η)
◁ CANES VENATICI 68
Phecda (γ)
M109

DRACO 58
+70°
+60°
14₅
13₅
12₅
Dubhe (α)
Plough
Merak (β)
M108
M97
χ
ψ
56
+40°
55
+30°
ν
ξ
LEO 86 ▽

FULLY VISIBLE 90°N–16°S

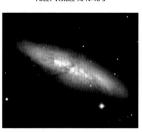

M82 *is a starburst galaxy where massive stars are being formed. A telescopic field of view will also show the spiral galaxy M81.*

OBJECT NAME	DESCRIPTION	MAG.
M81	*Spiral galaxy, 10 million lya.*	6.9
M82	*Peculiar galaxy, 10 million lya.*	8.4
OWL NEBULA (M97)	*Planetary nebula, 1,300 lya. Not visible with naked eye or binoculars, moderate telescope shows bluish disc.*	9.9
PINWHEEL GALAXY (M101)	*Spiral galaxy, 23 million lya.*	7.7
M109	*Barred spiral galaxy, 55 million lya. Small apertures reveal centre.*	9.8

STAR NAME	DESCRIPTION	MAG.
DUBHE (α)	Yellow giant (K0), 672 lya. Companion splits with large telescope.	1.9 + 4.8
MERAK (β)	Blue-white main sequence star (A1), 79 lya.	2.3
PHECDA (γ)	White main sequence star (A0), 84 lya.	2.4
MEGREZ (δ)	White main sequence star (A3), 81 lya.	3.3
ALIOTH (ε)	Blue-white star (A0), 81 lya.	1.8
MIZAR + ALCOR (ζ + 80)	Line-of-sight double formed by two main sequence stars (A2 + A5), each component a binary system, 87 + 81 lya.	2.2 + 4.0
ALKAID (η)	Blue-white main sequence star (B3), 101 lya.	1.9

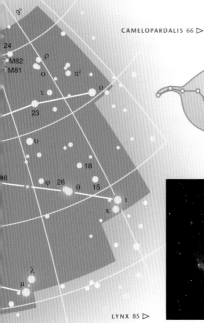

CAMELOPARDALIS 66 ▷

THE GREAT BEAR

LYNX 85 ▷

THE PINWHEEL GALAXY (M101) *is a face-on spiral galaxy visible through binoculars. Small telescopes show only the nucleus; larger apertures and/or photography will reveal the spiral arms.*

LEO MINOR 87
▽

M109 *is a barred spiral galaxy that lies close to the Gamma (γ) star Phecda, in the Big Dipper. This galaxy can be observed with modest instruments, but is too faint to be seen by the naked eye or binoculars.*

Camelopardalis

Camelopardalis (Cam)

NGC 2403 can be detected with binoculars under clear conditions, and appears as a hazy elliptical shape with smaller telescopes.

This constellation of the northern sky was introduced in 1613 by the Dutch astronomer and theologian Petrus Plancius. Although it covers a large area of the sky, it has no stars brighter than magnitude 4 and contains no bright clusters, planetary nebulae, or regions of nebulosity. The brightest star in the constellation, Beta (β), has two companions, one of which can be seen with good binoculars. The other fainter companion requires larger apertures. There are some galaxies present but they are faint and need a telescope of at least 100mm aperture to detect them, and greater aperture to reveal any detail. The constellation represents a giraffe – its long neck can be visualized as stretching around the North Celestial Pole toward Ursa Minor and Draco.

NORTHERN CELESTIAL HEMISPHERE

◁DRACO 58

FULLY VISIBLE 90°N–3°S

THE GIRAFFE

+70°

NGC 2403

+60°

NGC 1502, a small and bright cluster consisting of about 45 stars, is visible with binoculars.

LYNX 85 ▽

NAME	DESCRIPTION	MAG.
α	Very luminous blue-white supergiant (B0), 5,000 lya.	4.3
β	Yellow supergiant + two faint companions (G0), 1,000 lya.	4.0 + 7.4 + 11.4
11 + 12	Line-of-sight double (B3 + K0), 650 lya.	6.0 + 6.0
32	Blue-white stars (A0 + A0), 300 lya. Easy double for small telescopes.	5.3 + 5.7
COLLINDER 464	Large scattered open cluster of about 50 stars.	4.2
NGC 1502	Bright and small open cluster, 3,100 lya.	5.7
NGC 2403	Spiral galaxy, 12 million lya. Hazy glow in 100mm aperture.	8.4
IC 342	Barred spiral galaxy, 10 million lya. Requires moderate telescope.	9.1

IC 342 is a large galaxy, but its low surface brightness means that a large aperture telescope is needed.

URSA MINOR 60 ▷

32

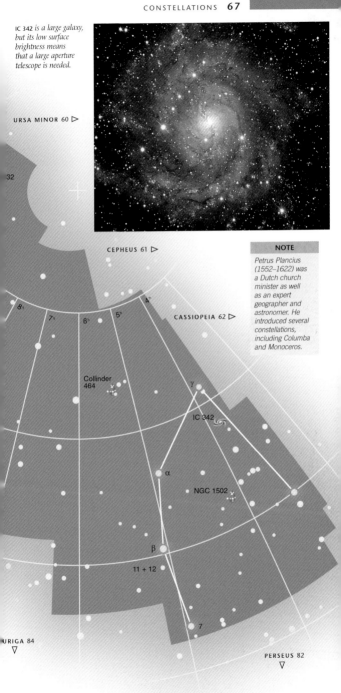

CEPHEUS 61 ▷

CASSIOPEIA 62 ▷

NOTE

Petrus Plancius (1552–1622) was a Dutch church minister as well as an expert geographer and astronomer. He introduced several constellations, including Columba and Monoceros.

8ʰ 7ʰ 6ʰ 5ʰ 4ʰ

Collinder 464

γ

IC 342

α

NGC 1502

β

11 + 12

7

URIGA 84
▽

PERSEUS 82
▽

Canes Venatici

Canum Venaticorum (CVn)

M94 is a fairly bright face-on spiral galaxy. It is easily visible with small apertures, and appears as a star-like nucleus with a surrounding halo.

Introduced as a new constellation by the Polish astronomer Johannes Hevelius, Canes Venatici represents the two hunting dogs, Asterion and Chara. The dogs are held on a leash by Boötes, the herdsman, as they pursue Ursa Major, the Great Bear. This constellation consists of faint stars, the brightest being of only magnitude 3. However, Canes Venatici does contain some galaxies within reach of amateur telescopes, and also M3, one of the finest globular clusters in the northern night sky.

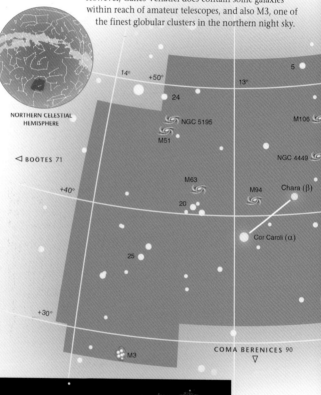

NORTHERN CELESTIAL HEMISPHERE

14ʰ   +50°   13ʰ   5

24   NGC 5195   M106

M51   NGC 4449

◁ BOÖTES 71

M63   M94   Chara (β)

+40°   20

Cor Caroli (α)

25

+30°

M3   COMA BERENICES 90
▽

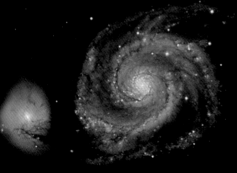

THE WHIRLPOOL GALAXY *(M51) has a smaller satellite galaxy, NGC 5195, which was in collision with the Whirlpool during the last 100 million years. Small telescopes reveal the nuclei of both galaxies, but much larger telescopes reveal structure in the spiral arms.*

M3 *is a globular cluster at the limit of naked-eye visibility, but can be seen on very dark, clear nights. It is an easy target for binoculars, but an aperture of at least 100mm is needed to resolve the stars.*

URSA MAJOR 64 ▷

THE HUNTING DOGS

LEO 86 ▽

FULLY VISIBLE 90°N–37°S

NOTE

The Whirlpool Galaxy was detected in 1773 by Charles Messier. It is connected to a neighbouring galaxy, NGC 5195 by an envelope of gas; their interaction has triggered a burst of star formation in NGC 5195.

THE SUNFLOWER GALAXY (M63) *gets its name from its appearance in larger telescopes, which reveal its patchy outer arms. In smaller instruments of about 100mm, however, it appears as a speckled elliptical haze.*

NAME	DESCRIPTION	MAG.
COR CAROLI (α)	Double star (A0), 110 lya. Easily split with small telescope.	2.9 + 5.6
CHARA (β)	Yellow main sequence star (G0), 27 lya.	4.2
M3	One of the best globular clusters, 34,000 lya.	6.3
WHIRLPOOL GALAXY (M51)	Spiral galaxy, 26 million lya. Visible with small telescope; it has an irregular satellite galaxy (NGC 5195) of 10.5 mag.	8.4
SUNFLOWER GALAXY (M63)	Spiral galaxy, 23 million lya. Elliptical shape apparent in small telescopes, but larger telescopes required for detail.	8.6
M94	Face-on spiral galaxy, 13 million lya. Nucleus and halo visible with small telescopes.	8.2
M106	Spiral galaxy, 20 million lya. Best viewed with larger instruments.	8.3
BOX GALAXY (NGC 4449)	Irregular galaxy, 11 million lya. Visible with small telescopes.	9.4

Corona Borealis

Coronae Borealis (CrB)

An ancient constellation, Corona Borealis represents the crown worn by the mythical Princess Ariadne of Crete on the occasion of her wedding to the god Bacchus (Dionysius). Corona Borealis is a faint constellation, but with a distinctive shape. Unfortunately, this constellation contains no objects visible to the amateur astronomer. It does, however, contain Abell 2065, a cluster of over 400 galaxies lying at a distance of about 1,500 million light years. The galaxies are no brighter than magnitude 16, and therefore need a powerful telescope for detection.

THE STARS OF *Corona Borealis are arranged in the distinctive shape of a semi-circle. Alpha (α) is the blue-white star near the centre, while Epsilon (ε), a red-orange giant, is seen towards the left of Alpha.*

NORTHERN CELESTIAL HEMISPHERE

FULLY VISIBLE 90°N–50°S

NOTE

According to myth, Ariadne's crown was thrown into the air by Bacchus, where its jewels turned into stars. Appropriately, its brightest star is named Gemma, Latin for "jewel".

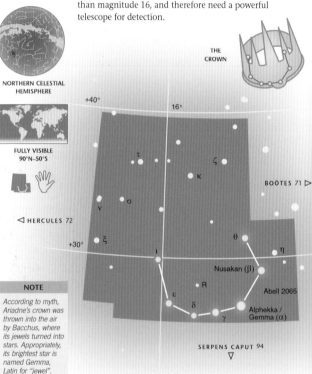

THE CROWN

BOÖTES 71 ▷

◁ HERCULES 72

Nusakan (β)

Abell 2065

Alphekka / Gemma (α)

SERPENS CAPUT 94 ▽

NAME	DESCRIPTION	MAG.
ALPHEKKA / GEMMA (α)	*Blue-white main sequence star (A0), 75 lya. Eclipsing binary, but variation too small for naked eye.*	2.2
NUSAKAN (β)	*Spectroscopic binary (F0), 114 lya.*	3.7
γ	*Blue-white sub-giant (B9), 145 lya.*	3.8
δ	*Orange giant (G4), 165 lya.*	4.6
ε	*Red-orange giant (K2), 230 lya.*	4.1
ζ	*Two blue-white stars (B6 + B7), 470 lya. Visible with small telescopes.*	5.0 + 6.0
σ	*Two yellow dwarf stars (F8 + G1), 70 lya; 1000-year orbiting period.*	5.6 + 6.6
R	*Yellow supergiant (C0), 7,000 lya.*	5.9–15
ABELL 2065	*Regular cluster of galaxies, 1,500 million lya.*	16

Boötes

Boötis (Boo)

This constellation was identified by the ancient Greeks as a herdsman driving the bear Ursa Major. According to Greek mythology, Boötes is the son of Zeus and Callisto. Zeus's jealous wife transformed Callisto into a bear out of revenge. Boötes nearly killed his mother Callisto when he was out hunting, but Zeus saved her by placing her in the sky as Ursa Major. Boötes lacks bright star clusters, nebulae, and galaxies, but does have some targets visible through moderately large telescopes.

THE HERDSMAN

NGC 5466, *a sparse globular cluster, is too faint to be seen by the naked eye or binoculars. However, small telescopes can detect it.*

NORTHERN CELESTIAL HEMISPHERE

FULLY VISIBLE
90°N–35°S

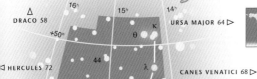

△ DRACO 58

URSA MAJOR 64 ▷

◁ HERCULES 72

CANES VENATICI 68 ▷

Nekkat (β)

Seginus (γ)

NGC 5653

NGC 5466

COMA BERENICES 90 ▷

Izar / Pulcherima (ε)

◁ CORONA BOREALIS 70

◁ SERPENS CAPUT 94

Arcturus (α)

NGC 5653 *imaged here in infrared by the Hubble Space Telescope. The red regions in the spiral arms are areas of star formation.*

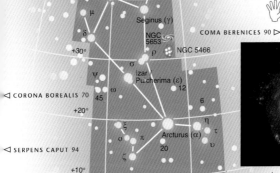

NAME	DESCRIPTION	MAG.
ARCTURUS (α)	Orange giant (K1), 37 lya. The fourth brightest star in sky.	-0.05
NEKKAT (β)	Yellow giant (G8), 219 lya.	3.5
SEGINUS (γ)	Blue-white giant (A7), 85 lya.	3.0
δ	White giant (B8), 117 lya.	3.5
IZAR / PULCHERIMA (ε)	Orange giant and blue main sequence companion (K0 + A2), 210 lya. Needs a high magnification to split.	2.5 + 4.9
κ	Double star (F0), 155 + 196 lya. Split easily by a small telescope.	5.6 + 6.6
NGC 5466	Globular cluster, 52,000 lya. Requires 150mm aperture to detect and 250mm to resolve member stars.	9.1
NGC 5653	Faint spiral galaxy, 161 million lya. Requires larger telescopes.	12.2

Hercules

Herculis (Her)

The fifth largest constellation in the night sky, Hercules, represents the Greek mythological hero responsible for killing the many-headed monster Hydra, the lion Leo, as well as a dragon in three of the twelve labours he was ordered to perform. Hercules is depicted kneeling on his right knee, his left foot resting on the head of the dragon, which is represented by the adjoining constellation Draco. The Hercules Cluster consists of galaxies too faint for modest telescopes but the constellation does contain M13, one of the finest globular clusters in the night sky.

M13 is a fine globular cluster that appears like a hazy star when seen through binoculars in dark skies. Small telescopes can resolve the outer-lying stars.

NORTHERN CELESTIAL HEMISPHERE

FULLY VISIBLE 90°N–38°S

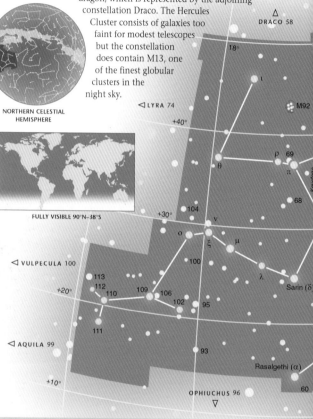

NAME	DESCRIPTION	MAG.
RASALGETHI (α)	*Red supergiant (M5), 400 lya. One of the largest stars known; multiple system.*	*2.7–4.0*
KORNEPHOROS (β)	*Yellow giant (G8), 148 lya.*	*2.8*
γ	*White giant (A9), 195 lya.*	*3.8*
SARIN (δ)	*Blue-white sub-giant (A3), 78 lya.*	*3.1*
RUTILICUS (ζ)	*Binary system (G0 + K0), 33 lya. Requires a telescope.*	*2.8 + 5.7*
MAASYM (κ)	*Telescopic double (G8), 388 lya.*	*5.3 + 6.5*
M13	*Brightest globular cluster in northern sky, 25,000 lya.*	*5.9*
M92	*Globular cluster, 29,000 lya. Good binocular target.*	*6.5*
NGC 6210	*Planetary nebula, 4,000 lya.*	*9.0*

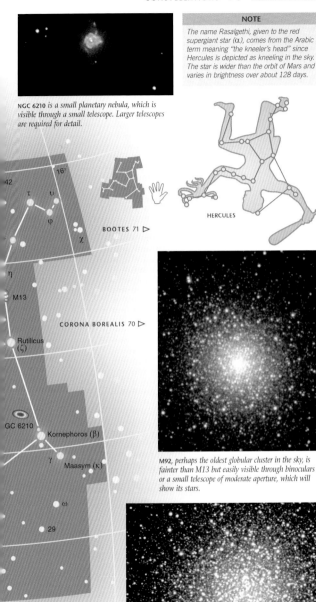

NOTE

The name Rasalgethi, given to the red
supergiant star (α), comes from the Arabic
term meaning "the kneeler's head" since
Hercules is depicted as kneeling in the sky.
The star is wider than the orbit of Mars and
varies in brightness over about 128 days.

NGC 6210 is a small planetary nebula, which is
visible through a small telescope. Larger telescopes
are required for detail.

HERCULES

BOOTES 71 ▷

CORONA BOREALIS 70 ▷

SERPENS CAPUT 94 ▷

M92, perhaps the oldest globular cluster in the sky, is
fainter than M13 but easily visible through binoculars
or a small telescope of moderate aperture, which will
show its stars.

M13 is seen through an increased
aperture here; this resolves more
of the stars within this cluster.
Larger telescopes reveal individual
stars nearer to the cluster's core.

Lyra

Lyrae (Lyr)

THE RING NEBULA
(M57), one of the best-
known objects in the
sky, is seen as a misty
elliptical disc through
a small telescope.
Larger apertures show
the nebula as a ring.

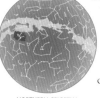

**NORTHERN CELESTIAL
HEMISPHERE**

The compact constellation of Lyra has been known since
ancient times, and represents the lyre, a stringed musical
instrument. According to Greek mythology, the lyre was
invented by Hermes, the Olympian god. He traded it with
Apollo, who later donated the lyre to his son Orpheus.
Orpheus played the lyre so beautifully that even animals
stopped to listen. Orpheus is now
represented by the constellation
Cygnus which lies next to Lyra. The
brightest star of Lyra is Vega, the star
that astronomers use to compare
the colour and brightness of all
other stars. The Solar System is
headed in Vega's direction at a
speed of 20 kilometres per second,
due to the Sun's orbit around the
centre of our galaxy.

◁ CYGNUS 76

RR

+40°

η

θ

THE RING NEBULA
is seen here imaged
at high resolution
by the Hubble
Space Telescope.
Unfortunately, this
level of detail cannot
be obtained with
amateur equipment.

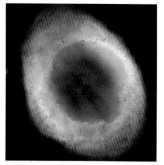

+30°

M56

VULPECULA 100
▽

M56 is a small
globular cluster too
faint for the naked eye
to see, and does not
have the bright core
most other globular
clusters show.
However, despite
its dimness and its
distance from the
Earth, it is not difficult
to resolve with
a small telescope.

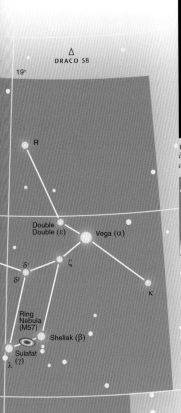

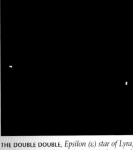

THE DOUBLE DOUBLE, *Epsilon (ε) star of Lyra, is visible as a double with the naked eye and a quadruple with a telescope.*

FULLY VISIBLE 90°N–42°S

THE LYRE

NOTE

The Pole Star is currently Polaris in Ursa Minor, but due to the Earth's slow wobble as it rotates each day, Vega, the fifth brightest star in the sky, will be the Pole Star in about 12,000 years' time.

NAME	DESCRIPTION	MAG.
VEGA (α)	*Blue-white main sequence dwarf star (A0), 25 lya.*	0.03
SHELIAK (β)	*Eclipsing binary (B8), 882 lya.*	3.3 – 4.4 + 7.2
SULAFAT (γ)	*Blue-white giant (B9), 635 lya.*	3.2
δ	*Naked-eye double, red supergiant and white dwarf (M4 + B2), 900 + 1,080 lya.*	5.6 + 4.2
DOUBLE DOUBLE (ε)	*Naked-eye double, telescopic quadruple, spectroscopic quintuple (A2 + A4 + A3 + A5), 161 lya.*	5.0 + 6.1+ 5.2 + 5.5
ζ	*Binocular double (A0 + F0), 152 lya.*	4.4 + 5.7
M56	*Globular cluster, 33,000 lya. Target for a small telescope.*	8.2
RING NEBULA (M57)	*Planetary nebula, 1,100 lya. Requires at least 75mm telescope.*	9.7

Cygnus

Cygni (Cyg)

THE NORTH AMERICAN NEBULA (NGC 7000) gets its name from its outline, which is surprisingly similar in shape to the continent.

This constellation represents the swan disguise that Zeus used when he visited the wife of the King of Sparta. Cygnus is an easily recognizable constellation lying against the richness of the Milky Way, and consequently, there are many targets for amateur astronomers. Cygnus lacks globular clusters and bright galaxies, but does contain nebulae and open clusters. The night sky in Cygnus is impressive when swept with binoculars or a telescope on low power, and it is possible to see the Great Rift – dark dust clouds within the Milky Way – with the naked eye.

NORTHERN CELESTIAL HEMISPHERE

FULLY VISIBLE 90°N–28°S

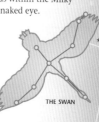

THE SWAN

◁ LACERTA 81

THE VEIL NEBULA (NGC 6992) is a supernova remnant in the southern part of Cygnus. It is visible with binoculars under ideal conditions.

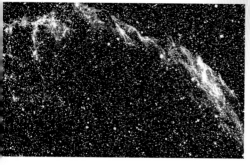

NOTE

According to myth, Zeus's union with Queen Leda of Sparta produced the twins Castor and Pollux, and Helen of Troy. The Swan's tail is marked by Alpha (α), named Deneb from an Arabic word meaning "tail".

OBJECT NAME	DESCRIPTION	MAG.
M29	Open cluster of about 20 stars, 4,000 lya.	7.1
M39	Open cluster of about 30 stars, 950 lya.	4.6
BLINKING PLANETARY (NGC 6826)	Planetary nebula, 3,200 lya. Visible with small telescopes, but larger apertures reveal detail within the disc.	9.8
VEIL NEBULA (NGC 6992)	Nebula, 2,000 lya.	7.0
NORTH AMERICAN NEBULA (NGC 7000)	Nebula, 1,500 lya. Visible with naked eye under clear conditions, easy for binoculars.	6.0

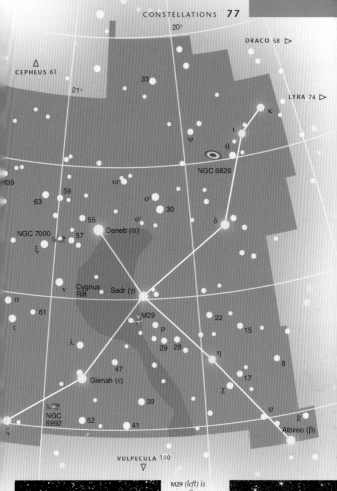

DRACO 58 ▷
△ CEPHEUS 61
LYRA 74 ▷

NGC 6826

139
63
59
30
55
Deneb (α)
NGC 7000
57
ξ
ν
Cygnus Rift
Sadr (γ)
M29
σ
61
τ
λ
P
29 28
η
22
15
47
Gienah (ε)
χ
17
8
39
NGC 6992
52
41
φ
2
ζ
Albireo (β)

VULPECULA 100 ▽

M29 *(left) is a small open cluster that is visible through binoculars and low-power telescopes.*

M39 *(right) is a sparse open cluster best seen with binoculars.*

STAR NAME	DESCRIPTION	MAG.
DENEB (α)	*Blue-white supergiant (A2), 3,200 lya.*	*1.2*
ALBIREO (β)	*Orange giant and blue-green companion (K5), 380 lya. Easily split with binoculars.*	*3.1 + 5.1*
SADR (γ)	*Yellow-white supergiant (F8), 1,500 lya.*	*2.2*
δ	*Blue-white giant and faint companion (A0), 171 lya. Visible with 100mm aperture or greater.*	*2.9 + 6.6*
GIENAH (ε)	*Orange giant (K0), 72 lya.*	*2.5*

Andromeda

Andromedae (And)

THE BLUE SNOWBALL *(NGC 7662), is visible through binoculars and small telescopes; its rounded outline is revealed by high magnification.*

According to Greek mythology, Andromeda was the daughter of Cassiopeia and Cepheus of Ethiopia. Cassiopeia had boasted that she was more beautiful than the daughters of the sea-god Poseidon. This angered Poseidon who sent Cetus, a sea monster, to attack Ethiopia. To appease Poseidon, Cassiopeia and Cepheus had Andromeda chained to a rock by the sea as a sacrifice to Cetus, but she was rescued by Perseus. Andromeda is a faint constellation, but famous due to the Andromeda Galaxy (M31), along with its satellite galaxies M32 and M110. Andromeda contains little of interest to the amateur astronomer by way of clusters or nebulae.

NORTHERN CELESTIAL HEMISPHERE

M32, a satellite galaxy of the Andromeda Galaxy, is visible with binoculars but appears as a star-like object. Very little detail can be seen with amateur telescopes.

OBJECT NAME	DESCRIPTION	MAG.
ANDROMEDA GALAXY (M31)	*Spiral galaxy, 2.4–3 million lya. Visible to naked eye under clear conditions.*	3.4
M32	*Almost spherical galaxy, 2.4–3 million lya. Dwarf elliptical companion to M31.*	8.2
M110	*Almost spherical galaxy, 2.4–3 million lya. Dwarf elliptical companion to M31.*	8.0
BLUE SNOWBALL (NGC 7662)	*Planetary nebula, 2,610 lya. Appears as a faint bluish disc.*	8.6

STAR NAME	DESCRIPTION	MAG.
ALPHERATZ (α)	Spectroscopic binary (A0), 97 lya.	2.1
MIRACH / MIRAAK (β)	Cool red giant (M0), 199 lya.	2.1
ALMACH/ ALMAAK (γ)	Orange and blue double (K2 + B9) with a fainter third star, 355 lya.	2.3 + 4.8
δ	Orange giant (K3), 101 lya.	3.3

NOTE

When Andromeda was chained and offered as a sacrifice to the sea-god Poseidon by her parents, it was the Greek hero Perseus who arrived just in time on the winged horse Pegasus and rescued her. He went on to marry her.

FULLY VISIBLE 90°N–37°S

23ʰ

0ʰ

3

8 7

ψ λ

κ ι ο

NGC 7662

ANDROMEDA

θ

σ

Alpheratz (α)

PEGASUS 102 ▷

M110, *a dwarf elliptical satellite galaxy of M31, is visible through binoculars under clear conditions.*

THE ANDROMEDA GALAXY *(M31) is our neighbouring galaxy and is the most distant object visible to the naked eye, appearing as an elongated smudge on a clear night.*

Triangulum

Trianguli (Tri)

This small northern constellation, one of the original 48 constellations listed by Ptolemy, consists of an elongated triangle of three insignificant stars. It does not contain any clusters or nebulae, but includes the nearby galaxy M33, the Triangulum Galaxy. About four times smaller (in radius) than our Milky Way Galaxy and the Andromeda Galaxy, M33 is the third largest member of the Local Group of galaxies. Since it is faint against the background sky, locating it with binoculars is best on a dark night.

THE TRIANGULUM or
Pinwheel Galaxy
(M33) appears larger
than the full Moon
but its low surface
brightness makes it
hard to see with the
naked eye.

**NORTHERN CELESTIAL
HEMISPHERE**

**FULLY VISIBLE
90°N–52°S**

NOTE
Triangulum was
known to the ancient
Greeks. Some say
it represents the
mouth of the river
Nile; others say it
represents the island
of Sicily. It was
sometimes called
"Deltotum" because
the Greek letter delta
is a triangle in its
capital form.

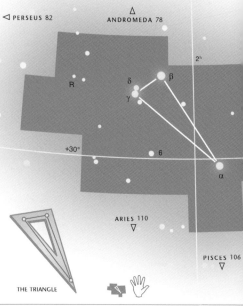

◁ PERSEUS 82

△ ANDROMEDA 78

R

δ β

γ

2ʰ

+30°

6

α

ARIES 110
▽

PISCES 106
▽

THE TRIANGLE

Lacerta

Lacertae (Lac)

Introduced in 1687 by the Polish astronomer Johannes Hevelius, Lacerta is an insignificant constellation. Since it is so small, it contains little of interest to the amateur astronomer. However, Lacerta is famed for the object BL Lacertae, earlier thought to be a variable star, but now known to be a distant elliptical galaxy, possibly containing a black hole at its core. It varies between magnitudes 12 and 16 and has given its name to a class of galaxies with active nuclei called BL Lac objects or "blazars". The Alpha (α) star of Lacerta is blue-white and of magnitude 2.5; the Beta (β) is a yellow giant of magnitude 4.4.

NGC 7243, a sparse
open cluster, is too
faint for the naked
eye. It is visible
with binoculars.

THE LIZARD

NGC 604 *is a bright emission nebula within the Triangulum Galaxy. It is so bright that it can sometimes be seen with binoculars even when the galaxy itself is invisible.*

EMISSION NEBULA, *NGC 604, is shown here in a high-resolution Hubble Space Telescope image.*

NAME	DESCRIPTION	MAG.
α	Yellow main sequence star (F6), 64 lya.	3.4
β	White giant (A5), 124 lya.	3.0
γ	Blue-white star (A1), 118 lya.	4.0
6	Yellow giant with companion (G5), 305 lya.	5.2 + 6.6
R	Red giant variable (M4) 1,300 lya. Brightness varies over 267 days.	5.4–12.6
TRIANGULUM / PINWHEEL (M33)	Large face-on spiral galaxy, 2.6 million lya. Low surface brightness; an aperture of 200mm is needed to observe fine detail.	5.7
NGC 604	Large emission nebula in M33, 2.6 million lya.	5.7

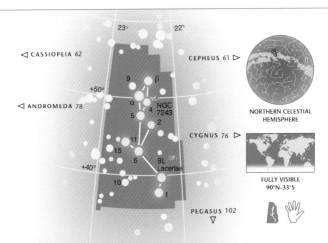

◁ CASSIOPEIA 62

CEPHEUS 61 ▷

◁ ANDROMEDA 78

CYGNUS 76 ▷

NORTHERN CELESTIAL HEMISPHERE

FULLY VISIBLE 90°N–33°S

PEGASUS 102 ▽

Perseus

Persei (Per)

NGC 884 *contains red giants that are easily detectable with low magnifications.*

The Greek mythological hero, Perseus, rescued Andromeda from the sea monster Cetus and killed Medusa. He now takes his place in the sky next to Andromeda and Cassiopeia, Andromeda's mother. This constellation lies against the rich background of the Milky Way, and so is ideal for sweeping with binoculars. The two open clusters NGC 869 and NGC 884 are visible to the naked eye on a dark, clear night, and make an excellent target for binoculars or a telescope with low magnification. Beta (β) is a famous eclipsing binary star with a magnitude variation that is easy to follow, dropping in brightness for 10 hours every two days and 21 hours.

NORTHERN CELESTIAL HEMISPHERE

FULLY VISIBLE 90°N–31°S

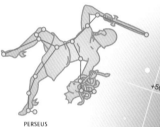

PERSEUS

◁ AURIGA 84

+50°

5

+40°

58

TAURUS 108 ▽

THE DOUBLE OPEN *clusters NGC 869 and NGC 884 are very close to each other, separated by only a few hundred light years.*

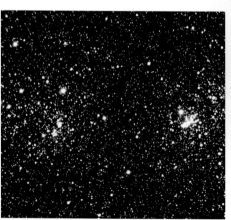

OBJECT NAME	DESCRIPTION	MAG.
DOUBLE CLUSTER, H AND X (CHI) (NGC 869 + 884)	Open clusters, 7,500 + 7,100 lya. Visible to naked eye, good binocular and small telescope target.	4.3 + 4.4
M34	Open cluster of about 80 stars, 1,500 lya.	5.2
THE LITTLE DUMBBELL (M76)	Planetary nebula, 3,400 lya. Visible through moderate-sized telescopes.	10.1

THE LITTLE DUMBBELL *(M76) is a very faint planetary nebula, named after its shape, which is similar to the Dumbbell Nebula in Vulpecula. A larger telescope, of at least 150mm aperture, is needed before it shows any discernible shape.*

M34, *though visible to the naked eye, is an ideal target for binoculars or small telescopes. It appears about the same size as the full Moon.*

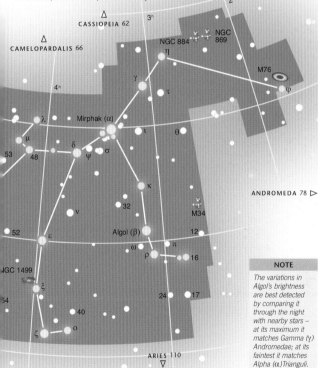

CASSIOPEIA 62

CAMELOPARDALIS 66

ANDROMEDA 78 ▷

ARIES 110

NOTE

The variations in Algol's brightness are best detected by comparing it through the night with nearby stars – at its maximum it matches Gamma (γ) Andromedae; at its faintest it matches Alpha (α) Trianguli.

STAR NAME	DESCRIPTION	MAG.
MIRPHAK (α)	*Yellow/white supergiant (F5), 592 lya.*	*1.8*
ALGOL (β)	*Famous eclipsing binary (B8), 92 lya.*	*2.1–3.3*
γ	*Yellow giant and eclipsing binary (G8), 256 lya.*	*2.9*
δ	*Blue giant (B5), 528 lya.*	*3.0*
ε	*Blue-white main sequence star (B0), 538 lya.*	*2.9*
ζ	*Blue supergiant and telescopic companion (B1), 980 lya.*	*2.9 + 9.5*
η	*Orange supergiant, multiple system (K0), 1,300 lya. Two companions visible through small telescope.*	*3.8 + 8.5 + 9.8*

Auriga

Aurigae (Aur)

NORTHERN CELESTIAL HEMISPHERE

FULLY VISIBLE 90°N–34°S

M37 is an open cluster with an apparent size in the sky of the Moon. It consists of about 150 stars. It appears as a hazy patch through binoculars, but telescopes can resolve individual stars, including red giants.

According to Greek legend, Auriga represents Erichthonius, a king of Athens who was an excellent charioteer. The star Gamma Aurigae used to be shared with the constellation Taurus, but is now assigned exclusively to Taurus as Beta (β) Tauri. The constellation's brightest star, Capella, represents Amaltheia who suckled the infant Zeus. The Milky Way runs through Auriga, and consequently, this constellation possesses some open clusters and regions of nebulosity. There are some galaxies too, but they are too faint for amateur instruments.

M36 is a small and bright open cluster, which is easily visible through binoculars. This cluster lends itself well to larger apertures and higher magnification.

THE CHARIOTEER

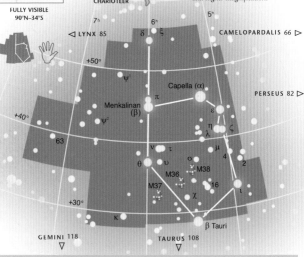

NAME	DESCRIPTION	MAG.
CAPELLA (α)	*Spectroscopic binary, two yellow giant stars (G8), 42 lya. The 6th brightest star in sky.*	*0.1*
MENKALINAN (β)	*Eclipsing binary, two blue-white stars (A2 + A2), 82 lya.*	*1.9–2.0*
δ	*Orange giant (K0), 142 lya.*	*3.7*
ε	*White supergiant (F0), 2,000 lya. Eclipsed by dust ring.*	*3.0*
ζ	*Eclipsing binary, orange giant and small blue-white star (K4 + B7), 790 lya.*	*3.7–4.0*
M36	*Open cluster, 4,200 lya.*	*6.0*
M37	*Open cluster, 4,600 lya.*	*5.6*
M38	*Open cluster, 4,500 lya. Requires low power, wide field of view.*	*6.4*

Lynx

Lyncis (Lyn)

This constellation, which lies in the northern sky, was introduced in 1687 by the Polish astronomer Johannes Hevelius, who wanted to fill the gap between Ursa Major and Auriga. Lynx contains few objects within easy reach of amateur astronomers, but it does have some interesting double and multiple stars to attract telescope users. In clear conditions, naked-eye observers will see little more than its brightest star, Alpha (α).

NGC 2419 *is an exceptionally distant globular cluster. The cluster is so far from the galactic disc that it is known as an "intergalactic wanderer".*

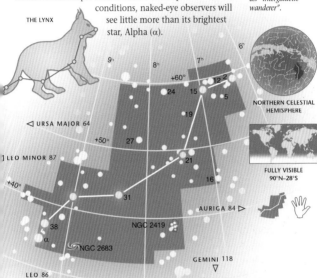

THE LYNX

NORTHERN CELESTIAL HEMISPHERE

FULLY VISIBLE 90°N–28°S

◁ URSA MAJOR 64

] LEO MINOR 87

LEO 86 ▽

CANCER 120 ▽

AURIGA 84 ▷

GEMINI 118 ▽

NGC 2419

NGC 2683

NOTE

It is claimed that this constellation was named Lynx because only lynx-eyed observers would be able to see its stars, all of which are quite faint and spread out.

NGC 2683 *is a nearly edge-on spiral galaxy that can be detected with an aperture of 150mm, but needs larger telescopes to reveal detail within the spiral arms.*

NAME	DESCRIPTION	MAG.
α	Red giant (K7), 222 lya.	3.1
5	Orange giant with an unrelated companion visible with small telescopes (K4), 680 lya. Large telescope reveals third star.	5.2 + 7.9 + 9.8
12	White main sequence star (A3), 230 lya. Second star visible with small telescope, third star with larger telescope.	5.0 + 5.5 + 6.1
19	Blue-white main sequence star and two fainter companions (B8 + A0), 468 lya. Target for small telescopes.	5.8 + 6.9 + 7.6
NGC 2419	Very distant globular cluster far from the galactic plane, 270,000 lya.	10.4
NGC 2683	Edge-on spiral galaxy, 16 million lya.	9.7

THE SPIRAL GALAXY
M65 is too faint for small binoculars, but is a popular target with amateur astrophotographers.

Leo

Leonis (Leo)

A large constellation, Leo represents the lion slain by the Greek hero Hercules, as one of his twelve labours. It is shaped like a lion, with a pattern of six stars called the Sickle, forming the lion's head and chest. Leo contains no nebulae or clusters, as it lies away from the plane of our galaxy, although it does contain a few galaxies within reach of amateur telescopes. Leo contains the dwarf star CN Leo, also known as Wolf 359, which is the fourth nearest star to our Sun, lying at a distance of only 7.8 light years. However, it is too faint for amateur astronomical observation.

NORTHERN CELESTIAL HEMISPHERE

THE LION

◁ VIRGO 88

M95 is a face-on barred spiral galaxy, visible only through moderately sized telescopes or better. Larger telescopes show details within the nucleus and spiral arms.

NAME	DESCRIPTION	MAG.
REGULUS (α)	*Blue-white main sequence star with an orange companion (B7 + K1), 77 lya.*	1.4 + 7.7
DENEBOLA (β)	*Blue-white main sequence star (A3), 35 lya.*	2.5
ALGIEBA (γ)	*Orange and yellow giants (K1 + G7), 126 lya.*	2.4 + 3.5
ZOSMA (δ)	*Blue-white main sequence star (A4), 58 lya.*	2.6
M65	*Spiral galaxy, 25 million lya. Barely visible with large binoculars.*	9.3
M66	*Spiral galaxy, 25 million lya. Barely visible with large binoculars.*	8.9
M95	*Barred spiral galaxy, 38 million lya.*	9.7
M96	*Spiral galaxy, 38 million lya.*	9.2
NGC 3628	*Edge-on spiral galaxy, 35 million lya.*	9.6

NGC 3344 *is a galaxy too faint to be seen by the naked eye or through binoculars. A large telescope with an aperture of 100mm or more is needed to observe any structure.*

Leo Minor

Leonis Minoris (LMi)

Introduced in the 17th century by Johannes Hevelius, this constellation represents a lion cub. It contains few objects of interest to amateur astronomers. Only one of its stars, the second brightest, has been assigned a Greek letter, β. The brightest star, 46, with magnitude 3.8, should have been assigned the letter α, but was forgotten by the English astronomer Francis Bailey when he assigned Greek letters to the constellation in 1845.

THE LITTLE LION

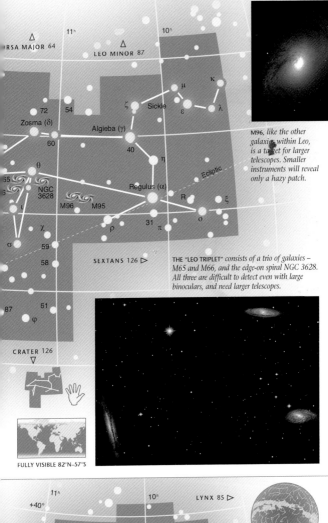

URSA MAJOR 64

LEO MINOR 87

11ʰ 10ʰ

72 54

ζ Sickle

μ κ

ε λ

Zosma (δ)

Algieba (γ)

60

40 η

θ

NGC
3628

M96 M95

Regulus (α)

Ecliptic

R ξ

χ

31 π ο

ι 59

ρ

σ

58

87 61

φ

SEXTANS 126 ▷

CRATER 126 ▽

M96, *like the other galaxies within Leo, is a target for larger telescopes. Smaller instruments will reveal only a hazy patch.*

THE "LEO TRIPLET" *consists of a trio of galaxies – M65 and M66, and the edge-on spiral NGC 3628. All three are difficult to detect even with large binoculars, and need larger telescopes.*

FULLY VISIBLE 82°N–57°S

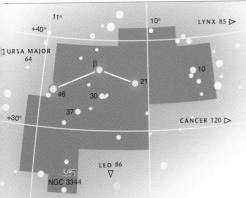

11ʰ 10ʰ

+40°

LYNX 85 ▷

URSA MAJOR 64

β

46 30 21

10

37

+30°

CANCER 120 ▷

LEO 86 ▽

NGC 3344

NORTHERN CELESTIAL HEMISPHERE

FULLY VISIBLE 90°N–48°S

Virgo

Virginis (Vir)

THE SOMBRERO GALAXY (M104) is not actually a member of the Virgo Cluster of galaxies, being some 20 million light years closer. It is elongated in shape.

The second largest constellation after Hydra, Virgo is the only female sign of the zodiac. Although associated with nearly every goddess in mythology, it represents the goddess of justice, with Libra, the scales of Justice, nearby. Virgo lacks bright star clusters and nebulae, but makes up for this with galaxies. When looking towards Virgo, one is looking out of our galaxy towards the Virgo Cluster, a cluster of galaxies some 55 million light years away that contains over 2,000 galaxies. Although many of the galaxies require powerful telescopes, some are visible with smaller amateur telescopes.

NORTHERN CELESTIAL HEMISPHERE

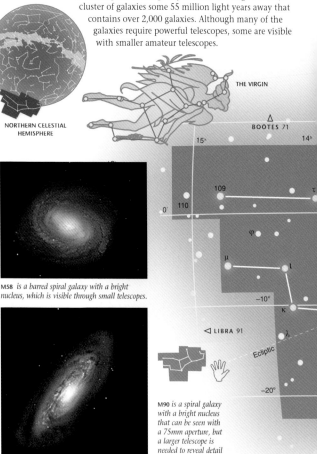

THE VIRGIN

BOOTES 71

M58 is a barred spiral galaxy with a bright nucleus, which is visible through small telescopes.

◁ LIBRA 91

M90 is a spiral galaxy with a bright nucleus that can be seen with a 75mm aperture, but a larger telescope is needed to reveal detail within the spiral arms.

STAR NAME	DESCRIPTION	MAG.
SPICA (α)	Blue-white main sequence star (B1), 260 lya.	1.0
ZAVIJAVA (β)	Yellow main sequence star (F8), 36 lya.	3.6
PORRIMA (γ)	Double star (F0 + F0), 39 lya. Too close for small instruments.	3.5 + 3.5
δ	Red giant (M3), 201 lya.	3.4
VINDEMIATRIX (ε)	Yellow giant (G9), 103 lya.	2.8

OBJECT NAME	DESCRIPTION	MAG.
M49	*Elliptical galaxy, 55 million lya. Brightest Virgo member.*	8.4
M58	*Barred spiral galaxy, 55 million lya.*	9.8
M59	*Elliptical galaxy, 55 million lya.*	9.6
M60	*Spherical galaxy, 55 million lya. Requires 75mm aperture.*	8.8
M61	*Large spiral galaxy, 55 million lya. Visible with 75mm aperture.*	9.7
M84	*Virtually spherical, 55 million lya.*	9.3
M86	*Elongated galaxy, 55 million lya.*	9.2
M87	*Giant spherical galaxy, 55 million lya. Strong radio source.*	8.6
M90	*Spiral galaxy, 55 million lya.*	9.5
SOMBRERO GALAXY (M104)	*Edge-on spiral galaxy, 35 million lya. Prominent dust lanes visible with 150mm aperture or more.*	8.5

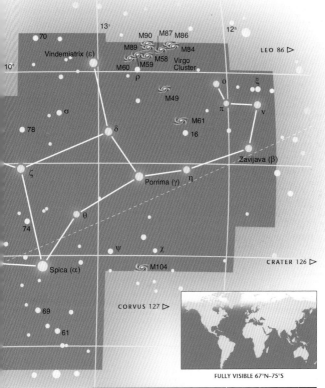

FULLY VISIBLE 67°N–75°S

THE VIRGO CLUSTER *in this amateur image shows a few of its over 2000 members. The brightest are within reach of amateur telescopes, and the whole area is popular with astrophotographers.*

Coma Berenices

Comae Berenices (Com)

THE BLACK EYE GALAXY (M64) gets its name from the dark obscuring dust silhouetted against its nucleus. Small telescopes show only the galaxy's shape, and larger telescopes detect the dust cloud.

This constellation represents the hair of Queen Berenice II of Egypt. According to legend, she cut off her hair and placed it in the temple of Aphrodite when her husband, King Ptolemy III, returned victorious from battle against the Assyrians. However, it was stolen from there and the court astronomer placated the Queen by telling her that the goddess had placed her hair in the stars of Coma Berenices. Although the stars of this constellation are faint, there are a number of objects, mainly galaxies, that are visible with binoculars and small telescopes.

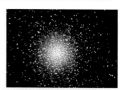
M53 is visible through binoculars; however, detail within the cluster can only be resolved with larger apertures.

NORTHERN CELESTIAL HEMISPHERE

FULLY VISIBLE
90°N–55°S

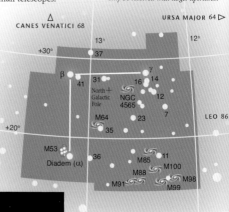

△ CANES VENATICI 68

URSA MAJOR 64 ▷

+30°

13ʰ 12ʰ

37

β 31 16 14 γ

41 North + Galactic Pole NGC 4565 12

+20° M64 23 7 LEO 86

35

M53 36 M85 11

Diadem (α) M88 M100

M91 M99 M98

◁ BOÖTES 71

VIRGO 88 ▽

BERENICE'S HAIR

M99, has a nucleus that is bright enough to be detected with small telescopes. However, the detail within the spiral arms is revealed only through more powerful telescopes.

NAME	DESCRIPTION	MAG.
DIADEM (α)	Close binary, two yellow-white stars (F5), 26-year period, 47 lya.	5.5 + 5.1
β	Yellow main sequence star (F9), 30 lya.	4.2
γ	Orange giant (K1), 170 lya.	4.4
M53	Globular cluster, 56,000 lya.	7.7
BLACK EYE GALAXY (M64)	Spiral galaxy, 15 million lya. Visible with large binoculars under clear conditions.	8.5
M85	Elliptical galaxy, 50 million lya. Small telescopes reveal shape.	9.1
M99	Face-on spiral galaxy, 50 million lya. 75mm aperture reveals nucleus.	9.8
M100	Face-on spiral galaxy, 50 million lya. Visible with 100mm aperture.	9.4

Libra

Librae (Lib)

Originally, the stars of Libra were called *Chelae*, Latin for "claw", and were considered a part of the constellation Scorpius. The ancient Greeks held the same view, but the Romans in the first century BCE assigned the stars to Libra. However, the star names still show the association with Scorpius as its claws – the three brightest stars are Zubenelgenubi, Zubeneschamali, and Zubenelakrab, which mean "southern claw", "northern claw", and "the scorpion's claw". Nowadays, Libra represents the scales of Justice.

NGC 5897, a sparse, loosely concentrated globular cluster, is a disappointing sight when viewed with smaller apertures.

SOUTHERN CELESTIAL HEMISPHERE

FULLY VISIBLE 60°N–90°S

THE SCALES

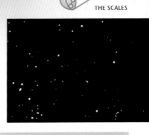

NOTE

Libra is a small and faint constellation, and apart from one unimpressive globular cluster, has nothing much to offer amateur astronomers with small telescopes.

THE STARS OF LIBRA include Alpha¹ and Alpha² ($\alpha^1 + \alpha^2$), collectively named Zubenelgenubi, the double star near the centre. Further south lies the orange star Sigma (σ).

NAME	DESCRIPTION	MAG.
ZUBENELGENUBI ($\alpha^1 + \alpha^2$)	Blue-white and white stars (A3 + F3), 77 lya. Split with binoculars.	2.7 + 5.2
ZUBENESCHAMALI (β)	White main sequence star (B8), 160 lya.	2.6
ZUBENELAKRAB (γ)	Orange giant (K0), 152 lya.	3.9
δ	Eclipsing binary (B9), with period of 2.327 days, 304 lya.	4.9–5.9
ε	Yellow sub-giant (F5), 105 lya.	4.9
ι^1	Quintuple system (B9), 377 lya. Three stars visible with large apertures; also forms a double with ι^2.	4.5 + 10.6 + 10.6
ι^2	White main sequence star (A2), 219 lya.	6.1
NGC 5897	Loose globular cluster, 40,000 lya.	8.6

Scorpius

Scorpii (Sco)

THE BUTTERFLY CLUSTER (M6) is a fairly bright and easily visible open cluster resembling the shape of a butterfly.

This constellation represents the scorpion that killed Orion. Since Orion sets before Scorpius, it seems that Scorpius is still chasing Orion through the night sky. The constellation resembles the shape of a scorpion with its raised tail marked by a curve of stars, and is quite striking on a clear dark night. A very rich area of the Milky Way runs through this constellation, including the centre of our galaxy. Consequently there are a variety of targets, especially star clusters, for small telescopes.

The brightest star, Antares, is a giant star about 600 million kilometres across and 9,000 times as luminous as the Sun. It is noticeably reddish in colour, rivalling the planet Mars, and varies in brightness between magnitudes 0.9 and 1.2 in a cycle lasting about four to five years. Close to Antares lies M4, the closest globular cluster to the Earth.

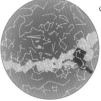

SOUTHERN CELESTIAL HEMISPHERE

FULLY VISIBLE 44°N–90°S

◁ SAGITTARIUS 136

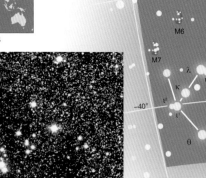

−30°

M6

M7

λ
υ

κ

ι²

ι¹

θ

−40°

◁ CORONA AUSTRALIS

M7 is a large and bright open cluster visible to the naked eye and an ideal target for binocular viewing.

OBJECT NAME	DESCRIPTION	MAG.
M4	*Large, loose globular cluster, 6,500 lya.*	5.9
BUTTERFLY CLUSTER (M6)	*Open cluster containing about 80 stars and obvious red giant, 2,000 lya.*	4.5
M7	*One of the best open clusters in the northern sky, 2,000 lya.*	3.3
M80	*Globular cluster, 32,000 lya. Appears as a fuzzy ball when viewed with binoculars.*	7.2
NGC 6231	*Open cluster, 780 lya. Individual stars visible with binoculars.*	5.9

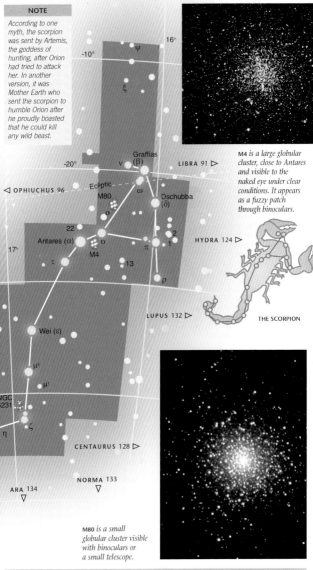

NOTE

According to one myth, the scorpion was sent by Artemis, the goddess of hunting, had tried to attack her. In another version, it was Mother Earth who sent the scorpion to humble Orion after he proudly boasted that he could kill any wild beast.

LIBRA 91 ▷

◁ OPHIUCHUS 96

HYDRA 124 ▷

LUPUS 132 ▷

CENTAURUS 128 ▷

ARA 134 ▽

NORMA 133 ▽

THE SCORPION

M4 is a large globular cluster, close to Antares and visible to the naked eye under clear conditions. It appears as a fuzzy patch through binoculars.

M80 is a small globular cluster visible with binoculars or a small telescope.

STAR NAME	DESCRIPTION	MAG.
ANTARES (α)	*Red supergiant (M1) with faint blue companion in 900-year orbit, 604 lya.*	*0.9 –1.2 + 5.4*
GRAFFIAS (β)	*Telescopic double (B + B), 530 + 1100 lya.*	*2.5*
DSCHUBBA (δ)	*Possibly a quadruple system (B0), 400 lya.*	*2.3*
WEI (ε)	*Sub-giant (K2), 65 lya. 40 times as luminous as the Sun.*	*2.3*
ζ	*Naked eye double, supergiant 280,000 times more luminous than the Sun and red giant companion (B1 + K4), 5,900 + 150 lya.*	*4.8 + 3.6*
η	*One of Scorpius' closest stars to the Earth (F1), 50 lya.*	*3.3*

Serpens

Serpentis (Ser)

THE EAGLE NEBULA
(M16), with its dark columns of dust shown in this very high resolution Hubble Space Telescope image, has become one of the most popular astronomical images of all time.

This is the only constellation that is made up of two parts – Serpens Cauda, the body of the serpent, and Serpens Caput, the serpent's head. The serpent is the symbol of Aesculapius, also known as Ophiuchus, the god of medicine. The constellation of Ophiuchus lies between the two parts of the serpent. In Serpens lies the large, bright Eagle Nebula (M16), which also contains an open cluster. The open cluster is visible with binoculars, but appears hazy due to the surrounding nebula. Larger aperture or long-exposure photography is needed to reveal detail within the nebula. Serpens is also home to M5, a bright globular cluster that can be seen with the naked eye under dark skies. Another naked-eye object is the open cluster IC 4756, an interesting target for binocular viewing.

NORTHERN CELESTIAL HEMISPHERE

M5 *is one of the finest globular clusters in the northern sky. It appears fuzzy through binoculars but starts to reveal stars when observed with larger telescopes.*

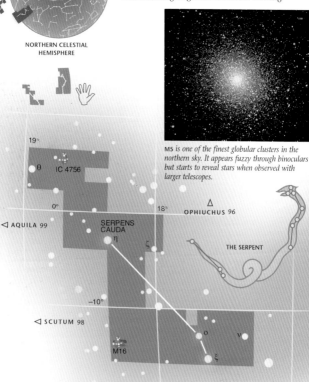

OBJECT NAME	DESCRIPTION	MAG.
M5	*Large and bright globular cluster, 24,000 lya. Naked eye object under favourable conditions.*	5.8
EAGLE NEBULA (M16)	*Nebula + open cluster, 8,000 lya. Cluster visible with binoculars; large telescope needed for nebula details.*	6.0
IC 4756	*Open cluster, 1,300 lya. Very clear with binoculars.*	5.4

STAR NAME	DESCRIPTION	MAG.
UNUKALHAI (α)	*Orange giant (K2), 72 lya.*	2.6
β	*Blue-white main sequence star (A2), with 10th mag. companion, 153 lya. Split by small telescopes.*	3.6
γ	*White main sequence star (F6), 36 lya.*	3.8
δ	*Long period binary (A9 + A7), 210 lya, orbital period in thousands of years. Split with small telescopes.*	4.2 + 5.2
ε	*Blue-white star (A2), 107 lya.*	3.7
ζ	*Yellow sub-giant (F2), 75 lya.*	4.6
η	*Orange giant (K0), 62 lya.*	3.2

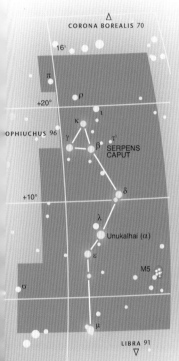

FULLY VISIBLE 74°N–64°S

NOTE

The upper part of the serpent contains Unukalhai (α), which means "the serpent's neck" in Arabic. In Greek mythology, serpents were a symbol of rebirth, since they shed their skins.

IC 4756 *is a scattered open cluster easily visible to the naked eye. Binoculars show the cluster particularly well, as does a telescope with a wide field and low magnification.*

THE EAGLE NEBULA *(M16) is an 800,000-year old nebula and cluster. The cluster stars appear embedded in a hazy mist when observed with binoculars.*

Ophiuchus

Ophiuchi (Oph)

M10 is a bright cluster, appearing about half the size of the full Moon. However, a moderate telescope is required to resolve details of the cluster.

The ancient constellation of Ophiuchus, straddling the celestial equator, depicts a man either holding a serpent (Serpens) on either side of his body, or with a serpent wrapped around him. It possibly represents the figure of Aesculapius (or Asclepius), the Greek god of medicine, who had the power to revive the dead. It is not a very bright constellation, but contains a number of interesting objects. It is especially rich in globular clusters – over 20 in number. This region of the night sky also contains large regions of nebulosity, popular with amateur astrophotographers. Its brightest star, Alpha (α), is also known as Rasalhague, which means "head of the serpent collector" in Arabic.

SOUTHERN CELESTIAL HEMISPHERE

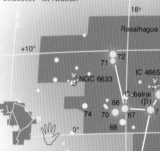

FULLY VISIBLE 59°N–75°S

◁ SERPENS CAUDA

REGIONS OF *nebulosity within Ophiuchus and Scorpius; the bright star visible below is Antares, the Alpha (α) star of Scorpio.*

OBJECT NAME	DESCRIPTION	MAG.
M10	*Large globular cluster, 14,000 lya.*	6.6
M12	*Large and bright globular cluster, 18,000 lya. Target for binoculars or small telescope.*	6.6
M19	*Globular cluster, 28,000 lya. Elongation visible through binoculars.*	7.2
NGC 6633	*Open cluster of about 30 stars, 950 lya. Good target for binoculars.*	4.6
IC 4665	*Open cluster of over 20 stars, 1,100 lya. Best seen with binoculars.*	4.2

STAR NAME	DESCRIPTION	MAG.
RASALHAGUE (α)	*White main sequence star (A5), 47 lya.*	*2.1*
CEBALRAI (β)	*Orange giant (K2), 82 lya.*	*2.8*
γ	*Blue-white main sequence star (A0), 95 lya.*	*3.7*
YED PRIOR (δ)	*Red giant (M1), 170 lya.*	*2.7*
YED POSTERIOR (ε)	*Yellow giant (G9), 108 lya.*	*3.2*
HAN (ζ)	*Blue main sequence star (O9), 458 lya.*	*2.5*
SABIK (η)	*Blue-white main sequence star (A2), 84 lya.*	*2.4*
ρ	*Multiple system (B2), 400 lya. Split with binoculars or small telescope.*	*5.0 + 5.7 + 6.7 + 7.3*
70	*Binary yellow and orange stars in 88-year orbit (K0 + K6), 16 lya. Easily split with small telescope.*	*4.2 + 6.0*

M12, *one of the brightest globular clusters in Ophiuchus, is slightly larger but fainter than M10. It was once believed to be an intermediate type between globular and dense open clusters, as it is not very concentrated.*

17ʰ

ι
κ

HERCULES 72 ▷

λ

SERPENS CAPUT 94 ▷

41

30 M10   M12

Yed Posterior (ε)   Yed Prior (δ)

υ

20   Han (ζ)

M107

SCORPIUS 92 ▷

THE SERPENT HOLDER

Sabik (η)

M9

φ   χ

ξ

ω   ψ

Ecliptic

ρ

M19   Antares

6   M62

◁ SAGITTARIUS 136

M19 *is a fairly rich and dense cluster. It is the most oblate (or "egg-shaped") globular cluster known, with its unusual shape discernible even with binoculars.*

Scutum

Scuti (Sct)

THE WILD DUCK CLUSTER (M11) appears as a hazy patch with binoculars, but a small telescope resolves the individual stars, revealing its shape.

In 1684, the Polish astronomer Johannes Hevelius introduced a constellation, *Scutum Sobiescianum*, which means Sobieski's Shield, to honour his patron, King John III Sobieski of Poland. Now known simply as Scutum, this small constellation is crossed by the Milky Way, which is why it contains rich star clouds, ideal for sweeping with binoculars. The Scutum Star Cloud is the brightest part of the Milky Way outside Sagittarius. The best target for amateur astronomers is the Wild Duck Cluster (M11), named after its fan shape that resembles a flock of ducks in flight when viewed with a small telescope. The variable Delta (δ) star has tiny changes in brightness that are too small and fast for amateur astronomers.

SOUTHERN CELESTIAL HEMISPHERE

FULLY VISIBLE
74°N–90°S

THE SHIELD

M26 is an open cluster consisting of about 30 to 40 stars, and being faint, it is best observed with larger apertures.

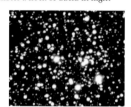

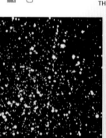

NGC 6712 is not visible with the naked eye or binoculars. A moderate telescope with 100mm aperture is required to detect it, while a larger telescope of 200mm reveals individual stars.

NAME	DESCRIPTION	MAG.
α	Orange giant (K3), 174 lya.	3.8
β	Yellow giant (G4), 690 lya.	4.2
γ	Blue-white main sequence star (A1), 290 lya.	4.7
δ	White giant (F2), 187 lya. Pulsating variable star.	4.6–4.8
WILD DUCK CLUSTER (M11)	Open cluster, 5,600 lya. A good target for binoculars, improves with larger apertures.	6.3
M26	Open cluster, 5,000 lya.	8.0
NGC 6712	Sparse globular cluster, 22,000 lya.	8.2
IC 1287	Nebula, 1,000 lya. Visible with 75mm aperture but a difficult target.	5.5
IC 1295	Planetary nebula, 3,600 lya. Best suited to larger telescopes.	12.5

Aquila

Aquilae (Aql)

This constellation of the northern sky was known as an eagle to observers over 3,000 years ago. According to mythology, the eagle, owned by the Greek god Zeus, kidnapped Ganymede (Aquarius) and brought him to Mount Olympus to serve as a cupbearer. It is a poor constellation for naked-eye objects, and the few open clusters and planetary nebulae are too faint to be observed with binoculars.

NGC 6781 is a faint, challenging planetary nebula that is best viewed with long-exposure photography.

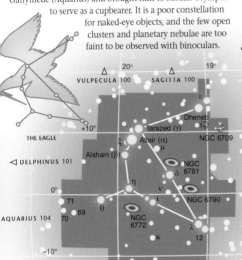

NORTHERN CELESTIAL HEMISPHERE

FULLY VISIBLE 78°N–71°S

NGC 6772 is a faint nebula in Aquila, which requires a large aperture or astrophotography to detect fine detail.

NGC 6790 is a small and bright nebula. Small telescopes of 75mm aperture can just detect the object, but larger apertures resolve fine detail.

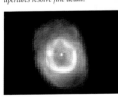

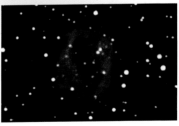

NAME	DESCRIPTION	MAG.
ALTAIR (α)	*White main sequence star (A7), 17 lya.*	0.7
ALSHAIN (β)	*Yellow sub-giant (G8), 45 lya.*	3.7
TARAZED (γ)	*Orange giant (K3), 460 lya.*	2.7
δ	*Yellow-orange star (F0), 50 lya.*	3.4
ε	*Orange sub-giant (K1), 155 lya.*	4.0
DHENEB (ζ)	*Blue-white star (B9), 83 lya.*	3.0
η	*Yellow-white supergiant (F6), variable with 7.2 day period, 1,200 lya.*	3.5-4.4
NGC 6772	*Faint planetary nebula, 4,100 lya. A challenge for larger telescopes.*	12.3
NGC 6781	*Faint planetary nebula, 2,500 lya.*	11.8
NGC 6790	*Planetary nebula, 10,000 lya.*	10.5

Sagitta

Sagittae (Sge)

M71 *appears as a fuzzy star when viewed through binoculars, and at least 150mm of aperture is needed before the stars are resolved.*

The third smallest constellation in the night sky, Sagitta has been known since ancient times. It represents an arrow, which, according to one Greek legend, is the arrow shot by Hercules to kill a vulture tormenting Chiron, the centaur. There is little of interest to the amateur astronomer in Sagitta, except the globular cluster M71, and even that is too faint at magnitude 8.5 for naked-eye observation. It lies midway along the arrow's shaft, 13,000 light years away.

NORTHERN CELESTIAL HEMISPHERE

FULLY VISIBLE
90°N–69°S

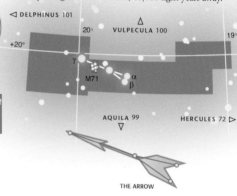

◁ DELPHINUS 101

VULPECULA 100

+20°

γ

M71

α

β

AQUILA 99

HERCULES 72 ▷

THE ARROW

Vulpecula

Vulpeculae (Vul)

M27 *is detectable as a bluish disc with binoculars; its dumbbell shape is revealed through a telescope.*

Introduced in the late 17th century by the Polish astronomer Johannes Hevelius who called it *Vulpecula cum Anser* (the Fox and Goose), Vulpecula lies to the south of Cygnus. It contains M27, the large and bright Dumbbell Nebula, about 1,000 light years away, with a magnitude of 7.4. M27 was discovered in 1764 by the French astronomer Charles Messier, and it is perhaps the best planetary nebulae for amateur observation. The open cluster, Brocchi's Cluster lies in the southern part of Vulpecula while the open cluster NGC 6882, lies in the north.

NORTHERN CELESTIAL HEMISPHERE

FULLY VISIBLE
90°N–61°S

THE FOX

+30°

21ʰ

20ʰ

31

NGC 6882

23

15

30

13

α

+20°

29

M27

12

Brocchi's Cluster

1

◁ PEGASUS 61

DELPHINUS 101

AQUILA 99

Delphinus

Delphini (Del)

This is a small constellation situated between Aquila and Pegasus and represents a dolphin. According to Greek mythology, dolphins were the messengers of the sea god Poseidon. The two brightest stars in Delphinus are Alpha (α) and Beta (β) – first named in a star catalogue compiled at the Palermo Observatory in 1814. When their common names, Sualocin and Rotanev, are read backwards they become Nicolaus Venator, which is the Latinized name of Niccolo Cattiatore, an assistant astronomer at the observatory who named the stars after himself.

NGC 6934 is a small globular cluster that only reveals its member stars when viewed with larger apertures.

NORTHERN CELESTIAL HEMISPHERE

FULLY VISIBLE 90°N–69°S

THE DOLPHIN

NOTE	THE BLUE FLASH
"Job's Coffin" is the name given to the asterism formed by the four brightest stars of this constellation, perhaps because of its box-like shape.	NEBULA (NGC 6905) is a faint planetary nebula which can be detected with only 100mm aperture, but its bluish colouring only becomes apparent with larger telescopes.

NAME	DESCRIPTION	MAG.
SUALOCIN (α)	*Blue-white main sequence star (B9), 241 lya.*	*3.8*
ROTANEV (β)	*Yellow binary (F5), 97 lya. Only splits with larger telescopes.*	*4.0 + 4.9*
γ	*Yellow and yellow-white stars (G5 + Γ8), 102 lya. Splits easily with small telescopes.*	*4.5 + 5.5*
δ	*White giant (A7), 204 lya.*	*4.4*
BLUE FLASH NEBULA (NGC 6905)	*Planetary nebula, 4,700 lya. Can be detected with a small telescope.*	*11.1*
NGC 6934	*Globular cluster, 49,000 lya. Detectable with small telescopes.*	*8.9*

Pegasus

Pegasi (Peg)

NGC 7332 (right) has a distinct peanut shape, and is brighter than NGC 7339 (left). Both galaxies can be detected with small telescopes.

NORTHERN CELESTIAL HEMISPHERE

FULLY VISIBLE 90°N–53°S

Famous as the winged horse in Greek mythology, Pegasus was born from Medusa's blood, after she was killed by the mythological Greek hero Perseus. Lying north of Aquarius and Pisces and adjoining Andromeda, the constellation represents the horse's upper body. Its most distinctive feature is the Square of Pegasus, made up of the four stars – Alpha (α), Beta (β), Gamma (γ), and Alpha (α) Andromedae. This constellation now has no Delta star, as it has been assigned to the constellation Andromeda. Pegasus is home to the bright globular cluster M15, one of the finest in the northern skies, which is visible with binoculars and small telescopes and can be also seen by the naked eye in favourable conditions. The yellow main sequence star 51 was the first to be found with a planet.

◁ ANDROMEDA 78

α Andromedae

Great Square of Pegasus

Algenib (γ)

◁ PISCES 141

NGC 7331, a barred spiral galaxy, has a structure similar to the Milky Way. Seen almost edge-on from the Earth, this galaxy is easily visible with moderate telescopes of 100mm aperture.

Equuleus

Equulei (Equ)

TO THE LEFT of the stars of Equuleus lies Enif (ε), which is an orange supergiant lying in Pegasus. It can be seen with the naked eye.

The second smallest constellation in the night sky (Crux is the smallest), Equuleus was mentioned, along with 48 other constellations, by the Greek astronomer Ptolemy in the second century CE. The constellation represents a foal or small horse that lies next to the winged horse, Pegasus. It includes double and multiple stars, and its brightest star is the yellow giant, Kitalpha, the Alpha (α) star, which has a magnitude of 3.9 and lies 186 light years away. There is little of interest in this constellation to the amateur astronomer in the way of deep-sky objects.

THE LITTLE HORSE

NAME	DESCRIPTION	MAG.
MARKAB (α)	*Blue-white giant (B9), 140 lya.*	*2.5*
SCHEAT (β)	*Red giant (M2), 199 lya. Varies with no period.*	*2.3–2.7*
ALGENIB (γ)	*Pulsating variable (B2), 333 lya.*	*2.8*
ENIF (ε)	*Orange supergiant and faint blue companion (K2), 670 lya.*	*2.4 + 8.4*
HOMAM (ζ)	*Blue-white main sequence star (B8), 209 lya.*	*3.4*
MATAR (η)	*Yellow giant (G2), 215 lya.*	*2.9*
51	*Yellow main sequence star (G2), 50 lya.*	*5.5*
M15	*Globular cluster, 33,000 lya.*	*6.2*
NGC 7331	*Edge-on barred spiral galaxy, 49 million lya.*	*9.5*
NGC 7332	*Flattened elliptical galaxy, 63 million lya.*	*10.9*

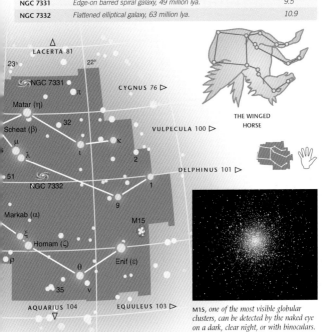

LACERTA 81

23ʰ 22ʰ

NGC 7331

Matar (η)

CYGNUS 76 ▷

32

Scheat (β)

VULPECULA 100 ▷

μ λ ι κ

2

51

NGC 7332

DELPHINUS 101 ▷

1

9

Markab (α)

M15

ξ

Homam (ζ)

ρ

θ Enif (ε)

35 ν

AQUARIUS 104 ▽ EQUULEUS 103 ▷

THE WINGED HORSE

M15, *one of the most visible globular clusters, can be detected by the naked eye on a dark, clear night, or with binoculars. The view improves with a larger aperture.*

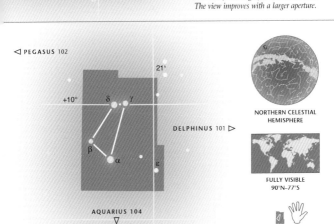

◁ PEGASUS 102

+10°

21ʰ

δ γ

β

α ε

DELPHINUS 101 ▷

AQUARIUS 104 ▽

NORTHERN CELESTIAL HEMISPHERE

FULLY VISIBLE 90°N–77°S

Aquarius

Aquarii (Aqr)

THE HELIX NEBULA *(NGC 7293) needs a telescope of moderate aperture to see any detail. Smaller instruments show it as a faint patch.*

Originally known to ancient civilizations as the Water, or the Sea, Aquarius is now known as the Water-bearer. According to Greek mythology, Aquarius represents Ganymede, a young shepherd taken by Zeus (Jupiter) to Mount Olympus to serve as cupbearer to the gods. The constellation has also been associated with the Sumerian myth of a global flood, a myth that could be the source of the biblical story of "Noah's Flood". Aquarius is located in the sky close to other aquatic constellations: Pisces (fish), Eridanus (river), and Delphinus (dolphin). It contains the globular clusters M2, an easy target for binocular viewing, and M72, which requires a more powerful instrument. The most spectacular object in Aquarius is the Helix Nebula, but it only appears as a faint patch through binoculars, and even then, clear dark skies are needed.

SOUTHERN CELESTIAL HEMISPHERE

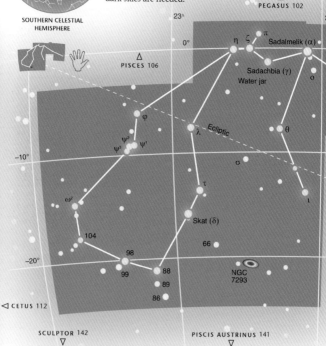

OBJECT NAME	DESCRIPTION	MAG.
M2	*Globular cluster, 35,000 lya. Easy binocular object.*	6.5
M72	*Globular cluster, 58,000 lya. Requires small telescope.*	9.5
SATURN NEBULA (NGC 7009)	*Planetary nebula, 2,400 lya. Bright blue disc, needs larger instruments to see detail.*	8.0
HELIX NEBULA (NGC 7293)	*Planetary nebula, 450 lya. Closest planetary nebula to the Earth, about half the apparent size of the Moon.*	8.0

M2 is an easy target for binocular viewing, but needs an aperture of 150mm before individual stars within the cluster can be clearly resolved.

NOTE

For southern-hemisphere observers, the Eta Aquarid meteor shower puts on a spectacular display in May with up to 50 meteors per hour. Each meteor is a tiny piece of Halley's comet.

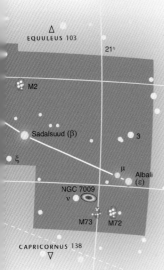

△
EQUULEUS 103

21ʰ

M2

Sadalsuud (β)

3

ξ

μ

Albali (ε)

NGC 7009
ν

M73 M72

CAPRICORNUS 138
▽

M72 is too faint for the naked eye and can just about be seen through binoculars. It appears hazy with moderate telescopes.

AQUARIUS

NGC 7009 was named the Saturn Nebula by the 19th century astronomer Lord Rosse, since its appearance in a telescope is similar to Saturn's.

FULLY VISIBLE 65°N–86°S

STAR NAME	DESCRIPTION	MAG.
SADALMELIK (α)	*Yellow supergiant (G2), 760 lya.*	*2.9*
SADALSUUD (β)	*Yellow supergiant (G0), 610 lya.*	*2.9*
SADACHBIA (γ)	*Blue-white main sequence star (B9), 158 lya.*	*3.9*
SKAT (δ)	*Blue-white main sequence star (A2), 160 lya.*	*3.3*
ALBALI (ε)	*Blue-white main sequence star (A1), 102 lya.*	*3.8*
ζ	*Binary, two white stars (F2 + F2), in an orbital period of 760 days, 103 lya. Can be split with small telescope.*	*4.4 + 4.5*

Pisces

Piscium (Psc)

Pisces has been known since ancient times as either a fish or pair of fishes. This constellation of the zodiac can be traced back to the Babylonians. According to Greek mythology, Pisces represents Venus (Aphrodite) and her son Cupid (Eros) who escaped the monster Typhon by disguising themselves as fishes. Although Pisces is a large constellation, it does not contain many objects of interest to the amateur astronomer. There are no open or globular clusters, but the constellation does contain M74, a face-on spiral galaxy that has a diameter of about 80,000 light years. The galaxy can be seen through a small telescope as a rounded, fuzzy patch, but larger apertures are needed in order to see any detail.

THE STARS OF PISCES include the white star seen in the centre of the image – Alpha (α), Alrescha, actually a pair of stars that are currently moving closer together. The orange star at the upper left is Alpha (α) Ceti.

NORTHERN CELESTIAL HEMISPHERE

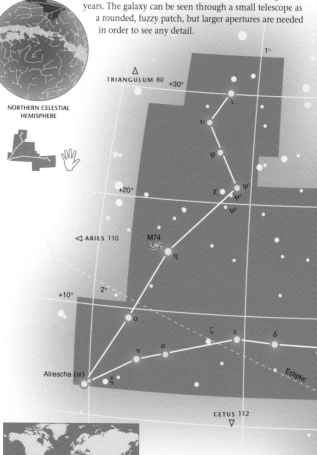

TRIANGULUM 80

◁ ARIES 110

M74

Alrescha (α)

CETUS 112

Ecliptic

FULLY VISIBLE 83°N–56°S

NAME	DESCRIPTION	MAG.
ALRESCHA (α)	*Double (A2), in an orbital period of 933 years, 140 lya, possible quadruple system. Needs 100mm aperture.*	4.2 + 5.2
β	*Blue-white main sequence star (B5), 493 lya.*	5.4
γ	*Yellow giant (G8), 179 lya.*	3.7
δ	*Orange giant (K4), 281 lya.*	4.4
ε	*Yellow giant (G9), 215 lya.*	4.3
ζ	*Double (F0), 148 lya. Can be split with a small telescope.*	5.2 + 6.4
η	*Yellow giant (G8), 294 lya. The brightest star in Pisces.*	3.6
M74	*Face-on spiral galaxy, 25 million lya.*	9.2

M74 is too faint to be seen with the naked eye, but a moderate aperture telescope will start to reveal its structure. Larger apertures are needed to see its spiral arms, which also show well on long-exposure photographs.

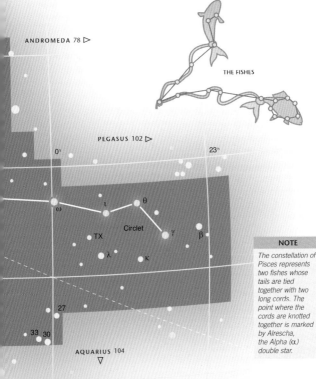

THE FISHES

ANDROMEDA 78 ▷

PEGASUS 102 ▷

0°

23ʰ

ω

ι

θ

Circlet

γ

β

TX

λ

κ

27

33 30

AQUARIUS 104
▽

ANDROMEDA 78 ▷

PEGASUS 102 ▷

AQUARIUS 104

NOTE

The constellation of Pisces represents two fishes whose tails are tied together with two long cords. The point where the cords are knotted together is marked by Alrescha, the Alpha (α) double star.

Taurus

Tauri (Tau)

THE PLEIADES (M45) *has six stars visible to the eye, but binoculars show dozens more, presenting a spectacular sight. Moderate telescopes or long-exposure photographs reveal the nebulosity.*

This is an ancient northern constellation of the zodiac, representing the bull disguise used by Zeus when he abducted Princess Europa of Phoenicia. Taurus lies between Aries and Gemini and contains a variety of objects, some visible to the naked eye and excellent targets for binoculars and small telescopes. The brightest star in Taurus is the giant Aldebaran, its red colour easily discernible to the naked eye. Taurus contains two open clusters: M45, the large, bright open star cluster also known as the Pleiades, or the Seven Sisters, and the far more scattered Hyades, which has about 200 stars.

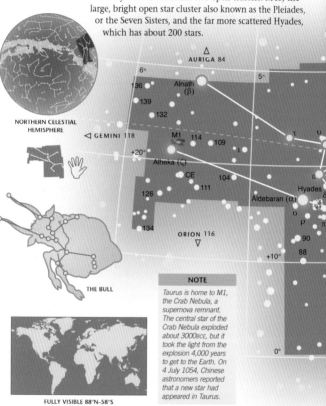

NORTHERN CELESTIAL HEMISPHERE

THE BULL

FULLY VISIBLE 88°N–58°S

NOTE

Taurus is home to M1, the Crab Nebula, a supernova remnant. The central star of the Crab Nebula exploded about 3000BCE, but it took the light from the explosion 4,000 years to get to the Earth. On 4 July 1054, Chinese astronomers reported that a new star had appeared in Taurus.

NAME	DESCRIPTION	MAG.
ALDEBARAN (α)	Variable red giant (K5), 65 lya. Possibly a six-star system.	0.75–0.95
ALNATH (β)	Blue-white giant (B7), 131 lya.	1.6
γ	Yellow giant (K0), 140 lya.	3.6
δ	Yellow giant (K0), 150 lya.	3.8
ε	Yellow giant (K0), 135 lya.	3.5
ALHEKA (ζ)	Close binary system (B2), 417 lya.	3.0
HYADES	Loose V-shaped open cluster, 150 lya.	0.5
CRAB NEBULA (M1)	Supernova remnant, 6,500 lya.	8.4
PLEIADES (M45)	Open cluster, 378 lya. Binoculars give best view.	4.17

PLEIADES STARS	DESCRIPTION	MAG.
ALCYONE (η)	*Blue-white giant (B7), 378 lya.*	2.8
ATLAS (27)	*Blue-white giant (B8), 378 lya.*	3.6
ELECTRA (17)	*Blue-white giant (B6), 378 lya.*	3.7
MAIA (20)	*Blue-white giant (B7), 378 lya.*	3.8
MEROPE (23)	*Blue-white giant (B6), 378 lya.*	4.2
TAYGETA (19)	*Blue-white giant (B6), 378 lya.*	4.3
PLEIONE (28)	*Blue-white giant (B8), 378 lya.*	5.1
CELAENO (16)	*Blue-white giant (B7), 378 lya.*	5.4
ASTEROPE (21 + 22)	*Blue-white giant (B8 + B9), 378 lya.*	5.6 + 6.4

Δ
PERSEUS 82

4"

THE PLEIADES *occupies an area four times the size of the Moon and represents the mythical Seven Sisters and their parents, Atlas and Pleione. Only six of the seven stars are visible to the naked eye and there are two myths to explain the "missing Pleiad". One myth is that the least bright star is Merope, who was the only sister to marry a mortal. The other is that it is Electra, who could not bear to watch the fall of Troy. In reality, however, the faintest star is named Asterope.*

Asterope (21+22)   Taygeta (19)
Maia (20)   Celaeno (16)
Pleione (28)   Alcyone (η)
Atlas (27)   Electra (17)
Merope (23)

Pleiades
(M45)

37

Ecliptic

ARIES 110 ▷

λ

5

σ

ξ

7

ο

ν

10

CETUS 112 ▷

THE HYADES, *a scattered open cluster, forms the easily recognizable V-shape of Taurus and is best viewed with binoculars. The bright red star is Aldebaran, but is not part of the cluster.*

ERIDANUS 114
▽

THE CRAB NEBULA *(M1) is not visible to the naked eye, and can only be seen with binoculars under excellent viewing conditions. A moderate telescope is needed to discern details.*

Aries

Arietis (Ari)

This constellation represents Aries, the golden-fleeced ram of ancient Greek mythology. Ancient astronomers visualized the figure of the crouching ram from the crooked line formed by three faint stars of the constellation: the Alpha (α), Beta (β), and Gamma (γ) stars. Viewed from the Earth, the Sun's position against the background stars is constantly changing, and each year the Sun crosses the celestial equator, moving from the southern celestial hemisphere to the northern celestial hemisphere. The point at which the Sun crosses the celestial equator is known as the vernal equinox or the First Point of Aries. However, due to the Earth's slow wobble on its axis (precession), the vernal equinox has now moved out of Aries and into neighbouring Pisces. Aries contains little of interest to amateur observers.

THE STARS OF ARIES *include Hamal (α), bottom centre of the image. Top left is the cluster Pleiades and the orange giant to the right of Hamal is Beta (β) Andromedae.*

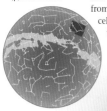

NORTHERN CELESTIAL HEMISPHERE

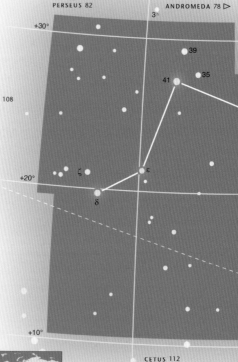

Δ
PERSEUS 82

ANDROMEDA 78 ▷

3ʰ

+30°

39

35

41

◁ TAURUS 108

ε

+20°

ζ

δ

+10°

CETUS 112
▽

FULLY VISIBLE 90°N–58°S

NGC 772 *is a difficult target that reveals little with a small telescope. Even larger telescopes do not show much more than the central regions.*

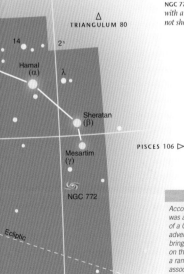

THE RAM

PISCES 106 ▷

NOTE

According to ancient Greek mythology, Aries was a ram with a golden fleece. Jason, the son of a Greek king, with the Argonauts, his fellow adventurers, embarked on an epic voyage to bring the fleece back to Greece from Colchis on the Black Sea. Aries was also identified as a ram by the ancient Egyptians, who associated it with their god Amon Ra.

NAME	DESCRIPTION	MAG.
HAMAL (α)	*Orange giant (K2), 66 lya.*	*2.0*
SHERATAN (β)	*Blue-white main sequence star (A5), 60 lya.*	*2.6*
MESARTIM (γ)	*Double star, (A0 + A1), 204 lya. Can be split with a small telescope.*	*4.7 + 4.6*
δ	*Red giant (K2), 168 lya.*	*4.3*
ε	*Two white stars (A2 + A2), 290 lya. Requires 100mm to split.*	*5.2 + 5.5*
λ	*White star with faint yellow companion (F0), 133 lya.*	*4.8 + 7.3*
NGC 772	*Spiral galaxy, 130 million lya. Small apertures show a hazy spot.*	*10.3*

Cetus

Ceti (Cet)

Although it is the fourth largest constellation in the sky, Cetus contains few bright deep-sky objects. It lies to the south of Pisces and Aries and is one of the original 48 Greek constellations listed by Ptolemy in his *Almagest*. In 1596, the Dutchman David Fabricius noticed what he thought was a new star in Cetus. In fact it was not a new star, but Omicron (o) which had increased in brightness. Also known as Mira, from the Latin for "wonderful", it was the first variable star to be discovered. Mira, which varies in brightness over a period of 331.96 days, is the prototype of a class of long-period variable stars. Such a change in brightness can be monitored with the naked eye.

M77 is the brightest of the Seyfert galaxies, a class of galaxies that have extremely bright centres. However, large telescopes are required to see its details.

SOUTHERN CELESTIAL HEMISPHERE

FULLY VISIBLE 65°N–79°S

THE SEA MONSTER

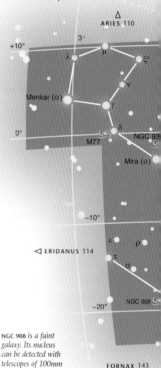

NGC 908 is a faint galaxy. Its nucleus can be detected with telescopes of 100mm aperture, but larger instruments are needed before any spiral arm detail can be observed.

OBJECT NAME	DESCRIPTION	MAG.
M77	Spiral galaxy, 40 million lya. Nucleus can be seen with binoculars.	8.8
NGC 246	Bright planetary nebula, 1,450 lya.	8.5
NGC 247	Edge-on spiral galaxy, 13 million lya.	8.9
NGC 908	Edge-on barred spiral galaxy, 65 million lya.	10.2
NGC 936	Barred spiral galaxy, 50 million lya. Requires 100mm aperture.	10.1

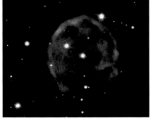

NGC 246 can be detected with binoculars. However, due to the low surface brightness of the object, a large telescope with at least 150mm aperture is required to observe detail.

NGC 247 is too faint for the naked eye, but can be detected with binoculars and requires larger telescopes for detail. It is a member of the Sculptor Group of galaxies.

NOTE

Cetus is represented as a sea monster. In Greek myth, Cetus was sent by the sea god Poseidon to devour the princess Andromeda, but was killed by the hero Perseus.

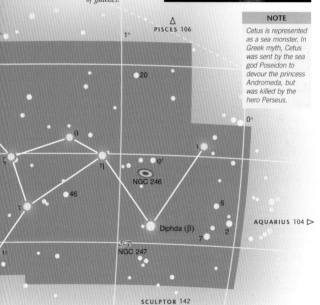

△
PISCES 106

1^h

20

0^h

θ

ζ

η

ι

φ¹

NGC 246

46

τ

6

Diphda (β)

7

2

AQUARIUS 104 ▷

υ

NGC 247

SCULPTOR 142
▽

STAR NAME	DESCRIPTION	MAG.
MENKAR (α)	Red giant (M2), 220 lya. Forms line-of-sight double with 5.6 mag. star.	2.5
DIPHDA / DENEB KAITOS (β)	Orange giant (K0), 96 lya. The brightest star in Cetus.	2.0
γ	Close double (A3 + F3), 82 lya. Splits with 75mm aperture.	3.5 + 6.2
δ	Blue-white sub-giant (B2), 650 lya.	4.1
ε	Yellow main sequence star (F5), 88 lya.	4.8
MIRA (ο)	Variable red giant (M7), 420 lya.	3.5–9.5

Eridanus

Eridani (Eri)

This constellation, which represents a river, is the sixth largest in the sky, and also the second longest. Various mythologies have identified Eridanus with different rivers, from the Nile to the Euphrates to the Po. However, as it consists of faint stars, the constellation is not given much notice. Although it covers a large area, it contains few bright deep-sky objects. There are no open or globular clusters visible with amateur instruments, but there are a few galaxies visible, and one planetary nebula that can be seen with binoculars under favourable conditions.

THE WITCH HEAD NEBULA *(IC 2118), so named for its resemblance to a witch's face, can be seen with the naked eye, but only under clear conditions and dark skies.*

SOUTHERN CELESTIAL HEMISPHERE

NGC 1300, an almost face-on barred spiral galaxy, can be detected with small telescopes as a hazy patch, but a telescope with a 250mm aperture will show its structure.

OBJECT NAME	DESCRIPTION	MAG.
NGC 1291	Barred spiral galaxy, 22 million lya. Visible with binoculars.	8.5
NGC 1300	Barred spiral galaxy, 46 million lya. Requires moderate telescope.	11.0
NGC 1532	Spiral galaxy, 54 million lya. NGC 1531 in same field of view.	11.1
NGC 1535	Planetary nebula, 1,700 lya.	9.6
WITCH HEAD NEBULA (IC 2118)	Nebula, 1,000 lya. The low surface brightness of the nebula demands low magnification if a telescope is used.	5.0

STAR NAME	DESCRIPTION	MAG.
ACHERNAR (α)	*Blue-white main sequence star (B5), 140 lya.*	*0.5*
CURSA (β)	*Blue-white giant (A3), 89 lya.*	*2.8*
ZAURAK (γ)	*Red giant (M0), 140 lya. One of the brightest in the sky.*	*2.9*
δ	*Orange sub-giant (K0), 28 lya.*	*3.5*
ϵ	*Orange main sequence star (K2), 11 lya. Orbited by a large planet.*	*3.7*
ZIBAL (ζ)	*Blue-white star (A5), 52 lya.*	*4.8*
AZHA (η)	*Orange giant (K1), 72 lya.*	*3.9*
ACAMAR (θ)	*Blue-white stars (A3 + A2), 160 lya. Can be split by small telescope.*	*3.2 + 4.3*
40 (o)	*Orange and white dwarfs (K1), 16 lya. Visible with small telescope.*	*4.4 + 9.5*

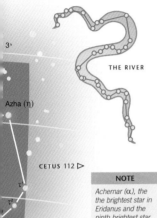

3ʰ

Azha (η)

THE RIVER

CETUS 112 ▷

τ^1

τ^2

FORNAX 143 ▷

FULLY VISIBLE 32°N–89°S

NOTE

Achernar (α), the the brightest star in Eridanus and the ninth brightest star in the sky, gets its name from an Arabic word that means "river's end"; it marks the constellation's southernmost tip.

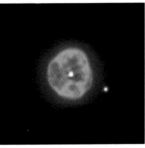

NGC 1535 *is a planetary nebula that is visible with binoculars. Larger telescopes and greater magnification is needed before either fine detail or the greenish colour can be observed.*

ι

amar

PHOENIX ▷
154

κ

φ

χ

Achernar (α)

NGC 1532 *has a nearby small elliptical galaxy, NGC 1531. NGC 1532 is visible with small telescopes, but the galaxy is faint and requires a larger telescope to bring out detail.*

Orion

Orionis (Ori)

THE ORION NEBULA *becomes more complex when viewed with binoculars. This amateur photograph reveals the structures within the nebula.*

The constellation of Orion is perhaps the best known since ancient times. The Syrians knew it as Al Jabbar, the Giant, and the ancient Egyptians as Sahu, the soul of Osiris. Its position on the celestial equator ensures that it can be seen from all over the world. Orion contains M42, the Orion Nebula, visible to the naked eye as a patch of light. This is a region of active star formation, with over 700 young stars, and the associated nebulosity is illuminated by four hot giant stars called the Trapezium (Theta). Orion contains several regions of nebulosity and is a very rewarding constellation for astrophotographers.

NORTHERN CELESTIAL HEMISPHERE

ORION

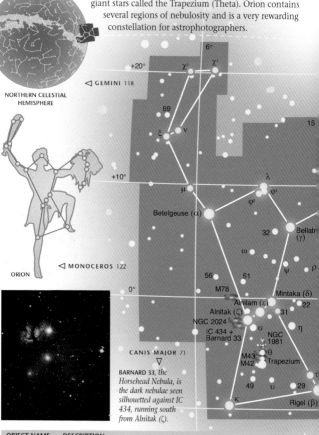

◁ GEMINI 118

◁ MONOCEROS 122

CANIS MAJOR 71
▽

BARNARD 33, *the Horsehead Nebula, is the dark nebulae seen silhouetted against IC 434, running south from Alnitak (ζ).*

OBJECT NAME	DESCRIPTION	MAG.
ORION NEBULA (M42 + M43)	Nebula, 1,500 lya. Can be seen with the naked eye as well as binoculars.	4.0 + 9.0
M78	Small faint reflection nebula and 10th mag. star, 1,600 lya.	8.3
BARNARD 33 + IC 434	Dark nebula + strip of nebulosity, 1,500 lya. Nebula shaped like the head of a horse, visible with small apertures, just below Alnitak.	
NGC 1981	Small open cluster of about 20 faint stars, 1,300 lya.	4.6
FLAME NEBULA (NGC 2024)	Bright nebula with dark dust lanes, 1,500 lya. Found next to Alnitak, easily visible with binoculars.	10.7

STAR NAME	DESCRIPTION	MAG.
BETELGEUSE (α)	*Red variable supergiant (M2), 800 times larger than the Sun, 427 lya.*	*0.0–1.3*
RIGEL (β)	*Hot blue hypergiant (B8) with two faint dwarf companions, 773 lya.*	*0.2 + 6.8*
BELLATRIX (γ)	*Blue giant (B2), 243 lya.*	*1.6*
MINTAKA (δ)	*Blue giant (O9), 2,000 lya. Companion needs binoculars/telescope.*	*2.2 + 6.9*
ALNILAM (ε)	*Blue supergiant (B0), 1,300 lya.*	*1.7*
ALNITAK (ζ)	*Blue supergiant (O9), 820 lya.*	*1.7 + 3.9*
η	*Double star, blue-white primary (B1), 900 lya.*	*3.8 + 4.8*
TRAPEZIUM (θ)	*Four stars seen with a small telescope (O, B), actually a 10-star system, 1,500 lya.*	*5.1 + 5.1+ 6.7 + 8.0*

FULLY VISIBLE 79°N–67°S

TAURUS 108 ▷

TRAPEZIUM, *the multiple star system of Theta (θ), can be seen illuminating the Orion Nebula. It is visible with small apertures.*

ERIDANUS 114 ▷

EPUS 144 ▽

5ʰ
1
Aldebaran
O¹
O²
π¹
π²
π³
π⁴
π⁵
π⁶

NOTE

Orion represents a giant hunter or warrior followed by his dogs, Canis Major and Canis Minor. According to Greek mythology, despite his hunting prowess, he was killed by a mere scorpion. In the sky, Orion is placed opposite Scorpius and, each night, the star appears to flee below the horizon as the scorpion rises.

WIDE-ANGLE VIEW *of Orion, showing the Orion Nebula, M42, below the blue giant belt star Alnitak (top of picture). Just below Alnitak can be seen the dark shape of Barnard 33, also known as the Horsehead Nebula.*

Gemini

Geminorum (Gem)

The constellation of Gemini represents Castor and Pollux, the twin sons of the Queen of Sparta. They sailed with Jason and the Argonauts on the quest for the Golden Fleece and were regarded as the patrons of seafarers. Castor and Pollux are the brightest stars in Gemini. Although they represent twins, the stars themselves are not related. Since only a small part of the Milky Way passes through Gemini, the constellation possesses few objects for amateur astronomers. The best object is the open cluster M35, a naked-eye object that appears as an elliptical, elongated patch of starlight through binoculars.

M35 *is an open cluster consisting of about 200 stars, some of which can be resolved with binoculars and instruments with small apertures.*

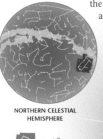

NORTHERN CELESTIAL HEMISPHERE

THE ESKIMO NEBULA *(NGC 2392), also known as the Clown Face Nebula, is not visible to the naked eye, but can be detected with small telescopes. Larger telescopes detect features that give it the appearance of a face, which explains its common names.*

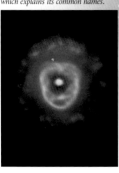

◁ LYNX 85

8ʰ

Castor (α)

ρ

τ

+30°

χ

σ

Pollux (β)

ι

φ

υ

◁ CANCER 120

κ

Wasat (δ)

+20°

NGC 2392

ζ

81

λ

+10°

3

CANIS MINOR 86
▽

OBJECT NAME	DESCRIPTION	MAG.
M35	*Open cluster, 2,800 lya.*	*5.1*
ESKIMO NEBULA (NGC 2392)	*Planetary nebula, 3,000 lya. Appears as a bluish disc in small telescopes, larger instruments required to discern detail.*	*9.1*
JELLYFISH NEBULA (IC 443)	*Nebula, 5,000 lya. A faint supernova remnant, suitable for larger apertures.*	*12.0*

NOTE

Although named after twins, Castor and Pollux are not identical. Castor is a multiple system of six stars, including a blue-white pair and a close pair of red dwarfs, while Pollux is an orange giant that lies closer to the Earth.

△
AURIGA 84

THE JELLYFISH NEBULA *(IC 443) is a faint supernova remnant near the bright Eta (η) star, Propus (top right). A pulsar has been recently discovered within the nebula.*

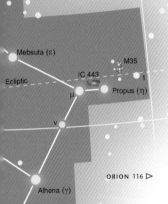

Mebsuta (ε)

M35

IC 443

Ecliptic

μ

1

Propus (η)

ν

ORION 116 ▷

Alhena (γ)

30

ζ

MONOCEROS 122
▽

THE TWINS

FULLY VISIBLE 90°N–55°S

STAR NAME	DESCRIPTION	MAG.
CASTOR (α)	*Multiple system (A0), 42 lya. Three stars visible with small telescope.*	*1.9 + 3.0*
POLLUX (β)	*Orange giant (K0), 34 lya. The brightest star in the constellation.*	*1.2*
ALHENA (γ)	*Blue-white sub-giant (A0), 105 lya.*	*1.9*
WASAT (δ)	*White star and orange dwarf (F0 + K3), 59 lya. Can be split with larger telescope.*	*3.5 + 8.2*
MEBSUTA (ε)	*Yellow supergiant (G8), 900 lya.*	*3.1*
ζ	*Variable (F7–G3), in a period of 10.15 days, 1,200 lya.*	*3.6–4.2*
PROPUS (η)	*Triple system, red and yellow giants (M3 + G0), 350 lya. One component is a variable, two stars visible with telescope.*	*3.1–3.9 + 6.5*

Cancer

Cancri (Cnc)

NORTHERN CELESTIAL HEMISPHERE

FULLY VISIBLE 90°N–57°S

PRAESEPE (M44), also called the Beehive Cluster, occupies an area three times the size of full Moon. It is visible to the naked eye.

According to Greek mythology, Cancer represents the crab that attacked Hercules during his fight with Hydra, but was crushed underfoot during the struggle. Cancer is the faintest of the twelve constellations of the zodiac, with no bright stars. The Milky Way does not run through Cancer, therefore, this constellation contains no nebulosity, globular clusters, or planetary nebulae within reach of amateur instruments. There are two open clusters: Praesepe (M44), which consists of a scattering of stars, and M67, which is smaller and more concentrated.

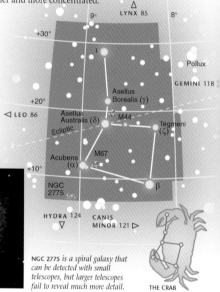

NGC 2775 is a spiral galaxy that can be detected with small telescopes, but larger telescopes fail to reveal much more detail.

THE CRAB

Canis Minor

Canis Minoris (CMi)

PROCYON, the Alpha (α) star, towards the top of the centre of this image, and Gomeisa, the Beta (β) star, below it, are the two brightest stars of Canis Minor.

This constellation represents the second of Orion's two hunting dogs. Although Canis Minor contains Procyon, the Alpha (α) star, which is the eighth brightest star in the night sky, it unfortunately contains nothing else of interest to the amateur astronomer. Procyon forms a glittering triangle with two other stars of first magnitude: Betelgeuse in Orion and Sirius in Canis Major.

THE LESSER DOG

STAR NAME	DESCRIPTION	MAG.
PROCYON (α)	*Yellow main sequence star and dwarf companion (F5), 11.4 lya. Too faint for amateur observation.*	0.4 + 10.7
GOMEISA (β)	*Blue-white main sequence star (B8), 170 lya.*	2.9

M67 is an open cluster that contains more stars than M44 but appears fainter. Binoculars show a hazy patch, but small telescopes reveal the individual stars, of which there are over 200.

NAME	DESCRIPTION	MAG.
ACUBENS (α)	White star (A5), 174 lya. Has a faint 12th mag. companion.	4.3
β	Orange giant (K4), 290 lya.	3.5
ASELLUS BOREALIS (γ)	White main sequence star (A1), 158 lya.	4.7
ASELLUS AUSTRALIS (δ)	Orange giant (K0), 136 lya.	3.9
TEGMENI (ζ)	Triple system (F8 + G0), 83 lya. Small telescope shows two stars, while larger telescope reveals three.	5.0 + 6.0 + 6.2
PRAESEPE (M44)	Open cluster of about 50 stars, 570 lya. Binoculars show patch.	3.7
M67	Open cluster, 2,500 lya.	6.1
NGC 2775	Spiral galaxy, 55 million lya.	10.3

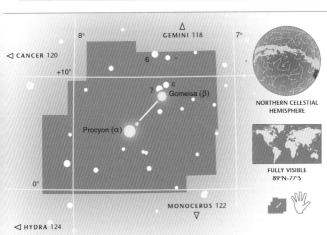

◁ CANCER 120

△ GEMINI 118

8ʰ   7ʰ

+10°

6

γ   ε
Gomeisa (β)

Procyon (α)

0°

NORTHERN CELESTIAL HEMISPHERE

FULLY VISIBLE
89°N–77°S

MONOCEROS 122
▽

◁ HYDRA 124

Monoceros

Monocerotis (Mon)

NGC 2237, the glowing Rosette Nebula, contains the open cluster NGC 2244. Large telescopes are needed to observe the surrounding nebulosity.

The origins of Monoceros, depicting the mythical unicorn, are unknown, but it first appeared in literature in the 17th century. The introduction of this constellation has been attributed to a German scientist Jakob Bartsch in 1624, as well as Dutch astronomer Petrus Plancius in 1613. Although rich in star clusters and nebulae because the Milky Way runs through it, Monoceros has no bright stars. The most well-known object within it is NGC 2237, the Rosette Nebula. The nebula is not visible to the naked eye and needs large telescopes to detect it. However, long-exposure photography reveals the beauty of this nebula, with its flower-like form, making it a popular target for amateur astrophotographers. NCC 2264, the Christmas Tree, is an open cluster that is visible with binoculars, and appears triangular when viewed through a small telescope.

SOUTHERN CELESTIAL HEMISPHERE

THE UNICORN

FULLY VISIBLE 78°N–78°S

M50 is best viewed with binoculars, which will resolve the brightest stars. The open cluster appears to be half the apparent width of the full Moon.

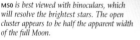

OBJECT NAME	DESCRIPTION	MAG.
M50	Open cluster of nearly 100 stars, 2,950 lya.	6.3
NGC 2232	Open cluster, 1,300 lya. Binoculars reveal about 20 stars.	3.9
NGC 2244 + ROSETTE NEBULA (NGC 2237)	Open cluster + nebula, 4,500 lya.	4.8
CHRISTMAS TREE (NGC 2264)	Open cluster, 2,600 lya.	3.8

NOTE

Monoceros is overshadowed by its neighbours, Orion, Gemini, and Canis Major, but it can be easily located as it lies on the celestial equator, flanked by the three brilliant first-magnitude stars – Betelgeuse, Procyon, and Sirius.

NGC 2244 *is the open cluster embedded within the Rosette Nebula. The nebula itself cannot be seen with the naked eye, but the cluster makes an excellent target for binoculars.*

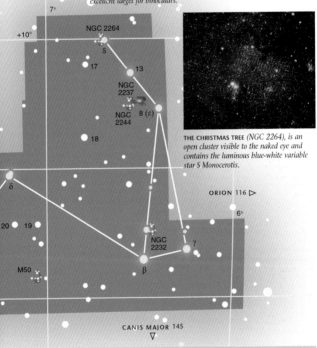

THE CHRISTMAS TREE *(NGC 2264), is an open cluster visible to the naked eye and contains the luminous blue-white variable star S Monocerotis.*

STAR NAME	DESCRIPTION	MAG.
α	Orange giant (K0), 144 lya.	3.9
β	Triple system (B3 + B3 + B3), 690 lya. Easily split by small telescopes.	4.6 + 5.0 + 5.4
γ	Orange giant (K3), 215 lya.	4.0
δ	Blue-white main sequence star (A2), 375 lya.	4.2
8 (ε)	Yellow and blue-white stars (A5 + F4), 128 + 79 lya. Line-of-sight double for small telescopes.	4.4 + 6.7
S	Multiple system of six stars (O7), variable, 2,600 lya.	4.7

Hydra

Hydrae (Hya)

M48, an open cluster appearing larger than a full Moon, is visible to the naked eye in clear, dark conditions. It is a good target for binocular viewing.

The constellation of Hydra is the largest in the sky. According to one legend, it represents the multi-headed monster killed by Hercules. According to another, Hydra was the water-snake banished by Apollo to the sky along with Corvus the crow, who angered Apollo by using Hydra as an excuse for his own delay in returning from fetching water. Although the constellation is large, its stars are faint and only its brightest star has been given a name, Alphard, which means "the solitary one" in Arabic. There are few astronomical objects in Hydra that can be observed clearly with amateur equipment.

SOUTHERN CELESTIAL HEMISPHERE

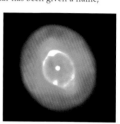

NGC 3242, a planetary nebula, can be detected with small telescopes, but larger instruments reveal its detail. It is also known as the Ghost of Jupiter due to its resemblance to the planet.

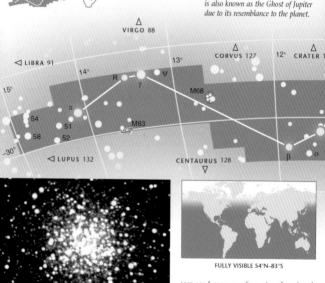

FULLY VISIBLE 54°N–83°S

M68 can be seen as a fuzzy star when viewed with binoculars. A larger instrument is needed in order to resolve the individual stars.

OBJECT NAME	DESCRIPTION	MAG.
M48	Open cluster of about 80 stars, 2,000 lya.	5.8
M68	Globular cluster, 31,000 lya.	8.2
M83	Face-on spiral galaxy, 15 million lya.	8.2
GHOST OF JUPITER (NGC 3242)	Planetary nebula, 2,600 lya. Appears as a small blue-green disc with a small telescope.	8.6

STAR NAME	DESCRIPTION	MAG.
ALPHARD (α)	Orange giant (K3), 177 lya.	2.0
β	Blue-white giant (B9), 365 lya.	4.3
γ	Yellow giant (G8), 132 lya.	3.0
δ	Blue-white main sequence star (A0), 180 lya.	4.1
ε	Yellow and blue system (G0), 135 lya. Actually a quintuple system, but needs larger telescope to split.	3.4 + 6.7
27	Yellow and white stars (G8 + F5), 202 + 244 lya.	5.0 + 6.9
54	Possible binary for small telescopes (F0 + G1), 55 lya.	5.3 + 7.4

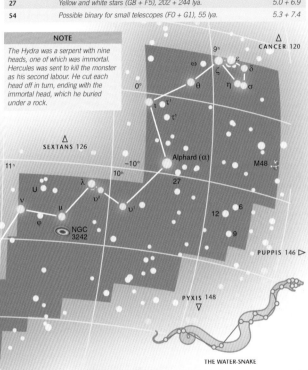

NOTE

The Hydra was a serpent with nine heads, one of which was immortal. Hercules was sent to kill the monster as his second labour. He cut each head off in turn, ending with the immortal head, which he buried under a rock.

△ CANCER 120

9ʰ
ω   ε   δ
ζ
0°   θ   η   σ
ι   τ²
τ³

△ SEXTANS 126

11ʰ   −10°   Alphard (α)   M48
10ʰ
U   λ   27
ν   μ   υ²   6
φ   υ¹   12   9
NGC 3242   PUPPIS 146 ▷

PYXIS 148 ▽

THE WATER-SNAKE

△ ANTLIA 148 ▽

M83, *a spiral galaxy, is only just visible with binoculars or small telescopes. Larger telescopes are needed to see fine detail within the galaxy.*

Sextans

Sextantis (Sex)

The constellation of Sextans was introduced in 1687 by the Polish astronomer Johannes Hevelius to represent the sextant, an instrument he used to measure star positions. Sextans lies away from the Milky Way and is a small, faint constellation, with no bright or named stars, clusters, or nebulosity. The few galaxies within reach of the amateur need larger telescopes for a detailed view.

THE SPINDLE GALAXY (NGC 3115) gets its name from its shape. It is a flattened elliptical galaxy that is best observed with larger apertures.

SOUTHERN CELESTIAL HEMISPHERE

FULLY VISIBLE
78°N–83°S

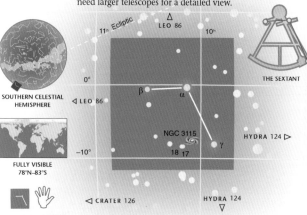

THE SEXTANT

Crater

Crateris (Crt)

According to legend, Crater was the cup associated with the story of Corvus the crow, and was placed in the night sky as a result of Apollo's anger with Corvus. Crater lacks bright stars, clusters, or nebulae, but has some galaxies that can be observed with large amateur telescopes.

NGC 3981, a spiral galaxy seen nearly edge-on from the Earth, is a difficult target due to its low surface brightness.

SOUTHERN CELESTIAL HEMISPHERE

FULLY VISIBLE
65°N–90°S

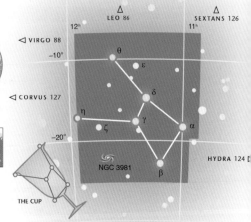

THE CUP

Corvus

Corvi (Crv)

In Greek mythology, Corvus was a crow sent by Apollo with a cup to fetch some water from a spring. However, Corvus stopped to eat figs and returned late, clutching a water-snake in its claws. It blamed the snake for blocking the spring and, angered at the lie, Apollo placed Corvus, the cup (Crater), and the water-snake (Hydra) in the sky. Corvus has no bright clusters or nebulae of interest to amateur astronomers. Although there are galaxies, they are too faint for most amateur telescopes. Corvus does, however, contain NGC 4038 and NGC 4039, a pair of colliding galaxies that can be seen by telescopes of moderate to large apertures.

NGC 4038 and NGC 4039 are a pair of interacting galaxies called the Antennae. The interaction has drawn out a long trail of gas, dust, and stars from each galaxy.

SOUTHERN CELESTIAL HEMISPHERE

FULLY VISIBLE
65°N–90°S

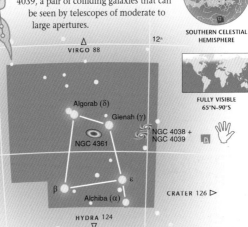

THE CROW

△ VIRGO 88

◁ VIRGO 88

−20°

Algorab (δ)

Gienah (γ)

NGC 4361

NGC 4038 + NGC 4039

β

ε

Alchiba (α)

CRATER 126 ▷

12ʰ

HYDRA 124 ▽

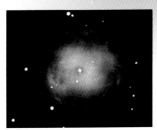

NGC 4361, a faint planetary nebula, has a distinct purple colour when viewed with larger amateur telescopes. Binocular-viewing needs clear skies.

A HUBBLE SPACE TELESCOPE high-resolution image shows the nuclei of the colliding galaxies NGC 4038 and NGC 4039, the Antennae.

NAME	DESCRIPTION	MAG.
ALCHIBA (α)	White main sequence star (F0), 48 lya.	4.0
β	Yellow giant (G5), 140 lya.	2.7
GIENAH (γ)	Blue-white giant (B8), 165 lya.	2.6
ALGORAB (δ)	Blue-white star and faint purplish companion (B9), 88 lya.	3.0 + 9.2
ANTENNAE (NGC 4038 + 4039)	Spiral galaxies, 45 million lya. Requires 150mm aperture to be seen in detail.	10.7
NGC 4361	Planetary nebula, 2,500 lya. Requires 150mm aperture for detail.	10.3

Centaurus

Centauri (Cen)

The constellation Centaurus represents the mythological figure of Chiron, who had the upper body of a man and four legs of a horse. He was killed by a poisoned arrow accidentally shot by Hercules. The Milky Way flows through Centaurus, enriching it with several interesting targets for amateur astronomers. The constellation is famous for Omega (ω) Centauri (NGC 5139), the Alpha (α) and Proxima Centauri system, and Centaurus A (NGC 5128). Although Omega (ω) Centauri bears a Greek letter, it is not a star, but the largest, brightest globular cluster of the night sky. Alpha (α) consists of two yellow and orange stars that orbit each other every 80 years; Proxima Centauri is the closest star to the Sun. Centaurus A is a well-known galaxy with a dark dust lane visible with larger apertures.

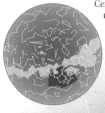

OMEGA (ω) CENTAURI (NGC 5139) appears as a patch larger than the full Moon. Stars can be individually resolved with small telescopes and binoculars.

SOUTHERN CELESTIAL HEMISPHERE

NOTE

Draw a line through Alpha (α) and Beta (β) Centauri to find the location of Crux, the Southern Cross. This will help to avoid confusion with the False Cross – Iota (ι) and Eta (η) Carinae, and Delta (δ) and Kappa (κ) Velorum.

THE CENTAUR

◁ LUPUS 132

CIRCINUS 152

OBJECT NAME	DESCRIPTION	MAG.
OMEGA (ω) CENTAURI (NGC 5139)	Largest and brightest globular cluster, 17,000 lya. Visible to the naked eye.	3.7
NGC 3766	Scattered open cluster of about 100 stars, 5,500 lya.	5.3
BLUE PLANETARY (NGC 3918)	Planetary nebula, 3,200 lya. Telescopic appearance similar to Jupiter, visible with binoculars.	8.4
NGC 4945	Barred spiral galaxy, 13 million lya.	8.4
CENTAURUS A (NGC 5128)	Lenticular galaxy, 11 million lya. Visible with binoculars; at least 100mm aperture is needed to see the dark dust band.	7.0
NGC 5460	Large open cluster of over 40 stars, 2,500 lya.	5.6

STAR NAME	DESCRIPTION	MAG.
RIGIL KENTAURUS (α)	*Double with Proxima Centauri as the third component (G2 + K1 + M5), 4.4 lya. The third brightest star in sky.*	-0.01 + 1.3 + 11.0
AGENA (β)	*Blue giant (B1), 525 lya.*	0.6
MENKENT (γ)	*Double (A0), 130 lya. Large telescope needed to split.*	2.9 + 2.9
δ	*Blue-white sub-giant (B2), 395 lya.*	2.6
ε	*Blue-white giant (B1), 375 lya.*	2.3

NGC 5128 *is a powerful radio source designated Centaurus A. It is possibly the result of a collision between an elliptical and a spiral galaxy.*

NGC 4945, *a barred spiral galaxy, is not visible to the naked eye, but is bright enough to be detected with good binoculars. Larger apertures are needed to resolve any detail.*

VELA 149 ▷

NGC 3918

CARINA 150 ▷

FULLY VISIBLE 25°N–90°S

NGC 3766 *is a fairly bright and scattered open cluster visible to the naked eye. It is best observed with binoculars or a low-power telescope.*

Crux

Crucis (Cru)

THE JEWEL BOX *(NGC 4755), also known as the Kappa (κ) Crucis cluster, is visible to the naked eye; binoculars or low-power telescopes shows its stars.*

The smallest constellation in the night sky, Crux is nevertheless one of the most famous and easily recognized star patterns of all. It was originally regarded by the ancient Greeks as a part of Centaurus, but it came to be recognized as a separate constellation in the late 16th century. The Milky Way is bright in this part of the sky, making the dark nebula Coalsack, a wedge-shaped cloud of dust and gas, easily visible by contrast. The Coalsack, however, has not been assigned a NGC or any other catalogue number.

SOUTHERN CELESTIAL
HEMISPHERE

THE SOUTHERN CROSS

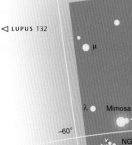

◁ LUPUS 132

13ʰ

μ

λ

Mimosa (β)

−60°

NGC 4755

◁ TRIANGULUM
AUSTRALE 153

Coalsack

◁ CIRCINUS 152

APUS 159
▽

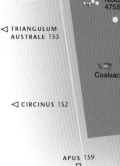

THE FOUR BRIGHTEST *stars of Crux form a distinctive cross for southern hemisphere observers – the Gamma (γ) star is noticeably a red giant compared to the other blue-white stars.*

NAME	DESCRIPTION	MAG.
ACRUX (α)	*Multiple system (B0 + B0 + B4), 321 lya.*	1.4 + 1.8
MIMOSA (β)	*Blue variable giant (B0), double star, 352 lya.*	1.3 + 11.4
GACRUX (γ)	*Red giant with two companions (M3), 88 lya.*	1.6 + 6.7 + 9.5
δ	*Blue-white sub-giant (B2), 364 lya.*	2.8
COALSACK	*Dark nebula, 550 lya. Possibly the closest such nebula to the Earth.*	
NGC 4103	*Open cluster of about 50 stars, 3,900 lya.*	7.4
NGC 4349	*Open cluster of about 30 stars, 5,500 lya. Telescope resolves stars.*	7.4
JEWEL BOX (NGC 4755)	*Open cluster, 7,800 lya. Best observed with binoculars or a wide-field telescope.*	4.2

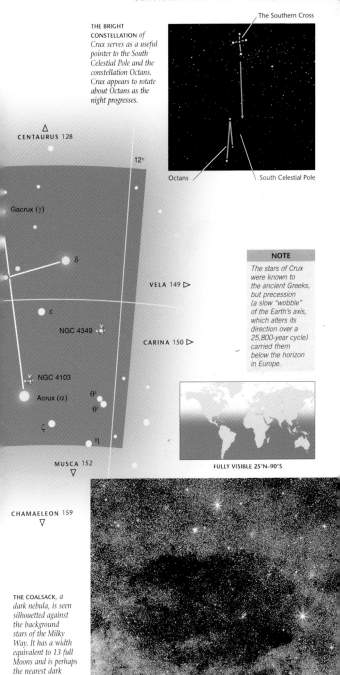

THE BRIGHT CONSTELLATION *of Crux serves as a useful pointer to the South Celestial Pole and the constellation Octans. Crux appears to rotate about Octans as the night progresses.*

The Southern Cross

Octans

South Celestial Pole

△ CENTAURUS 128

12ʰ

Gacrux (γ)

δ

ε

NGC 4349

NGC 4103

Acrux (α)

θ²

θ¹

ζ

η

VELA 149 ▷

CARINA 150 ▷

MUSCA 152 ▽

CHAMAELEON 159 ▽

NOTE

The stars of Crux were known to the ancient Greeks, but precession (a slow "wobble" of the Earth's axis, which alters its direction over a 25,800-year cycle) carried them below the horizon in Europe.

FULLY VISIBLE 25°N–90°S

THE COALSACK, *a dark nebula, is seen silhouetted against the background stars of the Milky Way. It has a width equivalent to 13 full Moons and is perhaps the nearest dark nebula to the Earth.*

Lupus

Lupi (Lup)

NGC 5882, *a faint planetary nebula, is shown here in the light of ionized oxygen. The nebula actually appears bluish when viewed without a filter.*

This is an ancient constellation, which for the Greeks and Romans represented a wolf speared by Centaurus. Lupus appears to be an insignificant constellation for it has no bright or named stars. However, it lies on the edge of the Milky Way, and therefore contains numerous objects that can be observed with amateur instruments. These include double stars that are easy to spot through a small telescope.

THE WOLF

SOUTHERN CELESTIAL HEMISPHERE

FULLY VISIBLE
34°N–90°S

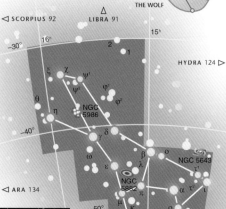

◁ SCORPIUS 92   △ LIBRA 91

HYDRA 124 ▷

◁ ARA 134

◁ NORMA 144

CENTAURUS 128 ▷

NGC 5643 *is a faint galaxy and requires large instruments to show any detail. Its active nucleus is a strong source of X-rays.*

NAME	DESCRIPTION	MAG.
α	Blue giant (B1), 548 lya.	2.3
β	Blue giant (B2), 524 lya.	2.7
γ	Blue-white star with very faint companion (B2), 570 lya.	2.8
δ	Blue giant (B1), 510 lya.	3.2
ε	Blue giant (B2), 504 lya.	3.4
ζ	Yellow main sequence star (G8), 116 lya.	3.4
η	Double star (B2). Difficult to split.	3.4 + 7.9
κ	Double star (B9 + A0), 188 lya. Easy to split with small telescope.	3.9 + 5.7
μ	Multiple star (B8), 290 lya. Large telescope can split brightest star.	4.3 + 6.9
NGC 5643	Faint face-on barred spiral galaxy, 47 million lya.	10.7
NGC 5882	Planetary nebula, 5,500 lya. Easy for apertures above 75mm.	10.5
NGC 5986	Globular cluster, 34,000 lya.	7.1

Norma

Normae (Nor)

Originally called *Norma et Regula*, the set square and ruler, this constellation was introduced in the 18th century by Nicolas Louis de Lacaille. It has no Alpha or Beta stars, as these were absorbed by neighbouring Scorpius when its boundaries were changed. The Milky Way runs through Norma, which lies across the galactic equator. Therefore, it is rich with star fields worth sweeping with binoculars, although its stars are faint and lost among the multitude of background stars.

NGC 6067 *is a small scattered open cluster close to the Kappa (κ) star and is easily observed with binoculars.*

SOUTHERN CELESTIAL HEMISPHERE

FULLY VISIBLE 29°N–90°S

NOTE

The most distinctive feature of Norma is a right-angled trio of three faint stars. However, they are somewhat difficult to identify against the rich Milky Way star fields.

THE LEVEL

SHAPLEY 1, *shown here, is a planetary nebula, and is a difficult target even for large telescopes.*

NAME	DESCRIPTION	MAG.
γ	*Line-of-sight double (F9 + G8), 1,400 + 92 lya.*	4.9 + 4.0
δ	*Blue-white star (A0), 125 lya.*	4.7
ε	*Binary star (B3 + A0) in a 13-year orbiting period, 400 lya.*	4.8 + 7.5
NGC 5946	*Globular cluster, 36,000 lya. Requires at least 100mm aperture.*	9.6
NGC 6067	*Scattered open cluster, 6,800 lya. Best viewed with binoculars.*	5.6
NGC 6087	*Scattered open cluster of about 40 stars, 3,000 lya. Best viewed with binoculars; contains S Normae, a yellow supergiant.*	5.4

Ara

Arae (Ara)

According to Greek mythology, Ara represents the altar upon which the Greeks swore allegiance before their battle against the Titans. This constellation lies against the background of the Milky Way, and consequently contains clusters within reach of amateur instruments. Although Ara contains nebulosity, the nebulae are best seen through long-exposure photography.

NGC 6397 is one of the closer globular clusters to the Sun, seen here as imaged by the Hubble Space Telescope.

SOUTHERN CELESTIAL HEMISPHERE

FULLY VISIBLE
22°N–90°S

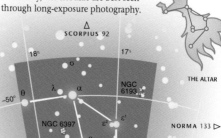

THE ALTAR

△ SCORPIUS 92

NORMA 133 ▷

◁ TELESCOPIUM 153

PAVO 162 ▽

NOTE

The celestial altar, Ara, is oriented with its top facing south. The Milky Way above it seems to be the "smoke" given off by the incense burning on the altar.

NGC 6362, a bright and compact globular cluster, can be detected with small telescopes, but only larger apertures will resolve the individual stars.

NGC 6193, an open cluster, is visible here with its associated nebulosity. The nebulosity is best revealed with long-exposure photography.

NAME	DESCRIPTION	MAG.
α	Blue-white star (B2), 241 lya.	2.8
β	Orange supergiant (K3), 600 lya.	2.8
γ	Blue supergiant with two faint companions (B1), 1,140 lya.	3.3 + 10.3 + 12.0
δ	Blue-white star (B8), 186 lya.	3.6
ζ	Orange giant (K5), 574 lya.	3.1
η	Orange giant (K5), 313 lya.	3.8
NGC 6193	Small open cluster of about 30 stars, 4,560 lya.	5.2
NGC 6362	Globular cluster, 23,000 lya.	8.3
NGC 6397	Globular cluster, 6,500 lya. Large and bright enough for binoculars.	5.8

Corona Australis

Coronae Australis (CrA)

An ancient constellation, known to Ptolemy in the second century BCE as a wreath, Corona Australis represents the crown placed in the sky by Bacchus after he had rescued his mother from the Underworld. The outline of the crown is formed by an arc of stars. Corona Australis sits at the edge of the Milky Way in the night sky, so deep-sky objects are heavily obscured by our galaxy's dust and gas. This small constellation contains stars of magnitude 4 and fainter.

NGC 6541, a globular cluster, requires a telescope of at least 150mm aperture before individual stars can be detected.

REGIONS OF REFLECTION NEBULOSITY, *NGC 6726, NGC 6727, and NGC 6729, lie near NGC 6723, the globular cluster shown in this image, which belongs to neighbouring Sagittarius.*

THE SOUTHERN CROWN

SOUTHERN CELESTIAL HEMISPHERE

FULLY VISIBLE 44°N–90°S

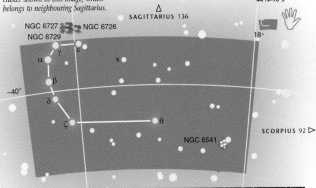

△ **SAGITTARIUS** 136

NGC 6727 ⬤⬤ NGC 6726
NGC 6729
γ ε
α κ
β
−40°
δ
ζ θ

SCORPIUS 92 ▷

NGC 6541

◁ **TELESCOPIUM** 153

18ʰ

A WIDE-FIELD VIEW *of the northwestern region of Corona Australis is shown here; the dark regions are where starlight is blocked by dust clouds.*

NAME	DESCRIPTION	MAG.
α	Blue-white main sequence star (A2), 130 lya.	4.1
β	Orange giant (K0), 510 lya.	4.1
γ	Yellow-white binary (F7) in 122-year orbital period, 58 lya.	4.8 + 5.1
δ	Orange giant (K1), 175 lya.	4.6
ε	Eclipsing binary with 14-hour period (F2), 98 lya.	4.7 – 5.0
κ	Line-of-sight double (B8 + B9), 1,700 + 490 lya.	5.9 + 6.5
NGC 6541	Globular cluster, 22,000 lya. Visible with small telescope.	6.7
NGC 6726 + NGC 6727 + NGC 6729	Nebulae with faint nebulosity, 420 lya. Best seen with large instruments.	7.2

Sagittarius

Sagittarii (Sgr)

THE LAGOON NEBULA (M8) is about three times the size of a full Moon. A telescope can reveal the dark dust lane that bisects it.

SOUTHERN CELESTIAL HEMISPHERE

An ancient constellation, Sagittarius represents the mythological figure of a centaur holding a raised bow and arrow. When viewing the constellation, one is looking directly towards the centre of our galaxy, about 26,000 light years away. Consequently, there are numerous star fields and clusters, including over 60 open and globular clusters. Sagittarius also contains regions of nebulosity, best appreciated with long-exposure photography.

Many of the clusters are, however, visible to the naked eye and it is a rewarding experience merely to sweep the constellation with binoculars on a clear night. A recognizable feature is the "Teapot", a pattern of ten stars that forms the outline of a teapot with a pointed lid and large spout.

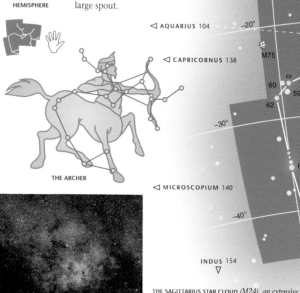

◁ AQUARIUS 104

◁ CAPRICORNUS 138

THE ARCHER

◁ MICROSCOPIUM 140

INDUS 154 ▽

THE SAGITTARIUS STAR CLOUD (M24), an extensive star field, is best viewed with binoculars. It is one of the brightest parts of the Milky Way and is visible to the naked eye.

OBJECT NAME	DESCRIPTION	MAG.
LAGOON NEBULA (M8)	Nebula, 5,000 lya. Naked-eye object; good for binoculars.	6.0
OMEGA NEBULA (M17)	Nebula, 4,000 lya. Binocular object; telescope preferred.	7.0
TRIFID (M20)	Nebula, 5,000 lya. Moderate telescope reveals detail.	7.6
M21	Open cluster of about 70 stars, 4,000 lya.	5.9
M22	Globular cluster, 10,000 lya. Telescope resolves stars.	5.0
M23	Scattered open cluster, 2,100 lya. Binocular object.	5.5
SAGITTARIUS STAR CLOUD (M24)	Extensive star field, visible with binoculars.	4.6

STAR NAME	DESCRIPTION	MAG.
RUKBAT (α)	*Blue-white main sequence star (B8), 170 lya.*	*4.0*
ARKAB (β)	*Naked-eye double (B8), 378 + 139 lya.*	*4.0 + 4.3*
ALNASL (γ)	*Orange giant (K0), 96 lya.*	*3.0*
KAUS MEDIA (δ)	*Orange giant (K2), 306 lya.*	*2.7*
KAUS AUSTRALIS (ϵ)	*Blue-white giant (B9) 145 lya. The brightest star in Sagittarius.*	*1.8*
ASCELLA (ζ)	*Short-period binary (A3 + A3) in a 21.1-year orbit, 120 lya.*	*3.2 + 3.4*
η	*Variable red-orange star and white companion (M3), 390 lya.*	*3.2 + 7.8*

AQUILA 99

SCUTUM 98 ▷

FULLY VISIBLE 44°N–90°S

OPHIUCHUS 96 ▷

M17
M18
M25 M24 M23
M21 M20
M22 Ecliptic
M28 M8
Milk Dipper
Teapot
Ascella (ζ) Kaus Media (δ)
M54
M70 M69 Alnasl (γ)
Kaus Australis (ε)

M22 *is a globular cluster that is visible to the naked eye on a dark moonless night. It is the third brightest globular cluster, but a moderate telescope is needed to resolve individual stars.*

CORONA AUSTRALIS 135   SCORPIUS 92 ▷

Rukbat (α)

Arkab (β¹+β²)

TELESCOPIUM 153

THE OMEGA NEBULA *(M17), is also known as the Horseshoe or Swan Nebula, and can be seen as a faint patch in binoculars. A larger telescope or photography is needed to reveal fine detail.*

Capricornus

Capricorni (Cap)

Depictions of a goat-fish have been found on Babylonian tablets over 3,000 years old, showing that Capricornus is perhaps the oldest constellation. The ancient Greeks identified it with the god Pan. According to legend, Pan and some other gods were attacked by the monster Typhon. In order to escape, Pan jumped into a river and turned his lower half into a fish. Capricornus contains little of interest to amateur astronomers, except for one globular cluster, M30, which has a number of stars extending from its very concentrated centre.

THE CAPRICORNUS STARS *are shown in this image. The white star left of the centre is Delta (δ), also known as Deneb Algedi. The orange star towards the bottom is Omega (ω).*

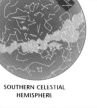

SOUTHERN CELESTIAL HEMISPHERE

FULLY VISIBLE 62°N–90°S

NOTE

The Alpha Capricornids meteor shower occurs between 15 July and 11 September, with a maximum activity of six to 14 meteors per hour around August 1. The meteors can be as bright as magnitude 2.

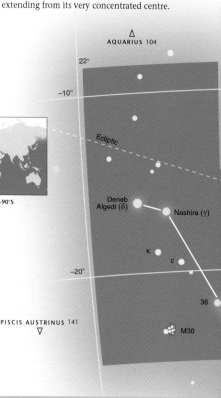

AQUARIUS 104

22ʰ

–10°

Ecliptic

Deneb Algedi (δ)

Nashira (γ)

κ

ε

–20°

36

PISCIS AUSTRINUS 141

M30

NAME	DESCRIPTION	MAG.
ALGEDI (α^1)	Optical double with Alpha (α^2), yellow supergiant (G3), 690 lya. Companion visible with small telescope.	4.3 + 9.2
ALGEDI (α^2)	Optical double (G6) with Alpha (α^1), companion also a double, 109 lya.	3.6 + 11.0
DABIH (β)	Yellow giant and blue-white main sequence companion (K0), 340 lya. Split with binoculars.	3.1 + 6.1
NASHIRA (γ)	White giant (A7), 140 lya.	3.7
DENEB ALGEDI (δ)	Eclipsing binary (A7), in a 24.5-hour period, 39 lya.	2.9 – 3.1
ε	Blue-white main sequence star (B3), 660 lya.	4.5
M30	Globular cluster, 30,000 lya.	7.5

M30 *is a globular cluster easily detected with binoculars or a small telescope. Larger apertures reveal chains of stars towards the north of the cluster.*

△
AQUILA 99

Algedi
(α¹ + α²)

ν

Dabih (β)

21ʰ

ρ

θ

η

24

ψ

ω

MICROSCOPIUM 140
▽

THE SEA GOAT

Microscopium

Microscopii (Mic)

Introduced in the 18th century by French astronomer Nicolas Louis de Lacaille, Microscopium is an insignificant constellation. The galaxies it contains are too faint for amateur viewing, with the exception of one galaxy, NGC 6925, which is of magnitude 11.3 and lies 150 million light years away; its shape is apparent with a 150mm aperture.

NGC 6925, *a faint and distant spiral galaxy, is seen edge-on from the Earth. It requires larger apertures before it reveals any detail.*

SOUTHERN CELESTIAL HEMISPHERE

FULLY VISIBLE 45°N–90°S

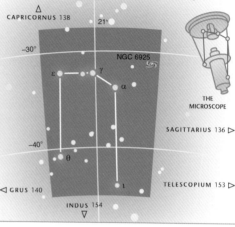

THE MICROSCOPE

SAGITTARIUS 136 ▷
TELESCOPIUM 153 ▷
◁ GRUS 140
INDUS 154
CAPRICORNUS 138

Grus

Gruis (Gru)

The constellation of Grus was introduced in the 16th century by two Dutch navigators, Pieter Dirkszoon Keyzer and Frederick de Houtman, and represents a crane. It lacks open clusters and nebulosity because it lies away from the plane of the Milky Way. There are three faint galaxies within reach of a more moderate telescope. Its brightest star is the Alpha (α) star, Alnair, which is of magnitude 1.7.

NGC 7582, *a barred spiral galaxy, is to the right of this image; it needs moderate to large telescopes to reveal detail.*

SOUTHERN CELESTIAL HEMISPHERE

FULLY VISIBLE 33°N–90°S

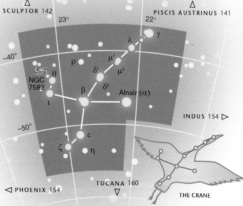

THE CRANE

SCULPTOR 142
PISCIS AUSTRINUS 141
INDUS 154 ▷
◁ PHOENIX 154
TUCANA 160

Piscis Austrinus

Piscis Austrini (PsA)

Often depicted as a fish drinking from the urn of nearby Aquarius, Piscis Austrinus is an ancient constellation and was known to Ptolemy in the second century CE. Piscis Austrinus has also been regarded as the parent of Pisces, which represent the two fishes. The constellation lacks bright clusters and nebulae, and most of its galaxies are too faint for most amateur telescopes, with the exception of NGC 7314, a spiral galaxy, although it requires large telescopes with an aperture of at least 200mm to reveal its true shape. However, the Alpha (α) star, Fomalhaut, at magnitude1.2, is not only the brightest star in the constellation but also ranks among the 20 brightest stars in the night sky. The constellation's Beta (β) and Gamma (γ) stars are both double stars.

NGC 7314, a spiral galaxy with an active nucleus, appears as a fuzzy patch when viewed with apertures of 150mm or so.

SOUTHERN CELESTIAL HEMISPHERE

FULLY VISIBLE 53°N–90°S

> **NOTE**
>
> *Represented in the constellation to the north is Aquarius, from whose urn water is said to flow into the mouth of the Southern Fish. The mouth is marked by the Alpha (α) star, named Fomalhaut, which means "fish's mouth" in Arabic.*

THE SOUTHERN FISH

△
AQUARIUS 104

23°
22°
NGC 7314
ε
λ
−30°
Fomalhaut (α)
δ
γ
β
τ
μ
ι

◁ **SCULPTOR 142**
GRUS 140
▽
MICROSCOPIUM 140 ▷

PHOENIX 154
▽

NAME	DESCRIPTION	MAG.
FOMALHAUT (α)	Blue-white main sequence star (A3), 25 lya. Possibly with a currently forming planetary system.	1.2
β	Possible binary system (A0), 148 lya.	4.9 + 7.9
γ	Sub-giant and dwarf companion (B9 + F5), 222 lya. Difficult for small telescopes.	4.5 + 8.0
δ	Giant and dwarf companion (G7 + G5), 170 lya.	4.2 + 9.9
NGC 7314	Spiral galaxy, 75 million lya. A target for larger telescopes.	10.9

Sculptor

Sculptoris (Scl)

This constellation appears to be insignificant, as it has no stars brighter than magnitude 4.3. However, when viewing Sculptor, the line of sight is directly out of our galaxy towards the South Galactic Pole and, therefore, not clouded by our galaxy's gas, dust, and stars. Consequently, this constellation contains some fine galaxies within reach of amateur telescopes. Sculptor was first visualized as a sculptor's workshop in the 1750s by French astronomer Nicolas Louis de Lacaille.

THE SCULPTOR GALAXY (NGC 253) is also known as the Silver Coin Galaxy. Large apertures reveal the structure of the spiral arms and the nucleus.

SOUTHERN CELESTIAL HEMISPHERE

FULLY VISIBLE 50°N–90°S

SCULPTOR

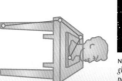

NGC 288 is a low-concentration globular cluster appearing as a hazy patch in small telescopes. Apertures of 100mm or above will show the individual members of the cluster.

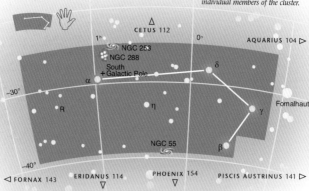

CETUS 112
AQUARIUS 104 ▷
NGC 253
NGC 288
South
+ Galactic Pole
δ
α
–30°
Fomalhaut
η
γ
R
NGC 55
–40°
β
◁ FORNAX 143   ERIDANUS 114   PHOENIX 154   PISCIS AUSTRINUS 141 ▷

NGC 55 is fainter than NGC 253, but this galaxy is still a rewarding target for small telescopes. Being edge-on, its elongation is visible in all apertures.

NAME	DESCRIPTION	MAG.
α	Blue-white giant (B7), 672 lya.	4.3
β	Blue-white main sequence star (B9), 178 lya.	4.4
γ	Orange giant (G8), 179 lya.	4.4
δ	Blue-white main sequence star (A0), 143 lya.	4.6
NGC 55	Edge-on barred spiral galaxy, 5 million lya. Larger apertures best.	8.2
SCULPTOR GALAXY (NGC 253)	Nearly edge-on spiral galaxy, 9 million lya. Small telescopes show elongation.	7.1
NGC 288	Globular cluster, 27,000 lya. Moderate instrument resolves stars.	8.1

Fornax

Fornacis (For)

A constellation introduced in the 18th century by Nicolas Louis de Lacaille, who gave it the original name of *Fornax Chemica*, the Chemical Furnace, Fornax is not rich in either stars or clusters. However, it is home to the Fornax Cluster, a cluster of galaxies about 75 million light years away from the Earth. The brighter galaxies within the cluster, notably NGC 1316 and NGC 1365, can be observed with amateur equipment.

NGC 1097 *galaxy is a strong radio source with a very bright and active nucleus. Larger telescopes resolve detail within the spiral arms.*

THE FURNACE

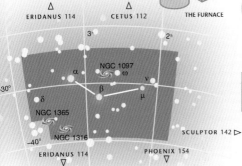

SOUTHERN CELESTIAL HEMISPHERE

FULLY VISIBLE 50°N–90°S

Caelum

Caeli (Cae)

Introduced in the 18th century by Nicolas Louis de Lacaille, Caelum represents an engraving tool. It contains little of interest to amateur astronomers. Alpha (α) is its brightest star, with a magnitude of 4.4.

THE CHISEL

THE SPARSE REGION *of Caelum has a white star in the centre, Alpha (α); the orange giant at the right is Alpha (α) Horologii.*

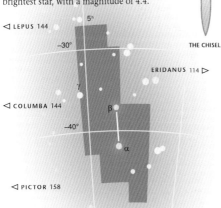

SOUTHERN CELESTIAL HEMISPHERE

FULLY VISIBLE 41°N–90°S

Lepus

Leporis (Lep)

An ancient southern constellation, Lepus represents a hare. It lies below Orion and is chased every night across the sky by Canis Major, the hunting dog. It is not a very bright constellation, but contains a few objects for amateurs, such as the bright globular cluster M79.

M79 *is a distant globular cluster, about 120 light years across; it can be detected with binoculars.*

SOUTHERN CELESTIAL HEMISPHERE

FULLY VISIBLE
62°N–90°S

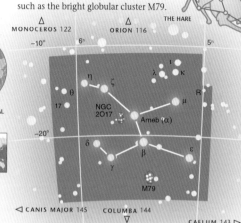

Columba

Columbae (Col)

NGC 1792 *is a spiral galaxy that appears elongated. Moderate-sized telescopes reveal fine detail.*

Representing the dove released from Noah's Ark, Columba is a small and faint constellation that was introduced in 1592 by the Dutch astronomer and theologian Petrus Plancius. Columba contains many faint galaxies, but most are too faint for most amateur telescopes.

SOUTHERN CELESTIAL HEMISPHERE

FULLY VISIBLE
46°N–90°S

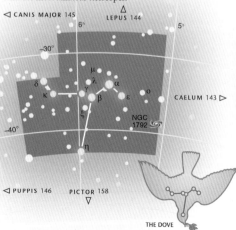

THE DOVE

Canis Major

Canis Majoris (CMa)

This is an ancient constellation, representing one of the two hunting dogs following Orion, the other being Canis Minor. Canis Major contains the brightest star in the sky, Sirius, which is outshone only by the Sun, Moon, Jupiter, Venus, and Mars. During the northern winter months, it can be seen in the sky at night, but each year after winter, starts to rise in the morning and is above the horizon only during the day. For Egyptians, this marked the start of the Nile's annual flooding and the beginning of their year.

M41 was known to the ancient Greeks. It is estimated to be around 200 million years old.

SOUTHERN CELESTIAL HEMISPHERE

FULLY VISIBLE 56°N–90°S

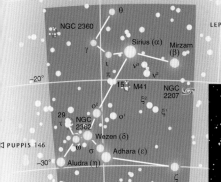

THE GREATER DOG

NGC 2207 is a spiral galaxy. An aperture of 150mm reveals an elongated nucleus. It has a companion galaxy, IC 2163, which is being distorted by it.

△
ORION 116

△
MONOCEROS 122

LEPUS 140 ▷

NGC 2360 is an open cluster and a good target for binocular viewing, consisting of about 80 stars.

◁ PUPPIS 146

COLUMBA 144
▽

NAME	DESCRIPTION	MAG.
SIRIUS (α)	Binary, main sequence star and faint white dwarf companion (A1), 8.6 lya.	-1.47 + 8.4
MIRZAM (β)	Blue giant (B1), 500 lya.	2.0
γ	Blue-white giant (B8), 402 lya.	4.1
WEZEN (δ)	White supergiant (F8), 1,800 lya.	1.8
ADHARA (ε)	Double (B2), 430 lya. Companion needs large telescope.	1.5 + 7.4
ζ	Spectroscopic binary and variable (B2), 336 lya.	3.0
ALUDRA (η)	Highly luminous blue supergiant (B5), 3,200 lya.	2.4
M41	Open cluster of about 50 stars, 2,300 lya. Visible to the naked eye.	4.5
NGC 2207	Spiral galaxy, 114 million lya.	10.7
NGC 2360	Open cluster of about 80 stars, 3,700 lya. Good binocular object.	7.2

Puppis

Puppis (Pup)

The ancient constellation of Argo Navis, named after the ship of the Argonauts, was divided into three in the 18th century by the French cartographer, Nicolas Louis de Lacaille. From Argo Navis he formed Carina (the keel), Vela (the sails), and Puppis (the stern). Puppis' bright stars do not carry the usual Greek letters of Alpha, Beta, and so on, as these stars were assigned to Carina. A rich part of the Milky Way passes through Puppis, which is why there are many star fields and clusters ideal for binocular viewing – there are over 70 open clusters within this constellation.

WIDE-ANGLE IMAGE *showing the two open clusters M46 and M47. Both clusters are visible to the naked eye, appearing as a faint knot in the background of the Milky Way.*

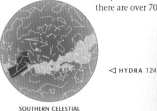

SOUTHERN CELESTIAL HEMISPHERE

◁ HYDRA 124

◁ PYXIS 148

◁ VELA 149

◁ CARINA 150

NGC 2451
NGC 2477
Naos (ζ)

Turais (ρ)
Aspidiske (ξ)

M93

M46

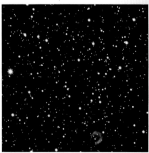

THE OPEN CLUSTER *M46, is visible to the naked eye, and appears as a hazy patch with binoculars. A telescope will resolve individual stars.*

M47, *an open cluster that is the same apparent size as a full Moon, contains about 30 stars, the brightest of which shine at magnitude 6.*

OBJECT NAME	DESCRIPTION	MAG.
M46	*Open cluster of 100 faint stars, 5,500 lya.*	*6.1*
M47	*Open cluster of about 30 stars, 1,500 lya.*	*4.4*
M93	*Open cluster of 80 faint stars, 3,600 lya. Requires binoculars.*	*6.2*
NGC 2451	*Open cluster, 720 lya. Requires binoculars.*	*3.7*
NGC 2477	*Open cluster, 4,200 lya. Binocular target.*	*5.8*

M93, a bright open cluster, is best seen with binoculars, and consists of about 80 faint stars. The two orange stars seen here are members of the cluster. M93's brightest stars are blue giants, and the cluster's age is estimated to be about 100 million years old.

CANIS MAJOR 145 ▷

7ʰ

FULLY VISIBLE 39°N–90°S

COLUMBA 144 ▷

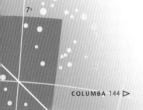

ν

ι

τ

THE STERN

NOTE

The stars in each of the three sections of the ancient Argo Navis retained their original Greek letters, and in the case of Puppis (representing the stern) the lettering now starts at Zeta (ζ), a star that is also known as Naos.

STAR NAME	DESCRIPTION	MAG.
NAOS / SUHAIL HADAR (ζ)	Blue-white supergiant (O5), 1,400 lya. One of the most luminous in the galaxy; hottest naked-eye star.	2.2
ν	Blue-white giant (B7), 600 lya.	3.1
ASPIDISKE(ξ)	Yellow supergiant (G3), 1,300 lya. Unrelated mag. 5.3 giant in binoculars field of view.	3.3
π	Orange giant, moderate-sized (K5), 1,100 lya.	2.7
TURAIS (ρ)	Yellow-white variable (K6), 3 hours 23 minutes period, 63 lya.	2.8–3.0

Pyxis

Pyxidis (Pyx)

NGC 2613 *is an edge-on barred spiral galaxy and a challenge for moderate instruments. The galaxy is a good target for long-exposure astrophotography and large telescopes.*

Representing a magnetic compass, Pyxis was introduced in the 18th century by French astronomer Nicolas Louis de Lacaille. The stars of Pyxis were originally part of the constellation Argo – a constellation that was broken up into Carina, Puppis, Vela and Pyxis. It contains no bright deep-sky objects within reach of small instruments.

SOUTHERN CELESTIAL HEMISPHERE

FULLY VISIBLE
52°N–90°S

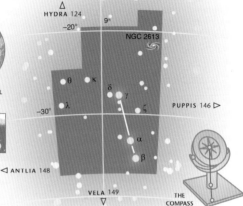

Antlia

Antliae (Ant)

NGC 2997 *is the brightest galaxy in Antlia and, being a face-on spiral galaxy, can be observed with moderate telescopes.*

Named by Nicolas Louis de Lacille, the 18th-century French astronomer, after the air pump invented by Robert Boyle, Antlia is a faint constellation. It contains no bright or named stars, lacks bright star clusters and nebulae, and is of little interest to those with binoculars or a small telescope. However, the constellation contains a cluster of galaxies, known as the Antlia Cluster, the brighter members of which can be observed with large telescopes. Its brightest star, Alpha (α), is an orange giant of magnitude 4.3.

SOUTHERN CELESTIAL HEMISPHERE

FULLY VISIBLE
49°N–90°S

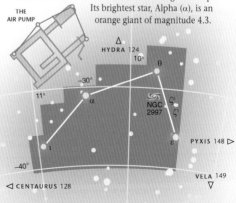

Vela

Velorum (Vel)

Vela was originally part of the constellation Argo Navis, which represented the ship used by Jason and the Argonauts. Argo Navis was broken up in the 18th century by Nicolas Louis de Lacaille into three new constellations: Puppis, Carina, and Vela; a fourth, Pyxis, was added later. The Milky Way runs through Vela and so the region is rich with over 40 star clusters and there are also large regions of nebulosity, best brought out with long-exposure astrophotography.

THE EIGHT-BURST NEBULA (NGC 3132), an easy target for amateur telescopes, appears as a disc larger than Jupiter through a small telescope.

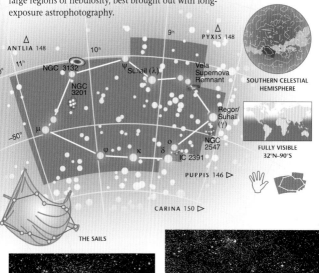

SOUTHERN CELESTIAL HEMISPHERE

FULLY VISIBLE 32°N–90°S

THE SAILS

NGC 3201, a globular cluster, can be detected with binoculars and small telescopes. Moderate instruments resolve the outer-lying members of the cluster.

THE VELA SUPERNOVA REMNANT, the largest supernova remnant visible to the naked eye, is the result of a supernova explosion that occurred about 10,000 to 12,000 years ago.

NAME	DESCRIPTION	MAG.
REGOR / SUHAIL (γ)	Two blue-white stars (WC8 + O9), primary is a Wolf-Rayet star, 840 + 1,600 lya. Can be split with binoculars.	1.8 + 4.3
δ	Blue-white main sequence star and faint companion (A0), 80 lya. Detectable with 100mm aperture.	1.9 + 5.1
κ	Blue-white main sequence star (B2), 539 lya.	2.5
SUHAIL (λ)	Orange supergiant (K5), 573 lya. Varies by 0.2 mag.	2.2
VELA SUPERNOVA REMNANT	Nebula, 6,000 lya.	12
EIGHT-BURST NEBULA (NGC 3132)	Planetary nebula, 2,600 lya. Disc very apparent in a small telescope.	9.2
NGC 3201	Globular cluster, 17,000 lya. 100mm aperture resolves stars.	6.8

Carina

Carinae (Car)

THE SOUTHERN PLEIADES *(IC 2602) is a prominent cluster containing eight stars. The brightest member of the cluster is Theta (θ), a dwarf star.*

The constellation of Carina originally formed part of the larger constellation Argo Navis, the ship of the Argonauts, which according to Greek legend, was the ship used by Jason during his search for the Golden Fleece. Argo Navis was broken up in the 18th century by Nicolas Louis de Lacaille, to form Carina (the keel), Vela (the sails), and Puppis (the stern). A rich part of the Milky Way runs through this magnificent constellation, which therefore contains many clusters and star fields, providing interesting targets for binoculars. Carina contains the variable star Eta (η), surrounded by the Eta Carinae Nebulae, a patch of glowing gas. Eta (η) is a variable star that at one time in 1843, reached magnitude -0.8, making it the second brightest star in the sky. It is now about magnitude 5 and visible to the naked eye, appearing more as an orange blob than a well-defined point.

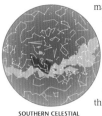

SOUTHERN CELESTIAL HEMISPHERE

NOTE

Carina represents the keel and hull of the Argo, the ship made for Jason by Argus, a divinely blessed shipwright, who in a fit of vanity, named it after himself. The blade of the ship's steering oar is marked by the star Canopus.

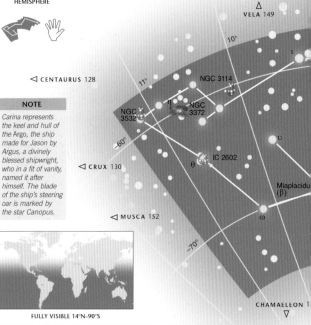

△ VELA 149

◁ CENTAURUS 128

NGC 3114

η NGC 3372

NGC 3532

−60°

11ʰ

10ʰ

◁ CRUX 130

IC 2602

θ

υ

Miaplacidu (β)

◁ MUSCA 152

ω

−70°

CHAMAELEON 1 ▽

FULLY VISIBLE 14°N–90°S

OBJECT NAME	DESCRIPTION	MAG.
NGC 2516	Large, bright open cluster of over 100 stars, 13,000 lya. Bright red giant in centre obvious with a small telescope.	3.8
NGC 3114	Open cluster, 28,000 lya. Needs wide field of view binoculars.	4.2
ETA CARINAE NEBULA (NGC 3372)	Bright diffuse nebula, 10,200 lya. Visible to naked eye; details can be seen with binoculars and small telescope.	1.0
NGC 3532	Open cluster of about 150 stars, with orange giants, 13,000 lya.	3.0
SOUTHERN PLEIADES (IC 2602)	Large, bright open cluster, 479 lya. Visible to naked eye.	2.7

STAR NAME	DESCRIPTION	MAG.
CANOPUS (α)	*White supergiant (F0), 313 lya. Second brightest star in the sky.*	*-0.6*
MIAPLACIDUS (β)	*Blue-white star (A0), 111 lya.*	*1.7*
AVIOR (ε)	*Orange giant (K0), 630 lya.*	*1.9*
η	*Variable blue star (F5), 7,500 lya. Four million times as luminous as Sun.*	*5.0*
θ	*Blue-white star (B0), 479 lya. The brightest member of IC 2602.*	*2.7*

NGC 3532 *is an open cluster visible to the naked eye, and located near the Eta Carinae Nebula. It is a rewarding target for binoculars or telescopes with a wide field of view.*

NGC 3372, *the large, diffuse Eta Carinae Nebula, surrounds the bright variable Eta (η) star of Carina, which lies in the brightest part of the nebula. The star appears as a hazy orange ellipse through a telescope.*

Musca

Muscae (Mus)

The constellation of Musca was introduced in the 16th century by the Dutch navigators Pieter Dirkszoon Keyser and Frederick de Houtman. It was originally called Apis, the Bee, but its name was later changed to Musca Australis to distinguish it from the Northern Fly. Its brightest star is the double star Alpha (α) at magnitude 2.7. Situated against the Milky Way, the constellation can be hard to identify.

NGC 4833 *is a compact globular cluster. It can be detected with binoculars and is fully resolved with telescopes of 100mm aperture or more.*

SOUTHERN CELESTIAL HEMISPHERE

FULLY VISIBLE 14°N–90°S

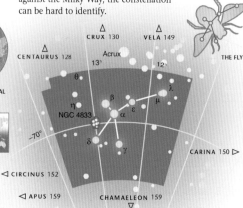

Circinus

Circini (Cir)

A small and insignificant constellation, Circinus was introduced in 1756 by Nicolas Louis de Lacaille. It lacks bright clusters, nebulae, or galaxies, but does contain NGC 5315, a faint and distant planetary nebula, which can be detected with a moderate telescope.

NGC 5315, *a planetary nebula, is about 4,000 to 13,000 lya, and is a strong radio source. Higher apertures reveal a blue-coloured disc.*

SOUTHERN CELESTIAL HEMISPHERE

FULLY VISIBLE 19°N–90°S

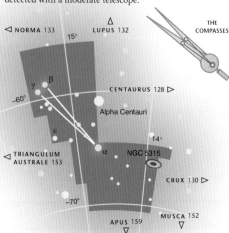

Triangulum Australe

Trianguli Australis (TrA)

This constellation is one of the dozen introduced in the 16th century by Dutch navigators Pieter Dirkszoon Keyser and Frederick de Houtman. Although easily recognized by its triangular shape, it is small constellation and contains little of interest to amateur astronomers apart from one open cluster, NGC 6025, which lies in the Milky Way. The cluster is about one-third the apparent width of the full Moon and is 2,700 light years away from the Earth.

NGC 6025, an open cluster containing about 50 stars, is visible with binoculars and small telescopes.

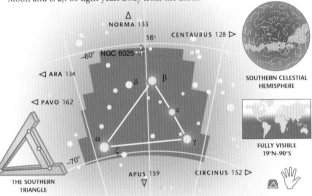

SOUTHERN CELESTIAL HEMISPHERE

FULLY VISIBLE 19°N–90°S

Telescopium

Telescopii (Tel)

Representing a telescope, Telescopium was introduced in the 18th century by French astronomer Nicolas Louis de Lacaille. It is faint and contains only one deep-sky object of interest to amateur astronomers, NGC 6584, which is easy to detect with powerful binoculars and appears as a small glow through instruments with small apertures. It lies 43,700 light years away.

NGC 6584, a globular cluster, appears as a small globe with small apertures. Individual stars can be resolved with larger telescopes.

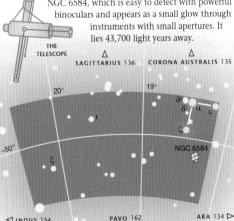

SOUTHERN CELESTIAL HEMISPHERE

FULLY VISIBLE 33°N–90°S

Indus

Indi (Ind)

NGC 7205 is a faint spiral galaxy that can be observed, without detail, using a 150mm aperture telescope.

The constellation of Indus represents a North American Indian, and was introduced in the 16th century by the Dutch navigators Pieter Dirkszoon Keyser and Frederick de Houtman. It has no star clusters or nebulae but contains some faint galaxies within reach of amateur telescopes. Its brightest star, Alpha (α), is of magnitude 3.1.

SOUTHERN CELESTIAL HEMISPHERE

FULLY VISIBLE
15°N–90°S

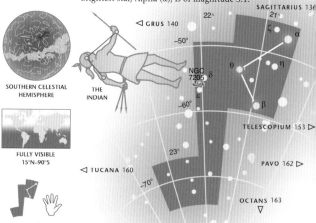

Phoenix

Phoenicis (Phe)

THE BRIGHT STAR at the top right, among the faint stars of Phoenix, is Achernar, the blue-white Alpha (α) star of Eridanus.

This constellation represents the mythological bird that rises from its own ashes. Introduced in the 16th century by Pieter Dirkszoon Keyser and Frederick de Houtman, Phoenix is a faint and insignificant constellation, containing little of interest for amateur astronomers.

SOUTHERN CELESTIAL HEMISPHERE

FULLY VISIBLE
32°N–90°S

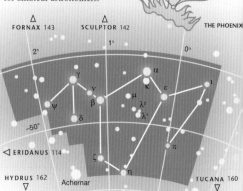

Horologium

Horologii (Hor)

A faint constellation introduced in 1750 by the French
astronomer Nicolas Loius de Lacaille, Horologium
represents a pendulum clock. The constellation contains
little of interest to the amateur astronomer.

NGC 1261, with a
magnitude of 8.4, is
the brightest deep-sky
object in Horologium
but a large telescope is
required to fully resolve
its member stars.

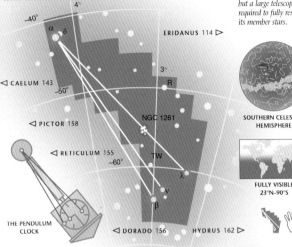

THE PENDULUM
CLOCK

SOUTHERN CELESTIAL
HEMISPHERE

FULLY VISIBLE
23°N–90°S

Reticulum

Reticuli (Ret)

During his survey of the southern sky, the French
astronomer Nicolas Louis de Lacaille used a grid, or reticule,
in the telescope eyepiece to measure stellar positions.
Lacaille introduced a new constellation into the sky,
Reticulum Rhomboidalis, now known as Reticulum, to
represent the reticule. The constellation contains some
faint galaxies. Its brightest star is Alpha (α), magnitude 3.5.

THE BARRED SPIRAL
galaxy NGC 1313 is
dominated by patches
of star formation,
apparent as clouds of
bluish stars.

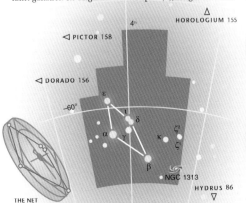

THE NET

SOUTHERN CELESTIAL
HEMISPHERE

FULLY VISIBLE
23°N–90°S

Dorado

Doradus (Dor)

AN IRREGULAR GALAXY, the Large Magellanic Cloud also shows evidence of being a barred spiral. It has over 10,000 million stars and is 20,000 light years across.

The constellation of Dorado was introduced in the 16th century by the Dutchmen, Pieter Dirkszoon Keyser and Frederick de Houtman. The constellation is home to the Large Magellanic Cloud (LMC), a satellite galaxy of our own Milky Way. The LMC is visible to the naked eye and is an excellent object for observation with any instrument. The LMC contains the Tarantula Nebula, another naked-eye target. This nebula is so large and bright that if it were placed in our galaxy at the location of the Orion Nebula, it would cast shadows on the Earth. The Tarantula Nebula is the only extra-galactic nebula that can be seen with the unaided eye.

SOUTHERN CELESTIAL HEMISPHERE

THE GOLDFISH OR SWORDFISH

◁ PICTOR 158

◁ CARINA 150

◁ VOLANS 158

MENSA 163 ▽

NGC 2100, one of the many clusters in the LMC, is so compact it resembles a globular cluster. It is typical of many of the LMC clusters and is visible with small telescopes.

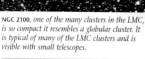

OBJECT NAME	DESCRIPTION	MAG.
LARGE MAGELLANIC CLOUD (LMC)	Irregular satellite galaxy of Milky Way, 163,000 lya.	0.9
NGC 1850	Open cluster, 163,000 lya. Easily visible with 100mm aperture.	8.4
TARANTULA NEBULA (NGC 2070)	Nebula in the LMC, 163,000 lya.	8.0
NGC 2100	Open cluster in the LMC, 163,000 lya.	9.6

STAR NAME	DESCRIPTION	MAG.
α	Blue-white giant (A0), 176 lya.	3.3
β	Yellow white supergiant variable (F6), with a period of 236 hours, 1,070 lya.	3.5 – 4.1
γ	Yellow giant (F4), 66 lya.	4.2
η	White main sequence star (A7), 145 lya.	4.3
R	Red giant variable (M8), with a period of 338 days, 204 lya.	4.8 – 6.6

△
CAELUM 143

HOROLOGIUM 155 ▷

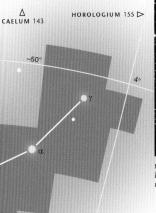

~-50°

4ʰ

γ

α

RETICULUM 155 ▷

NGC 1850 *is the brightest star cluster in the Large Magellanic Cloud. It is easily visible with a moderate telescope.*

FULLY VISIBLE 20°N–90°S

NOTE

A small galaxy in orbit around our own larger Milky Way, with a period of 1,500 million years, the Large Magellanic Cloud has one-tenth the mass of our galaxy and contains numerous clusters and bright nebulae.

HYDRUS 162
▽

THE TARANTULA NEBULA *(NGC 2070), also known as 30 Doradus (since it was originally thought to be a star), is larger than any nebula in our galaxy. Easily visible to the naked eye, it is a rewarding sight with any telescope.*

Pictor

Pictoris (Pic)

Introduced in the 18th century by the French astronomer
Nicolas Louis de Lacaille, Pictor is a faint constellation
lying south of Columba between Canopus in Carina and
the Large Magellanic Cloud. It contains a Beta (β) star,
which is surrounded by a disc of gas and dust that is
possibly the site of new planet formation.

SOUTHERN CELESTIAL
HEMISPHERE

FULLY VISIBLE
26°N–90°S

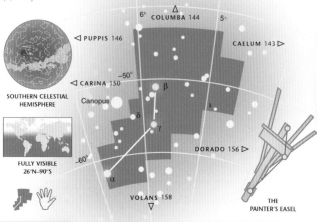

Volans

Volantis (Vol)

NGC 2442 *is a barred
spiral galaxy that
shows signs of having
been distorted by a
close encounter with
a passing galaxy.*

This constellation was introduced by the Dutch navigators
Pieter Dirkszoon Keyser and Frederick de Houtman towards
the end of the 16th century. The constellation has no
bright stars, clusters, or nebulae. However, its Gamma (γ)
double star of 3.8 and 5.7 magnitude
reveals its orange and yellow
colours through a small
telescope. The brightest galaxy
in Volans is best observed with
a large telescope.

SOUTHERN CELESTIAL
HEMISPHERE

FULLY VISIBLE
14°N–90°S

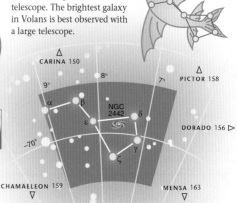

Chamaeleon

Chamaeleontis (Cha)

Named after the lizard that changes its skin colour to match its surroundings, Chamaeleon was introduced in the 16th century by Dutch navigators Pieter Dirkszoon Keyzer and Frederick de Houtman. A faint and insignificant constellation, it contains no bright nebulae, clusters, or galaxies. Its Delta (δ) double star is an orange giant and blue star, of magnitudes 5.9 and 4.4, and is easily visible with binoculars.

NGC 3195 is too faint to provide a detailed view with modest telescopes, but large telescopes or long-exposure photography will show structure within the disc.

THE CHAMELEON

△
MUSCA 152

△
CARINA 150

VOLANS 158 ▷

13ʰ 12ʰ 11ʰ 10ʰ 9ʰ 8ʰ

ε γ α

β δ

NGC 3195

-80°

◁ APUS 159

OCTANS 163
▽

MENSA 163 ▷

SOUTHERN CELESTIAL HEMISPHERE

FULLY VISIBLE
7°N–90°S

Apus

Apodis (Aps)

The constellation of Apus represents a bird of paradise, and was introduced as a new constellation in the 16th century by the Dutch navigators Pieter Dirkszoon Keyser and Frederick de Houtman. It lies in the most featureless area around the South Celestial Pole. It is insignificant and contains little of interest for the amateur astronomer. Its brightest star is Alpha (α), of magnitude 3.8. The Delta (δ) star is an optical double of two red giant stars.

APUS lies between Triangulum Australe (north) and Octans (south). Here the orange giant Alpha (α) of Triangulum Australe is at the top of the image.

THE BIRD OF PARADISE

△
TRIANGULUM AUSTRALE 153

△
CIRCINUS 152

17ʰ 16ʰ 15ʰ 14ʰ

-70°

ζ

β δ

γ α

η

MUSCA 152 ▷

-80°

CHAMAELEON 159
▽

SOUTHERN CELESTIAL HEMISPHERE

FULLY VISIBLE
7°N–90°S

Tucana

Tucana (Tuc)

Introduced as a new constellation by the Dutch navigators Pieter Dirkszoon Keyser and Frederick de Houtman towards the end of the 16th century, Tucana appears in Johann Bayer's celestial atlas published in 1603. It represents a toucan, a large-beaked bird native to South America. Although Tucana is a small constellation, sparse in clusters and nebulae, it contains two of the best deep-sky objects visible to amateur astronomers: the Small Magellanic Cloud (SMC) and 47 Tucanae (NGC 104), one of the globular clusters nearest to us. 47 Tucanae, originally catalogued as a star, is in fact the second brightest globular cluster in the night sky, shining at magnitude 4 and visible to the naked eye. The SMC is a satellite galaxy of the Milky Way and forms a distinctive wedge-shaped cloud in the southern skies.

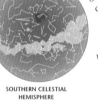

47 TUCANAE *(NGC 104), a globular cluster, has a diameter of 210 light years; packed in it is a mass that is over a million times larger than that of the Sun.*

SOUTHERN CELESTIAL HEMISPHERE

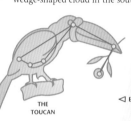

THE TOUCAN

△ PHOENIX 154

◁ ERIDANUS 114

–60°

◁ HOROLOGIUM 155

◁ HYDRUS 16

NGC 346, *a star-forming region about 200 light years across, is embedded in the SMC. Astronomers have identified a population of embryonic stars in its dark dust lanes, visible here in the centre.*

OBJECT NAME	DESCRIPTION	MAG.
47 TUCANAE (NGC 104)	Globular cluster, 14,700 lya.	4.0
SMALL MAGELLANIC CLOUD	Irregular galaxy, 210,000 lya. Visible to the naked eye, binoculars reveal clusters and nebulae.	2.3
NGC 346	Nebula + cluster, 210,000 lya. Clearly visible in binoculars.	7.0
NGC 362	Globular cluster, 29,000 lya. Binocular object.	6.6

FULLY VISIBLE 14°N–90°S

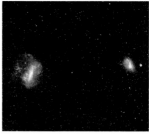

THE SMALL MAGELLANIC CLOUD *and 47 Tucanae (NGC 104), the globular cluster near it, are seen here in an amateur astrophotograph with a wide field view. To the naked eye, 47 Tucanae appears similar to a hazy star of magnitude 4, while SMC appears like an elongated patch of light seven times wider than the full Moon.*

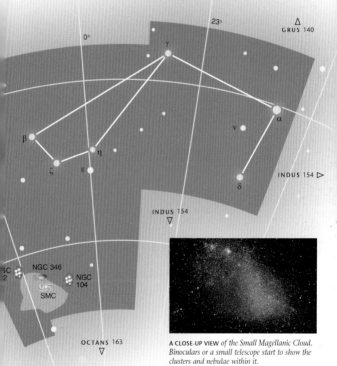

23ʰ

△ GRUS 140

0ʰ

γ

α

ν

β

ζ

η

ε

δ

INDUS 154 ▷

INDUS 154 ▽

NGC 346

NGC 104

SMC

OCTANS 163 ▽

A CLOSE-UP VIEW *of the Small Magellanic Cloud. Binoculars or a small telescope start to show the clusters and nebulae within it.*

STAR NAME	DESCRIPTION	MAG.
α	Orange giant (K3), 200 lya.	2.9
β	Multiple star system, two blue-white components (B9 + A2) visible with binoculars or small telescope, 140 + 172 lya.	4.4 + 4.5
γ	White giant (F1), 72 lya.	4.0
δ	Blue-white and yellow main sequence stars (B9 + G0), 267 lya.	4.5 + 8.9
κ	Binary star, yellow and orange (F5 + K1), 67 lya. Split by small telescopes.	5.1 + 7.3

Pavo

Pavonis (Pav)

NGC 6752 *is a globular cluster covering an area half the size of the full Moon. Although easily visible with binoculars, small telescopes are required to see detail.*

This is a recent constellation introduced by the Dutch navigators Pieter Dirkszoon Keyser and Frederick de Houtman in the late 16th century. It represents a peacock, which according to Graeco-Roman mythology, was the sacred bird belonging to Hera, the wife of Zeus. It contains NGC 6752, a globular cluster of magnitude 5.4, lying 15,000 light years away. Peacock, Pavo's brightest star, is of magnitude 1.9.

SOUTHERN CELESTIAL HEMISPHERE

FULLY VISIBLE
15°N–90°S

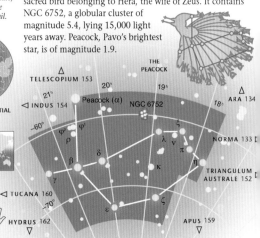

Hydrus

Hydri (Hyi)

THE STARS OF HYDRUS *are shown here; the red star near the centre is Gamma (γ), a red giant, which is of magnitude 3.2 and is 214 light years away.*

Representing a small water-snake, this constellation was introduced in the 16th century by Dutch navigators Pieter Dirkszoon Keyser and Frederick de Houtman. Its brightest star is the Beta (β) yellow giant, of magnitude 2.9.

SOUTHERN CELESTIAL HEMISPHERE

FULLY VISIBLE
8°N–90°S

Mensa

Mensae (Men)

The faintest of all the 88 constellations, Mensa contains little of interest. The constellation was introduced in the 18th century by the French astronomer Nicolas Louis de Lacaille and represents the Table Mountain at the Cape of Good Hope, from where he surveyed the southern sky. The yellow Alpha (α) star is its brightest at magnitude 5.1.

THE STARS OF MENSA *can be seen in the image above. The bright red giant towards the left of the image is Gamma (γ) of Hydrus.*

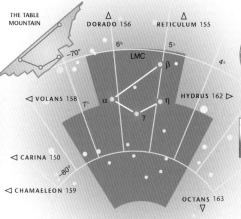

THE TABLE MOUNTAIN
△ DORADO 156
△ RETICULUM 155
6ʰ 5ʰ
−70° LMC
β 4ʰ
◁ VOLANS 158 α η
7ʰ γ HYDRUS 162 ▷
◁ CARINA 150 −80°
◁ CHAMAELEON 159
OCTANS 163 ▽

SOUTHERN CELESTIAL HEMISPHERE

FULLY VISIBLE
5°N–90°S

Octans

Octantis (Oct)

A faint and insignificant constellation, Octans was introduced in the 18th century by Nicolas Louis de Lacaille to represent the octant, the precursor to the sextant. Other than its location at the South Celestial Pole (SCP), it is of little interest to amateur astronomers. The yellow-white giant Sigma (σ) star is the nearest naked-eye star to the South Celestial Pole.

AMONG THE STARS *of Octans seen above is Epsilon (ε), the red star near the centre; the orange giant, far right, is Alpha (α) Trianguli Australis.*

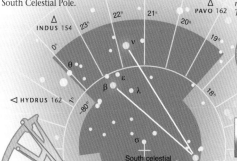

△ PAVO 162
△ INDUS 154
22ʰ 21ʰ
23ʰ 20ʰ
0° θ
ν 19ʰ
◁ HYDRUS 162 β ε
−80° λ 18ʰ
σ
South celestial pole
δ
THE OCTANT
◁ MENSA 163
CHAMAELEON 159 ▽

SOUTHERN CELESTIAL HEMISPHERE

FULLY VISIBLE
0°–90°S

NEBULA   GLOBULAR CLUSTER   GALAXY   STARS

Month by Month

This section of the book consists of sky charts showing you the position of the constellations and key deep-sky objects through every month of the year. Each chart shows the sky as it appears at 10pm Standard Time in mid-month and is accompanied by a brief description of the main features that will be visible at that time of year. Northern and southern hemispheres have separate charts; if you are sky-watching from the northern hemisphere use the first two pages of each month; if you are in the southern hemisphere, use the second two pages.

all 88 constellation patterns plotted on chart

introductory paragraph

ecliptic (useful for locating planets)

whole-sky chart

sides of chart show stars visible to east and west

cross on map indicates the zenith (point directly overhead)

centre of chart shows sky directly overhead

symbol for deep-sky object

chart shows stars brighter than magnitude 5.0

colour-coded lines indicate the position of the viewing horizon from different latitudes

Milky Way

table showing times when chart is applicable

cities representing range of latitudes

key to deep-sky objects

key to star magnitudes

The sky will look the same at 11 pm at the start of the month and at 9pm at the end of the month as it does at 10 pm in mid-month. To look at the sky at a different time, use charts for a different month: for every two hours before or after 10 pm, go one month backwards or forwards

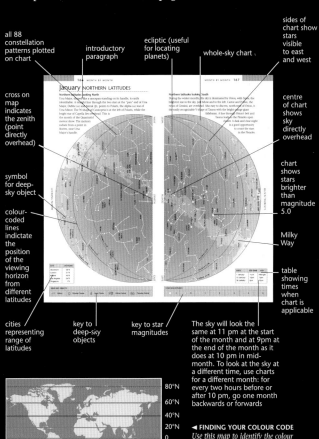

	80°N
	60°N
	40°N
	20°N
	0
	20°S
	40°S
	60°S

◄ **FINDING YOUR COLOUR CODE**
Use this map to identify the colour of the latitude line nearest to your geographical location. A 10 degree difference in latitude will have little effect on the stars you can actually see.

January NORTHERN LATITUDES

Northern latitudes looking North

Ursa Major, shaped like a saucepan standing on its handle, is easily identifiable. A straight line through the two stars at the "pan" end of Ursa Major, Dubhe (α) and Merak (β), points to Polaris, the Alpha (α) star of Ursa Minor. The W-shape of Cassiopeia is to the left of Polaris, while the bright star of Capella lies overhead. This is the month of the Quantratid meteor show. The meteors radiate from a point in Boötes, near Ursa Major's "handle".

LOOKING NORTH

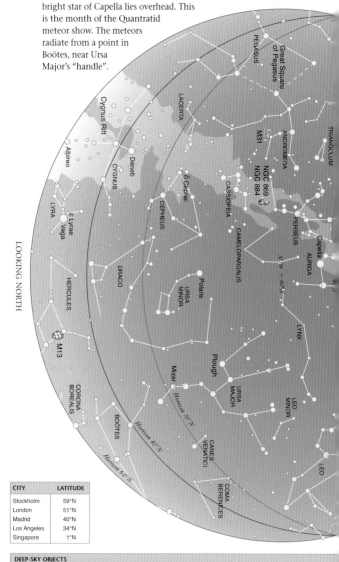

CITY	LATITUDE
Stockholm	59°N
London	51°N
Madrid	40°N
Los Angeles	34°N
Singapore	1°N

DEEP-SKY OBJECTS

	Galaxy		Globular Cluster		Open Cluster		Diffuse Nebula		Planetary Nebula

Northern latitudes looking South

During the winter months the sky is dominated by Orion, with Sirius, the brightest star in the sky, just below and to the left. Castor and Pollux, the twins of Gemini, are overhead. Also easy to discern, northwest of Orion, is the easily recognizable V-shape of Taurus with the bright orange giant Aldebaran. A line through Orion's belt and Taurus leads to the Pleiades open cluster. A dark and clear night is a good opportunity to count the stars in the Pleiades.

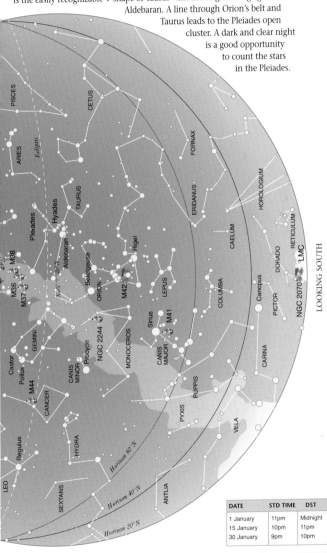

LOOKING SOUTH

DATE	STD TIME	DST
1 January	11pm	Midnight
15 January	10pm	11pm
30 January	9pm	10pm

STAR MAGNITUDES

| -1 | 0 | 1 | 2 | 3 | 4 | 5 |

January SOUTHERN LATITUDES

Southern latitudes looking North

The constellation Orion straddles the celestial equator, dominating the sky for southern as well as northern hemisphere observers. Sirius, in Canis Major, shines brightly to the right of Orion, nearly overhead, and the easily recognizable V-shape of Taurus can be found to Orion's lower left. The brightest star of Taurus, Aldebaran, shines with an orange hue. Below the V-shape of Taurus, to its left, the distinctive Pleiades star cluster is visible.

LOOKING NORTH

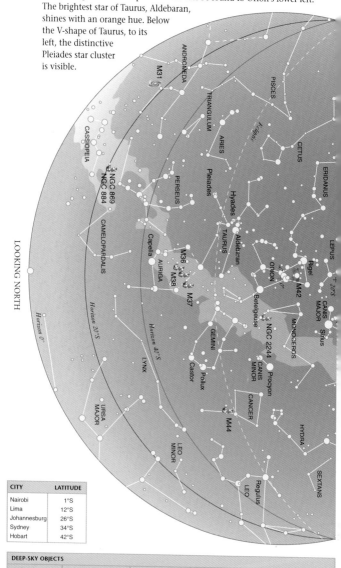

CITY	LATITUDE
Nairobi	1°S
Lima	12°S
Johannesburg	26°S
Sydney	34°S
Hobart	42°S

DEEP-SKY OBJECTS

	Galaxy		Globular Cluster		Open Cluster		Diffuse Nebula		Planetary Nebula

Southern latitudes looking South

Visible overhead are the bright stars of Rigel (Orion) and Sirius (Canis Major), and below them is Canopus, the Alpha (α) star of Carina, which is the second brightest star in the sky after Sirius. These three stars form a distinctive triangle in the sky. Observers can also view the Large Magellanic Cloud (LMC) and the Small Magellanic Cloud (SMC), two satellite galaxies of our own Milky Way, both of which can be found below Canopus.

LOOKING SOUTH

DATE	STD TIME	DST
1 January	11pm	Midnight
15 January	10pm	11pm
30 January	9pm	10pm

STAR MAGNITUDES

| -1 | 0 | 1 | 2 | 3 | 4 | 5 |

February NORTHERN LATITUDES

Northern latitudes looking North

The Pleiades cluster is high above the western horizon, with the recognizable V-shape of the horns of Taurus nearby. Capella in Auriga shines brightly, close to the zenith, and below it lies Cassiopeia. Looking northwards, Ursa Major and Ursa Minor are to the right of Cassiopeia; by following a curve through Ursa Major's tail, the bright star Arcturus can be located low down in the east. Cygnus and its brightest star Deneb are low on the northern horizon.

LOOKING NORTH

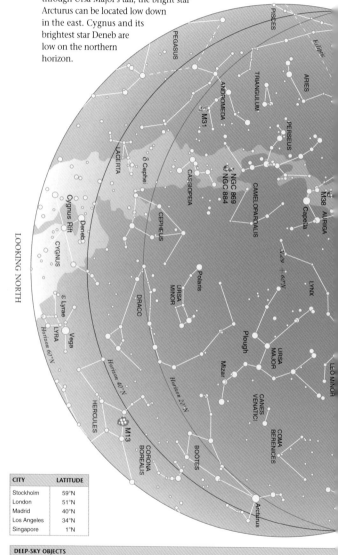

CITY	LATITUDE
Stockholm	59°N
London	51°N
Madrid	40°N
Los Angeles	34°N
Singapore	1°N

DEEP-SKY OBJECTS

Galaxy	Globular Cluster	Open Cluster	Diffuse Nebula	Planetary Nebula

Northern latitudes looking South

The southern sky in the winter months provides an excellent view of Taurus and Orion in the southwest. Taurus contains both the Pleiades and the Hyades clusters, easily observed with binoculars. The Orion Nebula is visible to the naked eye as a faint patch. Directly south and high above the horizon is the very bright star Sirius in Canis Major and only four degrees below it is the open cluster M41, visible with binoculars and small telescopes.

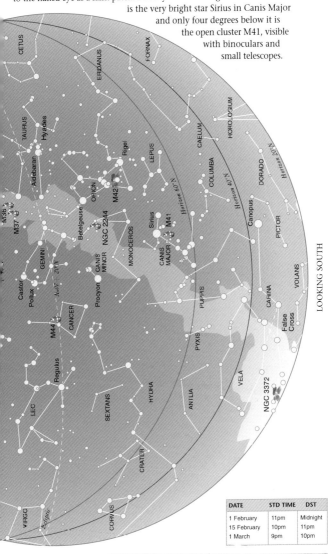

LOOKING SOUTH

DATE	STD TIME	DST
1 February	11pm	Midnight
15 February	10pm	11pm
1 March	9pm	10pm

STAR MAGNITUDES

| -1 | 0 | 1 | 2 | 3 | 4 | 5 |

February SOUTHERN LATITUDES

Southern latitudes looking North

A number of very bright stars can be seen in the summer northern sky. The well-known ones are Betelgeuse and Rigel in Orion, Aldebaran in Taurus, and Sirius in Canis Major. To the right of Orion is Procyon, while below Procyon are the Gemini twins of Castor and Pollux. Capella can be found lower down towards the northern horizon. Orion and Taurus, as always, provide a rewarding visual experience for users of binoculars and telescopes.

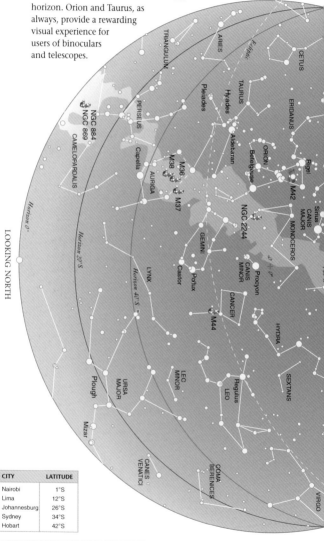

LOOKING NORTH

CITY	LATITUDE
Nairobi	1°S
Lima	12°S
Johannesburg	26°S
Sydney	34°S
Hobart	42°S

DEEP-SKY OBJECTS				
Galaxy	Globular Cluster	Open Cluster	Diffuse Nebula	Planetary Nebula

Southern latitudes looking South

The Milky Way runs from the southern horizon towards the zenith. Canopus in Carina lies high above the southern horizon, and above it, almost overhead, lies Sirius in Canis Major. Near the southeastern horizon lies Crux, and clear conditions should reveal the Coalsack, the dark dust cloud in Crux, as it blocks the light from the Milky Way stars behind it. High above the southern horizon are the Large and Small Magellanic Clouds (LMC, SMC).

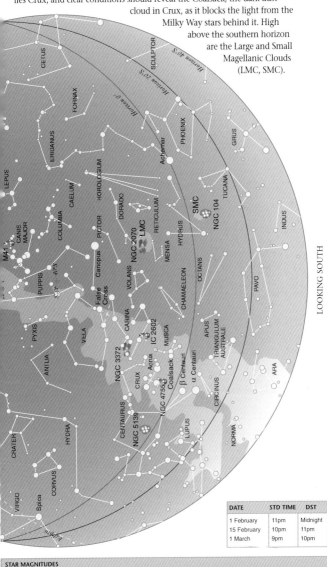

LOOKING SOUTH

DATE	STD TIME	DST
1 February	11pm	Midnight
15 February	10pm	11pm
1 March	9pm	10pm

STAR MAGNITUDES

| -1 | 0 | 1 | 2 | 3 | 4 | 5 |

March NORTHERN LATITUDES

Northern latitudes looking North

Ursa Major, high in the northern sky, is upside down. The two stars at the end of the "pan" point to Polaris, the Pole Star, in Ursa Minor. As the night progresses, all stars appear to revolve around Polaris. Towards the west, Capella is easy to find, and beyond it, the constellation of Taurus. A curve through Ursa Major's tail will lead to Arcturus, the brightest star in the east. As spring is approaching, the winter constellations set earlier each night in the west.

LOOKING NORTH

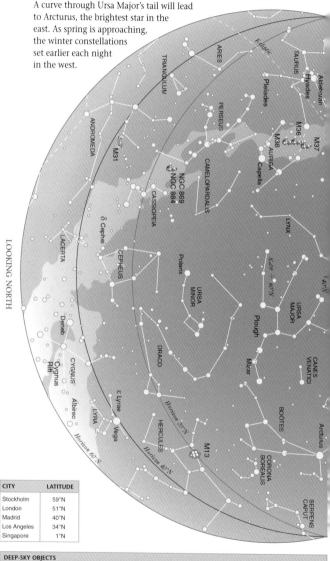

CITY	LATITUDE
Stockholm	59°N
London	51°N
Madrid	40°N
Los Angeles	34°N
Singapore	1°N

DEEP-SKY OBJECTS

Galaxy	Globular Cluster	Open Cluster	Diffuse Nebula	Planetary Nebula

Northern latitudes looking South

Leo and Gemini lie in the south and quite high up. The two stars of Gemini, Castor and Pollux, are high in the southwest. Orion and Sirius are slowly sinking below the western horizon, whereas towards the east rises Spica in Virgo, and further east is Arcturus. Cancer lies below Gemini, and contains the bright open cluster M44, also known as Praesepe or the Beehive. Although visible to the naked eye, its member stars can be seen only with binoculars.

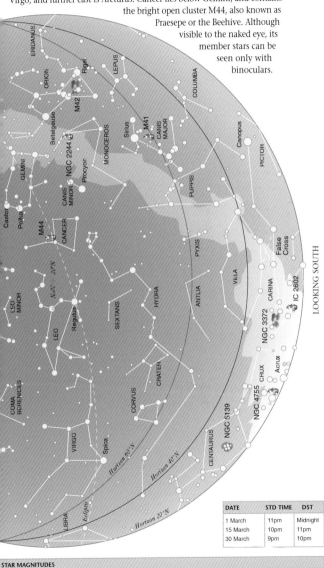

DATE	STD TIME	DST
1 March	11pm	Midnight
15 March	10pm	11pm
30 March	9pm	10pm

STAR MAGNITUDES

| -1 | 0 | 1 | 2 | 3 | 4 | 5 |

March SOUTHERN LATITUDES

Southern latitudes looking North

Orion, Taurus, and Auriga are setting in the west, taking with them the bright stars Betelgeuse, Rigel, Aldebaran, and Capella. Early in the evening Capella can be found near the northwest horizon. Sirius is the brightest star and is high in the northwest; below it and to the right (east) is Procyon, and below Procyon are Castor and Pollux, the twins of Gemini. Cancer is fairly high above the horizon, and the Praesepe Cluster (M44) can also be observed.

LOOKING NORTH

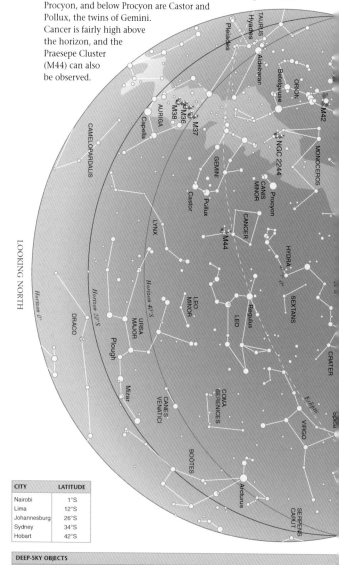

CITY	LATITUDE
Nairobi	1°S
Lima	12°S
Johannesburg	26°S
Sydney	34°S
Hobart	42°S

DEEP-SKY OBJECTS

Galaxy	Globular Cluster	Open Cluster	Diffuse Nebula	Planetary Nebula

Southern latitudes looking South

It is autumn in the southern hemisphere, and the Milky Way runs from the southeast horizon through the zenith (overhead). Canopus shines brilliantly to the south, while the cross of Crux is visible towards the east. Between Canopus and the southern horizon lie the Large and Small Magellanic Clouds (LMC, SMC), which make for excellent viewing with binoculars or telescopes. Below Crux is the constellation Centaurus, with its bright Alpha (α) and Beta (β) stars.

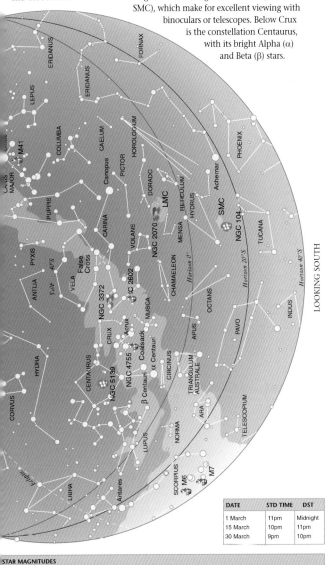

LOOKING SOUTH

DATE	STD TIME	DST
1 March	11pm	Midnight
15 March	10pm	11pm
30 March	9pm	10pm

STAR MAGNITUDES

| -1 | 0 | 1 | 2 | 3 | 4 | 5 |

April NORTHERN LATITUDES

Northern latitudes looking North

Ursa Major is nearly overhead, and upside down. The two pointer stars at the end of Ursa Major's "saucepan" point straight down to Polaris. By tracing a curve through Ursa Major's "handle", Arcturus, the brightest star in the spring sky, can be found. The Lyrid meteor shower appears this month, peaking on 21 April, with its radiant point located close to Vega in Lyra. The shower has, at the most, only 10 meteors an hour.

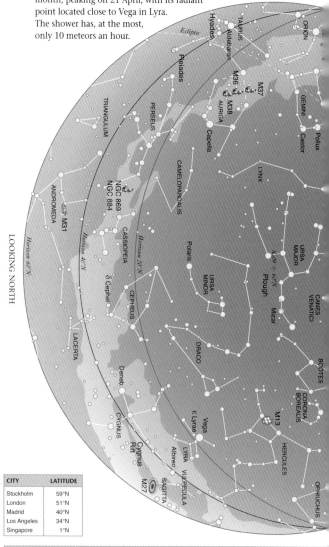

LOOKING NORTH

CITY	LATITUDE
Stockholm	59°N
London	51°N
Madrid	40°N
Los Angeles	34°N
Singapore	1°N

DEEP-SKY OBJECTS

Galaxy   Globular Cluster   Open Cluster   Diffuse Nebula   Planetary Nebula

Northern latitudes looking South

The constellation of Leo is high in the southern sky and contains the bright star Regulus. This star can be found by drawing a line through Ursa Major's pointer stars, away from Polaris. In the southeast, left of Leo, is the bright star Arcturus. Towards the west, Castor and Pollux, the brilliant stars of Gemini, can be seen. The bright winter constellation of Orion and its neighbour Sirius are slowly sinking into the west.

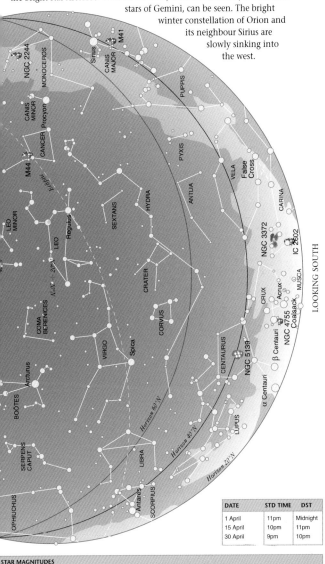

LOOKING SOUTH

DATE	STD TIME	DST
1 April	11pm	Midnight
15 April	10pm	11pm
30 April	9pm	10pm

STAR MAGNITUDES

-1	0	1	2	3	4	5

April SOUTHERN LATITUDES

Southern latitudes looking North

The most distinctive constellation of the northern sky as seen from southern latitudes is Leo. As it is a constellation introduced by ancient northern hemisphere observers, Leo appears upside down when viewed from the southern hemisphere. The star Arcturus is prominent in the east and Spica lies high above. Regulus, Leo's brightest star, shines high in the north, while in the west, the winter constellations sink into the twilight.

LOOKING NORTH

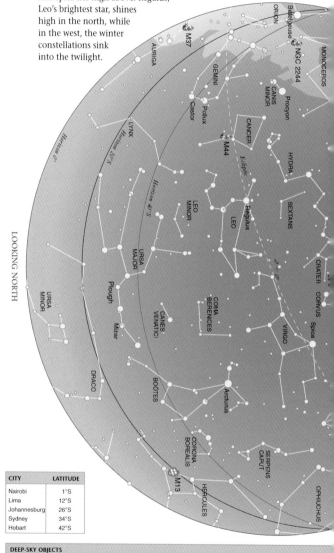

CITY	LATITUDE
Nairobi	1°S
Lima	12°S
Johannesburg	26°S
Sydney	34°S
Hobart	42°S

DEEP-SKY OBJECTS

Galaxy	Globular Cluster	Open Cluster	Diffuse Nebula	Planetary Nebula

Southern latitudes looking South

Canopus, the brightest star in Carina, dominates the southwest. Below it and towards the left are the Large and Small Magellanic Clouds (LMC, SMC), satellite galaxies of the Milky Way. Sirius, the brightest star in the sky, is west of Canopus. Towards the southeast lies Scorpius and the bright orange giant Antares. Crux, the Southern Cross, is high in the south, and below it are the Alpha (α) and Beta (β) stars of Centaurus. To the right of Crux are Vela and Carina.

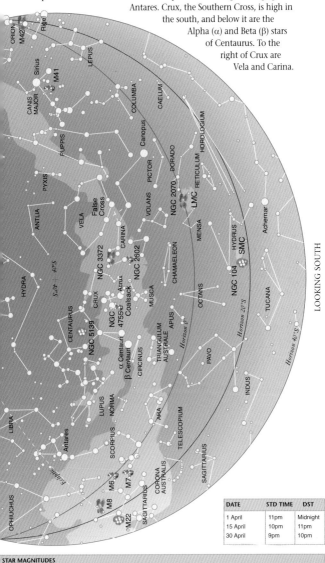

LOOKING SOUTH

DATE	STD TIME	DST
1 April	11pm	Midnight
15 April	10pm	11pm
30 April	9pm	10pm

STAR MAGNITUDES

-1	0	1	2	3	4	5

May NORTHERN LATITUDES

Northern latitudes looking North

Summer is approaching the northern hemisphere. Lyra, starting to climb towards the northeast, contains the bright star Vega. Cassiopeia, with its distinctive W-shape, lies along the northern horizon. Polaris can be found by following a straight line through the two end stars of Ursa Major's "pan". Cepheus lies between Polaris and Cassiopeia. The brilliant star Capella hangs low on the northwest horizon, to the left (west) of Cassiopeia.

LOOKING NORTH

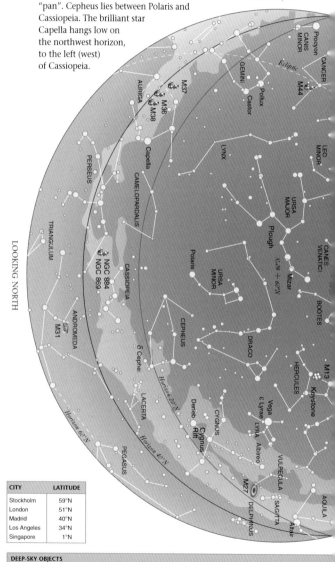

CITY	LATITUDE
Stockholm	59°N
London	51°N
Madrid	40°N
Los Angeles	34°N
Singapore	1°N

DEEP-SKY OBJECTS

| | Galaxy | | Globular Cluster | | Open Cluster | | Diffuse Nebula | | Planetary Nebula |

Northern latitudes looking South

The bright star Arcturus in the constellation Boötes tends to dominate the sky. Arcturus can be found by continuing along the curve of Ursa Major's "handle". By continuing further past Arcturus, the bright star Spica in Virgo will be reached. Eastwards of Arcturus is Hercules, and within Hercules lies the prominent globular cluster M13. This cluster is just visible to the naked eye under clear conditions, but it is an easy target for binoculars.

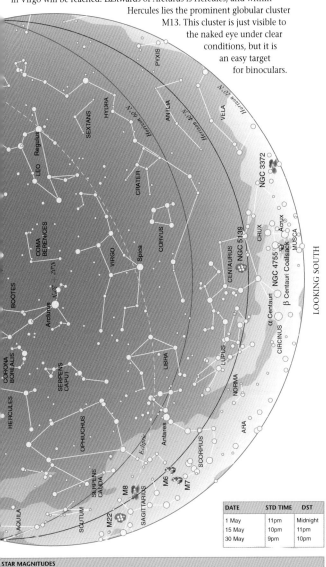

LOOKING SOUTH

DATE	STD TIME	DST
1 May	11pm	Midnight
15 May	10pm	11pm
30 May	9pm	10pm

STAR MAGNITUDES

| ○ -1 | ○ 0 | ○ 1 | ◦ 2 | · 3 | · 4 | · 5 |

May SOUTHERN LATITUDES

Southern latitudes looking North

Towards the north, Arcturus, one of the most brilliant stars in the sky, can be seen. Overhead lies Spica in Virgo. Below and to the left of Arcturus and Spica is Leo, prominent in the northwest, and its brightest star Regulus. Vega in Lyra lies low down in the northeast, and can be reached by drawing a straight line from Spica through Arcturus.

To the right (east) of Arcturus and Spica are the faint constellations Ophiuchus and Serpens.

LOOKING NORTH

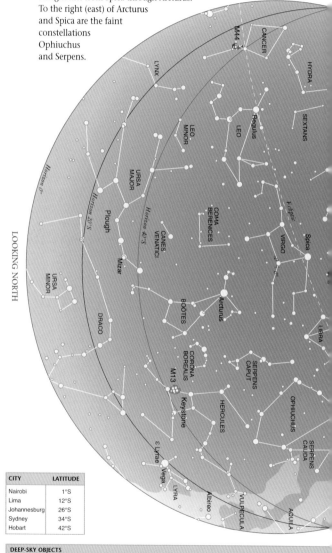

CITY	LATITUDE
Nairobi	1°S
Lima	12°S
Johannesburg	26°S
Sydney	34°S
Hobart	42°S

DEEP-SKY OBJECTS

Galaxy   Globular Cluster   Open Cluster   Diffuse Nebula   Planetary Nebula

Southern latitudes looking South

Crux appears upright and points down to Octans further south. Towards the zenith and within Centaurus is the bright globular cluster, Omega (ω) Centauri (NGC 5139), visible to the naked eye as a hazy star. As the night progresses, Scorpius and Sagittarius rise in the east, both worth sweeping with binoculars. The Eta Aquarids meteor shower starts in late April and peaks in the first week of May; about 35 bright meteors an hour can be seen.

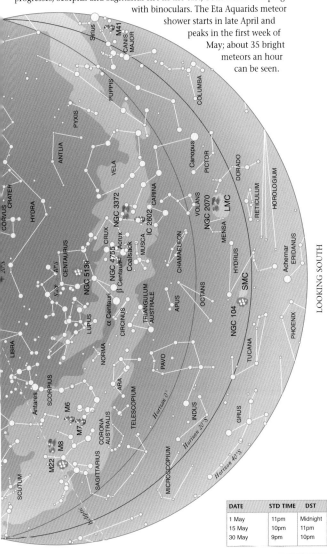

LOOKING SOUTH

DATE	STD TIME	DST
1 May	11pm	Midnight
15 May	10pm	11pm
30 May	9pm	10pm

STAR MAGNITUDES

	-1		0		1		2		3		4		5

June NORTHERN LATITUDES

Northern latitudes looking North

Summer constellations start to rise earlier each night in the east. Vega in Lyra rides high in the northeast, and below it rise Cygnus and the Milky Way. In the northwest, Ursa Major is standing on its "pan", with Leo to its left (west). Cassiopeia can be found lower down near the northern horizon. The Milky Way in the east should be scanned with binoculars, as it contains numerous star fields and clusters within reach of amateur observers.

LOOKING NORTH

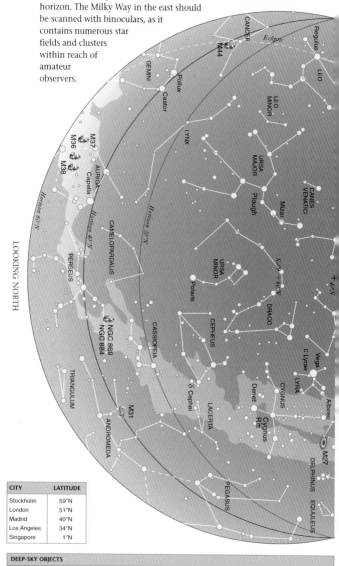

CITY	LATITUDE
Stockholm	59°N
London	51°N
Madrid	40°N
Los Angeles	34°N
Singapore	1°N

DEEP-SKY OBJECTS

Galaxy	Globular Cluster	Open Cluster	Diffuse Nebula	Planetary Nebula

Northern latitudes looking South

Arcturus, in Boötes, is high in the sky directly south, and below it is Spica, the most glittering star in Virgo. Lower down, near the southern horizon, Scorpius puts in an appearance, but how much of it is visible depends on the latitude – the further south, the more of this constellation is clearly seen. Scorpius' brightest star, Antares is visible low down, and can be clearly seen as an orange star. Leo is setting in the west, taking with it the bright star Denebola.

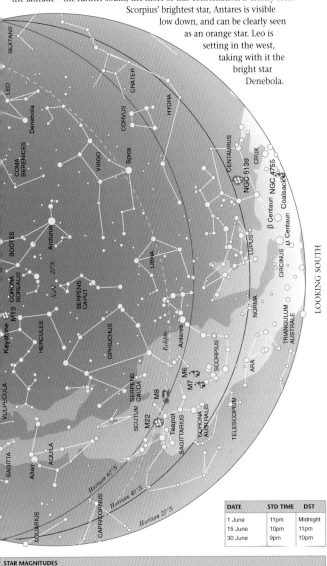

LOOKING SOUTH

DATE	STD TIME	DST
1 June	11pm	Midnight
15 June	10pm	11pm
30 June	9pm	10pm

STAR MAGNITUDES

| -1 | 0 | 1 | 2 | 3 | 4 | 5 |

June SOUTHERN LATITUDES

Southern latitudes looking North

High above the northern horizon, the bright star Arcturus is clearly visible. To its lower right is the constellation Hercules, containing the globular cluster M13, which is visible to the naked eye. Scorpius is overhead, high above the northern horizon, containing rich star fields and clusters, along with the orange star Antares. Towards the east, near the horizon, is Vega in Lyra, and further east is Altair in Aquila. The brightest star in the west is Spica in Virgo.

LOOKING NORTH

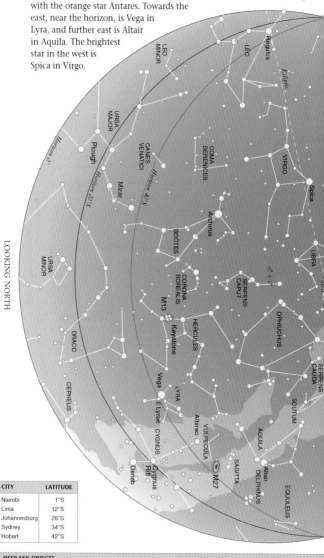

CITY	LATITUDE
Nairobi	1°S
Lima	12°S
Johannesburg	26°S
Sydney	34°S
Hobart	42°S

DEEP-SKY OBJECTS

 Galaxy   Globular Cluster   Open Cluster   Diffuse Nebula   Planetary Nebula

Southern latitudes looking South

The bright supergiant Antares is almost directly overhead. To its right, in the west, the brightest star seen is Spica in Virgo. The Milky Way runs from east to west and passes nearly overhead. The cross-shape of Crux lies southwest of Antares and Scorpius, and between Crux and Scorpius are the two bright stars Alpha (α) and Beta (β) Centauri. Below Crux lie the Large and Small Magellanic Clouds (LMC, SMC). In clear conditions, the Tarantula Nebula (NGC 2070) can be observed.

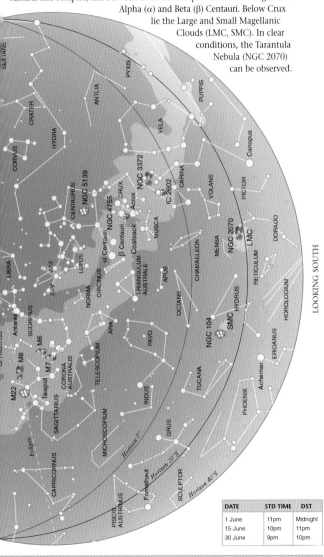

LOOKING SOUTH

DATE	STD TIME	DST
1 June	11pm	Midnight
15 June	10pm	11pm
30 June	9pm	10pm

STAR MAGNITUDES

| -1 | 0 | 1 | 2 | 3 | 4 | 5 |

July NORTHERN LATITUDES

Northern latitudes looking North

Ursa Major and Ursa Minor are central to the sky in this month. The bright star Arcturus lies in the west. Overhead Vega shines brightly, dominating the sky. The distinctive shape of Cassiopeia lies towards the east, along with Cygnus, a region rich with star fields that is worth viewing with binoculars. On a dark night, it is possible to see the faint stars of Draco winding between Ursa Major and Minor. The Summer Triangle of Deneb, Vega, and Altair dominates.

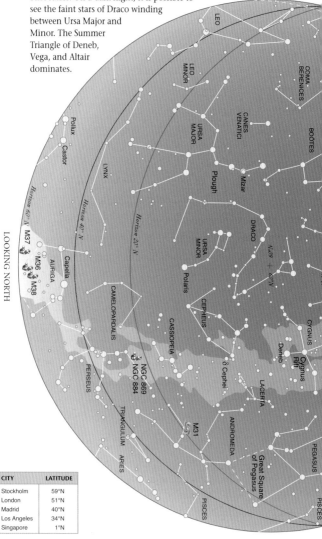

LOOKING NORTH

CITY	LATITUDE
Stockholm	59°N
London	51°N
Madrid	40°N
Los Angeles	34°N
Singapore	1°N

DEEP-SKY OBJECTS

🌀 Galaxy	🌐 Globular Cluster	✸ Open Cluster	🌫 Diffuse Nebula	👁 Planetary Nebula

Northern latitudes looking South

Near the southern horizon lies Scorpius and its most glittering star, Antares. Northerly latitudes allow Antares to move along the horizon as the night progresses. The region around Antares is rich with star clusters that are visible even with small amateur instruments. The Milky Way runs from the southern horizon upwards and towards the east (left). To the left of Scorpius is Sagittarius, and the view here is focused towards the centre of our Milky Way galaxy.

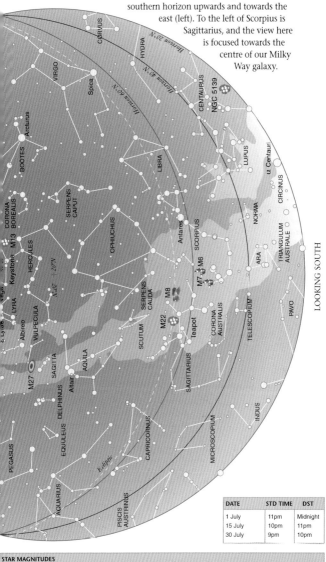

LOOKING SOUTH

DATE	STD TIME	DST
1 July	11pm	Midnight
15 July	10pm	11pm
30 July	9pm	10pm

STAR MAGNITUDES

-1   0   1   2   3   4   5

July SOUTHERN LATITUDES

Southern latitudes looking North

The sky is dominated by five bright stars: the orange supergiant Antares, high up in Scorpius, and the white stars Altair, Vega, Arcturus, and Spica running from east to west (right to left) in the constellations Aquila, Lyra, Boötes, and Virgo. The constellations Scorpius, Sagittarius, and Ophiuchus are nearly overhead, and are areas rich with clusters and regions of nebulosity. Binoculars and small telescopes can provide a rewarding view of this region.

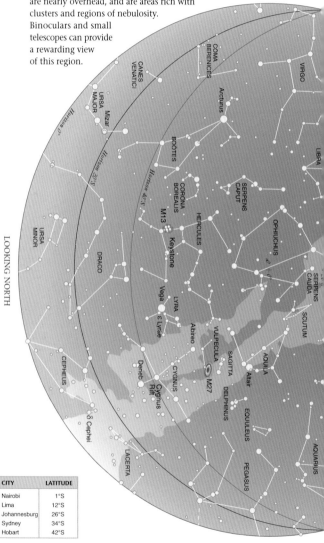

LOOKING NORTH

CITY	LATITUDE
Nairobi	1°S
Lima	12°S
Johannesburg	26°S
Sydney	34°S
Hobart	42°S

DEEP-SKY OBJECTS

Galaxy   Globular Cluster   Open Cluster   Diffuse Nebula   Planetary Nebula

Southern latitudes looking South

Scorpius and Sagittarius are nearly overhead, containing rich star fields and a good target for a low-power instrument like binoculars. Centaurus and Crux can be found heading towards the western horizon. If the sky is clear and dark, the Milky Way running through Crux can be seen to have a dark patch – this is the Coalsack, a region of cloudy dust obscuring the stars behind it. Other dark dust lanes can be seen running the length of the Milky Way.

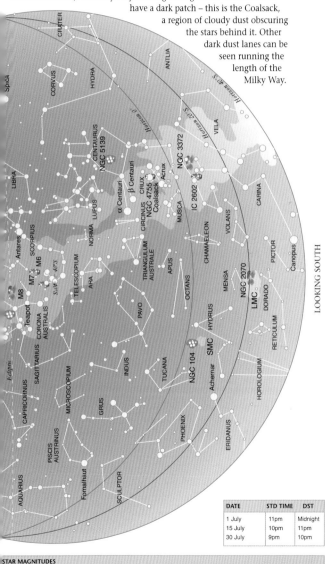

LOOKING SOUTH

DATE	STD TIME	DST
1 July	11pm	Midnight
15 July	10pm	11pm
30 July	9pm	10pm

STAR MAGNITUDES

● -1	● 0	● 1	● 2	• 3	· 4	· 5

August NORTHERN LATITUDES

Northern latitudes looking North

Towards the northwest is Ursa Major and in the northeast is Cassiopeia, with Polaris between them. Overhead is a triangle of three bright stars, Deneb in Cygnus, Vega in Lyra, and Altair in Aquila, known as the Summer Triangle. 12 August is the peak of the Perseid meteor shower, with bright meteors that can leave trails after flaring up. About 75 meteors an hour may be visible. The radiant point is near the Double Cluster (NGC 869 + 884) in Perseus.

LOOKING NORTH

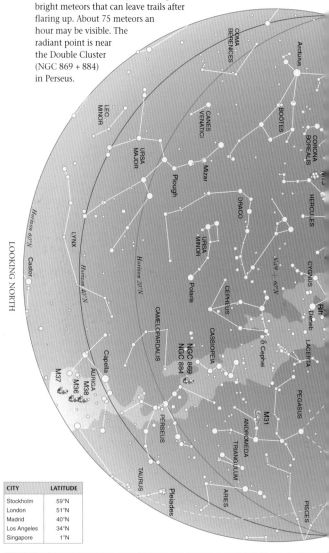

CITY	LATITUDE
Stockholm	59°N
London	51°N
Madrid	40°N
Los Angeles	34°N
Singapore	1°N

DEEP-SKY OBJECTS

| | Galaxy | | Globular Cluster | | Open Cluster | | Diffuse Nebula | | Planetary Nebula |

Northern latitudes looking South

The Milky Way shines from the southwest to the southeast, running through Cygnus. If the night is clear and very dark, structure can be seen within the Milky Way, including a dark region known as the Cygnus Rift, which divides the Milky Way into two. Below the Milky Way and towards the southern horizon reside the zodiacal constellations of Aquarius, Scorpius, Capricornus, and Sagittarius. The red giant Antares can be seen setting in the southwest.

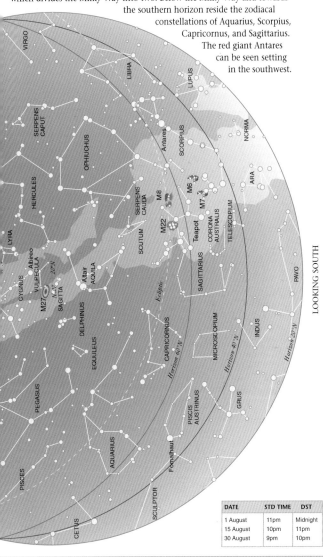

LOOKING SOUTH

DATE	STD TIME	DST
1 August	11pm	Midnight
15 August	10pm	11pm
30 August	9pm	10pm

STAR MAGNITUDES

| -1 | 0 | 1 | 2 | 3 | 4 | 5 |

August SOUTHERN LATITUDES

Southern latitudes looking North

The Summer Triangle formed by three bright stars, Deneb in Cygnus, Vega in Lyra, and Altair in Aquila, dominates the northern sky. To the left (west) of Vega is the constellation Hercules, containing M13, the largest northern globular cluster. M13 is difficult to see with the naked eye, but is an excellent target for binoculars or any telescope. High in the west is the orange giant Antares in Scorpius. The Milky Way stretches upwards from the northern horizon.

LOOKING NORTH

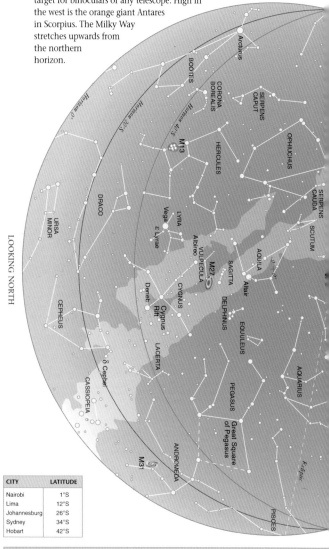

CITY	LATITUDE
Nairobi	1°S
Lima	12°S
Johannesburg	26°S
Sydney	34°S
Hobart	42°S

DEEP-SKY OBJECTS

Galaxy	Globular Cluster	Open Cluster	Diffuse Nebula	Planetary Nebula

Southern latitudes looking South

On a clear dark night, the Milky Way shines brightly from the northern to the southern horizon and the constellations of Sagittarius and Scorpius are high in the sky. The whole region is ideal for sweeping with binoculars. Towards the east, the bright star Fomalhaut can be found, and below it and slightly to the right is Achernar. Spica is setting in the west, while halfway between Scorpius and the southern horizon, Crux, the Southern Cross, is easily recognized.

LOOKING SOUTH

DATE	STD TIME	DST
1 August	11pm	Midnight
15 August	10pm	11pm
30 August	9pm	10pm

STAR MAGNITUDES

| -1 | 0 | 1 | 2 | 3 | 4 | 5 |

September NORTHERN LATITUDES

Northern latitudes looking North

The northern sky is sparse in bright stars during autumn. Cygnus is nearly overhead, and beneath it towards the west is Vega. The W-shape of Cassiopeia is standing on its end towards the northeast. Between Cassiopeia and Vega lie Cepheus and its Delta (δ) star, a variable with a five-day period that can be observed with the naked eye.

Ursa Major is lower down near the northern horizon, with the two pointer stars at the end of its "pan" pointing up to Polaris.

LOOKING NORTH

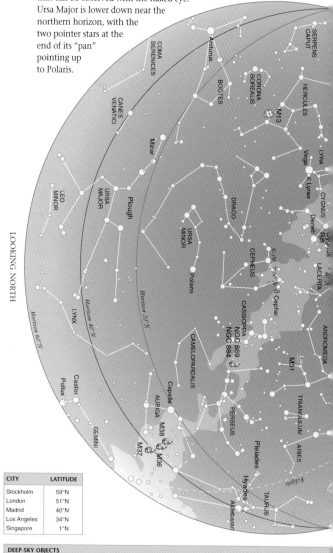

CITY	LATITUDE
Stockholm	59°N
London	51°N
Madrid	40°N
Los Angeles	34°N
Singapore	1°N

DEEP-SKY OBJECTS

Galaxy	Globular Cluster	Open Cluster	Diffuse Nebula	Planetary Nebula

Northern latitudes looking South

Cygnus and Vega are nearly overhead and due south of them is the bright star Altair in Aquila. Vega, Deneb, and Altair form the Summer Triangle. The Milky Way runs through this part of the sky and further south, leads to Sagittarius, near the southwestern horizon. On a dark night, one can detect dark rifts and dust lanes in the Milky Way. Just above the southern horizon is Fomalhaut, which can be used to find Aquarius and Capricornus.

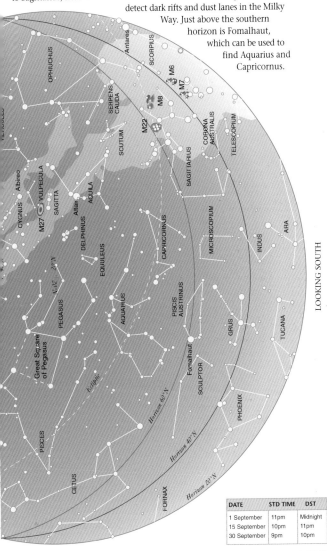

LOOKING SOUTH

DATE	STD TIME	DST
1 September	11pm	Midnight
15 September	10pm	11pm
30 September	9pm	10pm

STAR MAGNITUDES

| -1 | 0 | 1 | 2 | 3 | 4 | 5 |

September SOUTHERN LATITUDES

Southern latitudes looking North

The Summer Triangle formed by the bright stars Deneb, Vega, and Altair dominates the northern view. Between Deneb and Altair, one can find the constellation Vulpecula, which contains the planetary nebula M27. The rich part of the Milky Way, in Cygnus, lies close to the northern horizon and is not well placed for viewing. Sagittarius, however, is placed high in the sky towards the west, and is rich with star fields and star clusters.

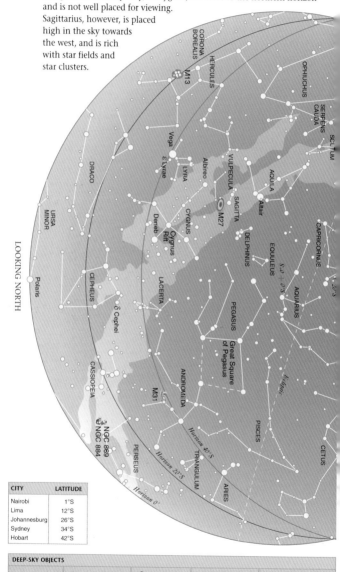

LOOKING NORTH

CITY	LATITUDE
Nairobi	1°S
Lima	12°S
Johannesburg	26°S
Sydney	34°S
Hobart	42°S

DEEP-SKY OBJECTS

Galaxy	Globular Cluster	Open Cluster	Diffuse Nebula	Planetary Nebula

Southern latitudes looking South

Towards the southeast, the brightest star is Achernar. Slightly above it and to the right is the Small Magellanic Cloud (SMC). This is a naked-eye object, as is the globular cluster 47 Tucanae (NGC 104) next to it. The Milky Way runs from the southern horizon and passes directly overhead. The southern part contains Crux, an easily recognized cross; a dark dust cloud called the Coalsack can also be seen. In the southwest, Scorpius is setting with its bright star, Antares.

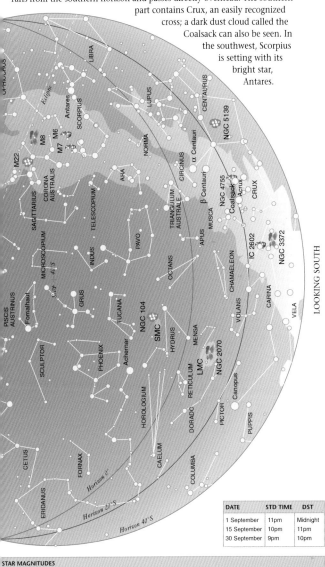

LOOKING SOUTH

DATE	STD TIME	DST
1 September	11pm	Midnight
15 September	10pm	11pm
30 September	9pm	10pm

STAR MAGNITUDES

| -1 | 0 | 1 | 2 | 3 | 4 | 5 |

October NORTHERN LATITUDES

Northern latitudes looking North

The Milky Way can be seen from horizon to horizon, passing overhead. The Summer Triangle, consisting of Deneb, Vega, and Altair lies towards the west (left). Taurus rises in the northeast, a sign of impending winter. Just above Taurus are the Pleiades (M45), a pleasant sight through binoculars. The Orionids meteor shower peaks on 21 October, with at most about 25 meteors an hour. The radiant point is within northern Orion and is best observed after midnight.

LOOKING NORTH

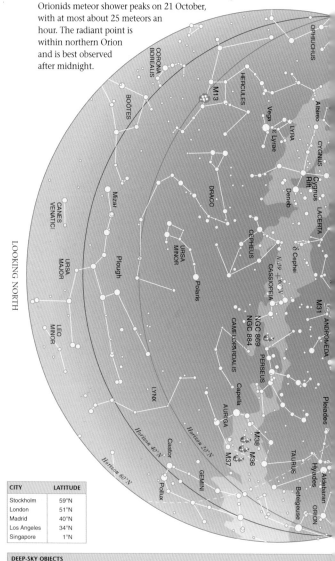

CITY	LATITUDE
Stockholm	59°N
London	51°N
Madrid	40°N
Los Angeles	34°N
Singapore	1°N

DEEP-SKY OBJECTS

Galaxy	Globular Cluster	Open Cluster	Diffuse Nebula	Planetary Nebula

Northern latitudes looking South

The Summer Triangle (Vega, Deneb, and Altair) continues to dominate the sky, but other autumnal constellations make a stronger appearance. Pegasus is high in the southern sky, below and to the right of Cassiopeia and Andromeda, which contains the spiral galaxy M31 – the Andromeda Galaxy. Under clear conditions, this galaxy can be detected with the naked eye, particularly if peripheral vision is used, and binoculars will find it easily.

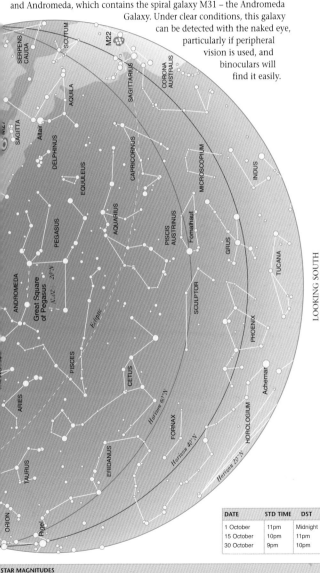

LOOKING SOUTH

DATE	STD TIME	DST
1 October	11pm	Midnight
15 October	10pm	11pm
30 October	9pm	10pm

STAR MAGNITUDES

| -1 | 0 | 1 | 2 | 3 | 4 | 5 |

October SOUTHERN LATITUDES

Southern latitudes looking North

Pegasus is central in the northern sky, with Andromeda below it and to the right (east), providing a good opportunity to see M31. Andromeda lies above the well-known W-shape of Cassiopeia. Directly overhead, the constellation of Aquarius can be seen. Towards the northwest, the Summer Triangle (Vega, Deneb, and Altair) is setting.

As the night progresses, the orange giant Aldebaran and the other stars of Taurus start to rise above the northeast horizon.

LOOKING NORTH

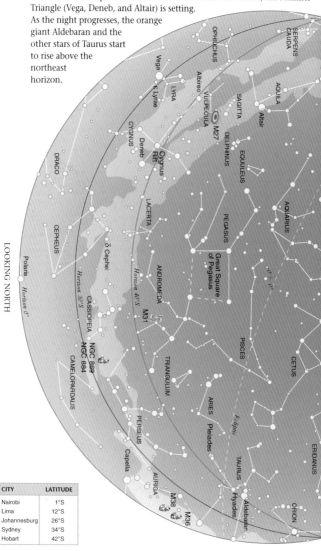

CITY	LATITUDE
Nairobi	1°S
Lima	12°S
Johannesburg	26°S
Sydney	34°S
Hobart	42°S

DEEP-SKY OBJECTS

 Galaxy   Globular Cluster   Open Cluster   Diffuse Nebula   Planetary Nebula

Southern latitudes looking South

In the southern hemisphere it is spring and the winter constellations are slowly slipping from view, to be replaced with a sparsely populated sky. In the west, towards the south, the Small Magellanic Clouds (SMC) is high enough above the horizon to give a rewarding sight for binoculars or telescopes. In the southeastern sky, Achernar is high, with Canopus rising below it. The western horizon sees the setting of Ophiuchus, Scorpius, and Sagittarius.

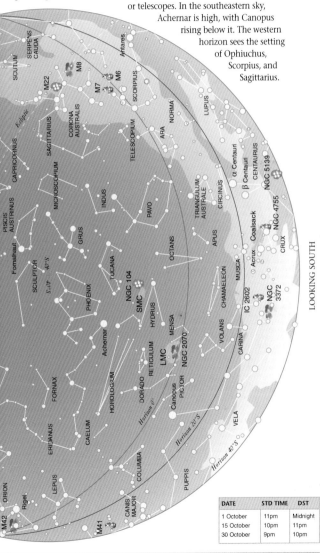

LOOKING SOUTH

DATE	STD TIME	DST
1 October	11pm	Midnight
15 October	10pm	11pm
30 October	9pm	10pm

STAR MAGNITUDES

| -1 | 0 | 1 | 2 | 3 | 4 | 5 |

November NORTHERN LATITUDES

Northern latitudes looking North

The Milky Way runs from east to west, passing overhead. High above the northern horizon, the constellations Andromeda and Perseus can be found, just above Cassiopeia. Under clear conditions, the Andromeda Galaxy (M31) can be detected with the naked eye. Ursa Major is low on the northern horizon, with Polaris in Ursa Minor above it. Towards the northeast, the star Capella glitters, and below Capella are Castor and Pollux, the twin stars of Gemini.

LOOKING NORTH

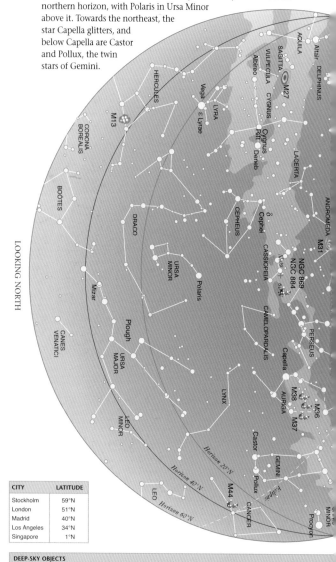

CITY	LATITUDE
Stockholm	59°N
London	51°N
Madrid	40°N
Los Angeles	34°N
Singapore	1°N

DEEP-SKY OBJECTS

Galaxy	Globular Cluster	Open Cluster	Diffuse Nebula
Planetary Nebula			

Northern latitudes looking South

As winter approaches, the winter constellations of Orion and Taurus arrive, rising in the east. The Pleiades star cluster rises before the other stars of Taurus and can be viewed with binoculars. Perseus and Andromeda are high in the sky, almost overhead, while Aquarius and Capricornus set in the west and Cetus lies south. Around this time, the Taurid and Leonid meteor showers put on a display with about 10 meteors an hour during their peak activity.

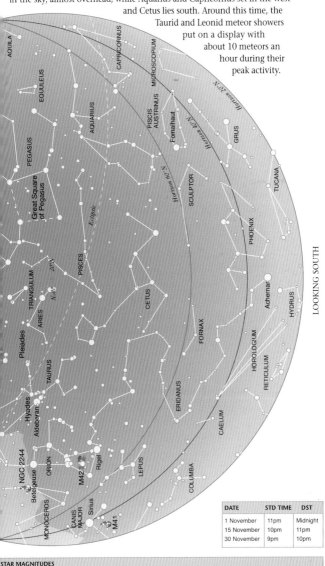

LOOKING SOUTH

DATE	STD TIME	DST
1 November	11pm	Midnight
15 November	10pm	11pm
30 November	9pm	10pm

STAR MAGNITUDES

| -1 | 0 | 1 | 2 | 3 | 4 | 5 |

November SOUTHERN LATITUDES

Southern latitudes looking North

Directly overhead lies the constellation Cetus, and further south below it are the constellations Pisces and Aries. Perseus, Andromeda, and Cassiopeia can be found lower down, close to the northern horizon, with the Great Square of Pegasus stretching across most of the northwestern sky. At this time, summer is approaching the southern hemisphere, heralded by the rising of Taurus and Orion in the northeast, with Orion located further east than Taurus.

LOOKING NORTH

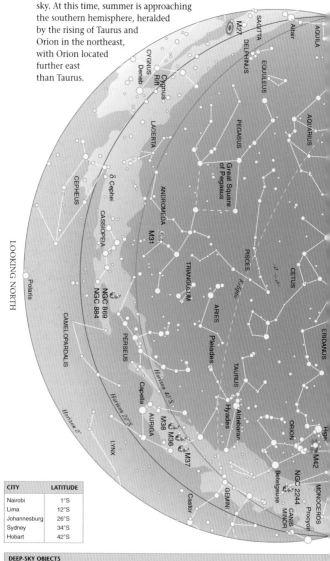

CITY	LATITUDE
Nairobi	1°S
Lima	12°S
Johannesburg	26°S
Sydney	34°S
Hobart	42°S

DEEP-SKY OBJECTS

Galaxy	Globular Cluster	Open Cluster	Diffuse Nebula	Planetary Nebula

Southern latitudes looking South

The Large and Small Magellanic Clouds (LMC, SMC) are well placed for naked-eye viewing, and in dark conditions the Tarantula Nebula in the Large Magellanic Cloud is clearly visible. Many of the constellations that can be seen are recent introductions, dating back to the 16th century, and lack bright objects of interest. An exception is Tucana, high in the sky, seen not only with the Small Magellanic Cloud, but also with the cluster 47 Tucanae (NGC 104).

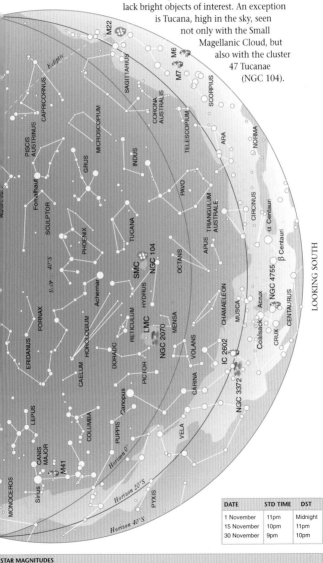

LOOKING SOUTH

DATE	STD TIME	DST
1 November	11pm	Midnight
15 November	10pm	11pm
30 November	9pm	10pm

STAR MAGNITUDES

| -1 | 0 | 1 | 2 | 3 | 4 | 5 |

December NORTHERN LATITUDES

Northern latitudes looking North

Capella is nearly overhead, and above it lies Taurus. Below and to the right (east) of Capella are Castor and Pollux, the two bright stars of Gemini. Just to the left of Capella lies Perseus, which contains the Double Cluster (NGC 869 + 884), two open star clusters just visible to the naked eye. Vega is low on the northwestern horizon, along with Deneb in Cygnus and Hercules. Cassiopeia is high in the northwest, and above it is Andromeda.

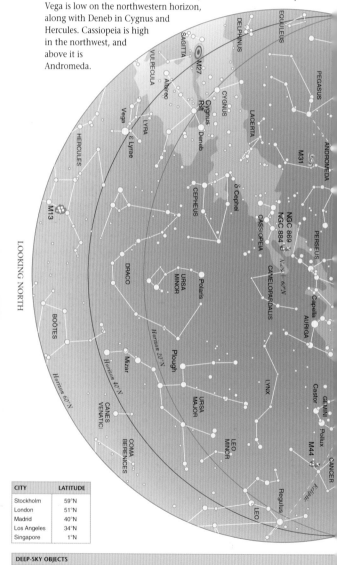

LOOKING NORTH

CITY	LATITUDE
Stockholm	59°N
London	51°N
Madrid	40°N
Los Angeles	34°N
Singapore	1°N

DEEP-SKY OBJECTS

| | Galaxy | | Globular Cluster | | Open Cluster | | Diffuse Nebula | | Planetary Nebula |

Northern latitudes looking South

The winter southern sky is spectacular, with the bright constellations of
Orion and Taurus. A dark winter sky is ideal for observing the Orion Nebula,
located below the three prominent blue-white stars that mark Orion's
"belt". Above Orion is the V-shape of Taurus, containing the scattered
stars of the Hyades cluster, while above
the V-shape is the Pleiades (M45)
open cluster. Binoculars can
reveal the richness of
the sky in Taurus
and Orion.

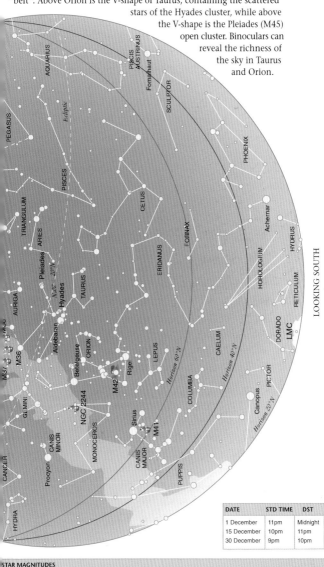

LOOKING SOUTH

DATE	STD TIME	DST
1 December	11pm	Midnight
15 December	10pm	11pm
30 December	9pm	10pm

STAR MAGNITUDES

| -1 | 0 | 1 | 2 | 3 | 4 | 5 |

December SOUTHERN LATITUDES

Southern latitudes looking North

Overhead the sky appears sparse, with the faint stars of Eridanus and Cetus. However, towards the east, the sky is rich with glittering stars and objects. Sirius is the brightest star high in the east, and to its left is Orion. As the night progresses, Castor and Pollux in Gemini climb higher, and just above them, to the right, Procyon journeys northwards.

Near the northern horizon Capella shines brightly, and to the left of the star, Perseus can be found, just above Cassiopeia.

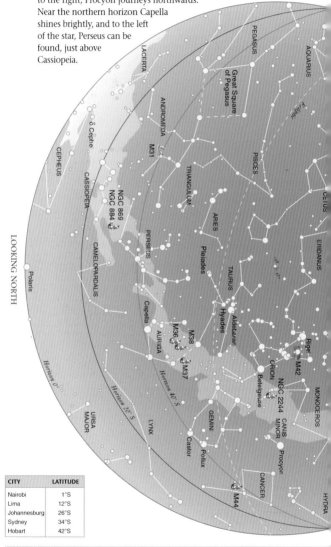

LOOKING NORTH

CITY	LATITUDE
Nairobi	1°S
Lima	12°S
Johannesburg	26°S
Sydney	34°S
Hobart	42°S

DEEP-SKY OBJECTS

Galaxy	Globular Cluster	Open Cluster	Diffuse Nebula	Planetary Nebula

Southern latitudes looking South

The southeastern summer sky contains a band of bright stars, three of which form a triangle: high up, in Orion, is Rigel, with Sirius below it, and to the right of Sirius is Canopus. High in the sky above the southern horizon the Large and Small Magellanic Clouds (LMC, SMC) are well placed for viewing. Binoculars and telescopes provide a rewarding view of the Clouds, and it should also be possible to discern the Tarantula Nebula (NGC 2070).

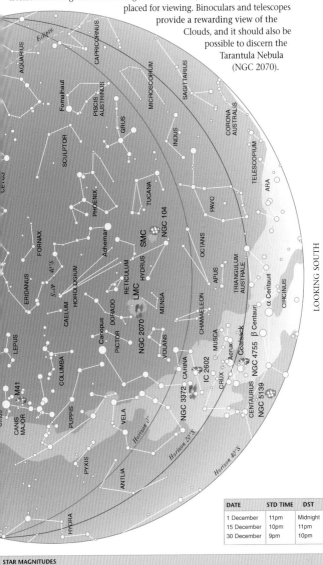

LOOKING SOUTH

DATE	STD TIME	DST
1 December	11pm	Midnight
15 December	10pm	11pm
30 December	9pm	10pm

STAR MAGNITUDES

| ● -1 | ● 0 | ● 1 | ● 2 | ∘ 3 | · 4 | · 5 |

Glossary

Many of the terms defined here are illustrated in the general introduction (pp. 8–26). Words in *italics* are defined elsewhere in the glossary.

ABSOLUTE MAGNITUDE A measure of the actual brightness of an object, defined as the *apparent magnitude* it would have at a distance of 32.6 *light years*.

APERTURE The diameter of the main mirror or lens in a telescope or binoculars. A large aperture telescope can see more detail and detect fainter objects than a small aperture telescope.

APPARENT MAGNITUDE The brightness of a celestial object as seen from the Earth. This depends on the object's real brightness and its distance from the Earth.

ASTERISM A pattern of *stars* where the *stars* are either a part of a *constellation*, or are members of several *constellations*. An example is the Plough in Ursa Major.

ASTEROID A rocky body orbiting the Sun with a diameter less than 1,000 km.

ASTRONOMICAL UNIT (AU) A measure of distance convenient for use within the Solar System, defined as the mean distance between the Earth and the Sun (149,597,970 km).

ASTROPHOTOGRAPHY Photography of celestial objects in the night sky; also includes photography of the Sun and *eclipses*.

BINARY STAR Two *stars* in mutual *orbit* around a common centre of mass, and bound together gravitationally.

CELESTIAL EQUATOR The celestial equivalent of the Earth's equator. The celestial equator marks a line where the plane of the Earth's equator meets the *celestial sphere*.

CELESTIAL POLE The celestial equivalent of the Earth's poles. The night sky appears to rotate on an axis through the celestial poles.

CELESTIAL SPHERE The imaginary sphere that surrounds the Earth, and upon which all celestial objects appear to lie.

CEPHEID VARIABLE A type of *variable star* with a regular pattern of brightness changes linked to the *star's* actual *luminosity*. Such *stars* are used as distance indicators.

CHARGE-COUPLED DEVICE (CCD) A light-sensitive silicon chip used as an alternative to photographic film.

COMET An icy body orbiting the Sun that may develop a glowing tail as it passes through the inner Solar System.

CONJUNCTION An alignment of objects in the night sky, with one passing in front of the other, particularly when a planet lines up with the Sun as viewed from the Earth.

CONSTELLATION An area of the night sky with boundaries that are determined by the International Astronomical Union; constellations are 88 in number.

DECLINATION The celestial equivalent of latitude on the Earth. It is the angle between a celestial object and the *celestial equator*, measured in degrees. The *celestial equator* has a declination of 0 degrees, and the *celestial poles* are at 90 degrees.

DEEP-SKY OBJECT A deep-sky object is any celestial object external to the Solar System, but excluding *stars*.

DIFFUSE NEBULA A cloud of gas and dust illuminated by *stars* embedded within it.

DOUBLE STAR Two *stars* that are not physically associated with each other but appear close together through line-of-sight from the Earth.

DWARF STAR A *star* that has lost most of its mass towards the end of its evolutionary development.

ECCENTRICITY A measure of the circularity of a body's *orbit*. An eccentricity of 0 means a circular orbit, with larger values indicating more elongated ellipses up to a theoretical maximum of 1.

ECLIPSE An alignment of a planet or moon with the Sun, which casts a shadow on another body. During a lunar eclipse, the Earth's shadow is cast on the Moon. During a solar eclipse, the Moon's shadow is cast on the Earth.

ECLIPTIC The plane of the Earth's *orbit* around the Sun, or the projection of that plane onto the *celestial sphere*.

ELONGATION The angular separation between the Sun and a planet as viewed from the Earth. Also used as the time of maximum angular separation (greatest elongation) between the inner planets, Mercury or Venus, and the Sun.

GALAXY A huge mass of *stars*, gas, and dust, containing from millions to billions of *stars*. Galaxies vary in size and shape, with diameters that range from thousands to hundreds of thousand of *light years*.

GIANT STAR A *star* that has expanded dramatically as it nears the end of its life-cycle.

GLOBULAR CLUSTER A sphere of *stars*, bound together gravitationally, and containing from tens of thousands to hundreds of thousands of *stars*.

LIBRATION A monthly variation in the parts of the Moon's surface visible from the Earth, due to the slight *eccentricity* and tilt of the Moon's *orbit*.

LIGHT YEAR The distance light can travel during the course of one year, that is, 9,460,700,000,000 km (5,878,600,000,000 miles).

LIMB The outer edge of a moon's or a planet's observed disc.

LOCAL GROUP A small cluster of over 30 galaxies which includes our own *galaxy*, the *Milky Way*.

LONG-EXPOSURE PHOTOGRAPHY Photography of the night sky where the camera shutter remains open, often for hours, in order to record very faint objects.

LUMINOSITY A measure of the amount of light that is produced by a celestial object.

MAGNITUDE The brightness of a celestial object, measured on a numerical scale, where brighter objects are given small or negative magnitude numbers, and fainter objects are given larger magnitude numbers.

MARE (plural: maria) Dark, low-lying areas of the Moon, flooded with lava, derived from the Latin word for "sea".

METEOR A small rock that burns due to friction as it enters the Earth's atmosphere.

METEORITE A *meteor* that reaches the Earth's (or another planet's) surface.

MILKY WAY A faint band of light visible on clear dark nights, consisting of millions of *stars*; the common name for our *galaxy*.

MULTIPLE STAR A system of *stars* that are bound together gravitationally and are in mutual *orbits*. Multiple *stars* consist of at least three *stars* and up to about a dozen *stars*.

NEBULA A cloud of gas and dust, visible by either being illuminated by embedded *stars* or nearby *stars*, or by obscuring starlight.

OPEN CLUSTER A group of up to a few hundred *stars* bound by gravity; found in the arms of a *galaxy*.

OPPOSITION The time when an outer planet lies on the exact opposite side of the Earth from the Sun. The planet is at its closest to the Earth and therefore appears brightest at this time.

ORBIT The path followed by a planet, *asteroid* or *comet* around the Sun, or a moon around its parent planet.

PARALLAX The apparent shift in an object's position as it is viewed from two different locations. The amount of shift depends on the distance of the object, and the distance between the two locations.

PHASE Illumination of the Moon or an inner planet, as seen from the Earth. At full phase, the side of the object facing the Earth is fully illuminated; at new phase, the object is fully in shadow; crescent, half phase, and gibbous phase are in between.

PLANETARY NEBULA A shell of gas thrown off by a *star* towards the end of its evolutionary development. In a small telescope, the shell resembles a planet's disc.

PRECESSION A gradual shift in the direction of the Earth's axis of rotation. It currently points towards the *star* Polaris, but it wanders over a 25,800-year cycle.

RADIO SOURCE A celestial object that appears bright when viewed with instruments that detect radio waves.

REFLECTING TELESCOPE (reflector) A type of telescope that collects and focuses light by using a mirror.

REFRACTING TELESCOPE (refractor) A type of telescope that collects and focuses light by using a lens.

REGOLITH The loose material or "soil" on the surface of a moon or planet.

RESOLVE The ability to detect detail within celestial objects, for example, craters on the Moon, or splitting *double stars*. The greater the *aperture* of a telescope, the greater its resolving power.

RETROGRADE MOTION A reversal of the usual eastward motion of a planet relative to background *stars*; occurs as it reaches *opposition*.

RETROGRADE ROTATION The rotation of a planet or moon in the opposite direction to its *orbit*. All of the planets *orbit* the Sun in the direction of the Sun's rotation: anti-clockwise when viewed from above the Sun's north pole. Most planets also rotate (spin) anti-clockwise. Venus, Uranus and Pluto have retrograde rotation: clockwise compared with their anti-clockwise *orbits*.

RIGHT ASCENSION The celestial equivalent of longitude on the Earth. It is measured in hours (one hour is 15 degrees) from the point where the Sun crosses the *celestial equator* in March.

SOLAR WIND A continuous flow of charged particles (electrons and protons) outward from the sun.

SPECTRAL TYPE A code assigned to a *star* based on the characteristics of its *spectrum*. Hot young *stars* are types O, B and A, older cooler *stars* are types F, G, K, and M.

SPECTRUM The range of wavelengths of light emitted by a celestial object, as well as any emission and absorption lines. The spectrum identifies the chemical and physical properties of the celestial object.

STAR A large sphere of gas that emits heat and light as a result of thermonuclear reactions within its core.

SUPERGIANT STAR A *star* at least ten times more massive than the Sun. Supergiants are at the end of their evolutionary development, and can be hundreds of times larger than the Sun, and thousands of times brighter.

SUPERNOVA An exceptionally violent explosion of a *star* during which it sheds its outer atmosphere; it outshines its host *galaxy*

SUPERNOVA REMNANT The outer layers of a *star* that have been ejected during a *supernova* explosion, travelling at high speed through space.

TERMINATOR The edge of the sunlit area of a moon or planet's surface, where the surface falls into shadow.

TRANSIT A planet's motion in front of the Sun, or a moon in front of its parent planet, as viewed from the Earth.

VARIABLE STAR A *star* that appears to change its brightness. This can be caused by physical changes within the *star*, or by the *star* being eclipsed by a companion.

WOLF-RAYET STAR A hot, massive *star* that produces a strong stellar wind.

ZODIAC The area of the sky, 9 degrees either side of the *ecliptic plane*, through which the Sun, the Moon and the planets move.

GREEK LETTERS

As a naming convention, some stars are assigned Greek letters according to their brightness (used in this book).

α	alpha	ν	nu
β	beta	ξ	xi
γ	gamma	ο	omicron
δ	delta	π	pi
ε	epsilon	ρ	rho
ζ	zeta	σ	sigma
η	eta	τ	tau
θ	theta	υ	upsilon
ι	iota	φ	phi
κ	kappa	χ	chi
λ	lambda	ψ	psi
μ	mu	ω	omega

Index

Acknowledgments

Dorling Kindersley would like to thank Planetary Visions for their work as picture researchers and administrators and Cathy Meeus and Kenny Grant for additional editorial and design assistance.

PICTURE CREDITS
Picture librarians: Richard Dabb, Lucy Claxton

Abbreviations key: a = above, b = bottom, c = centre, f = far, l = left, r = right, t = top.

The publishers would like to thank the following for their kind permission to reproduce the photographs.

Alex and Mike Beck 58tl; Anne Beiter 90tl; Adam Block 53tr; 58tl; 59cra, bl; 61tr; 63cla, br; 67tr; 73tr, br; 74tl; 78tl; 81tr; 83tl; 85br; 86bl; 88cfl, bl; 90cra, tl; 93br; 99br; 101tr; 102cfl; 103cfr; 105bct; 112bl; 113tl; 115cfr; 118tl, bl; 120cfl; 124cra; 126cfl; 127clb; 128tl; 145cla; Bruce Bohannan 64cfr; Todd Boroson 107cra; Cornell University 42bc; 43bc; Duke Creighton 127clb; Jeff Cremer 113tl; Richard Crisp 61rb; 66tl; 72tl; Russell Croman 22br; 68bl; 69crb, tr; 85tr; 88tl; 98tl; 100cfl; 127tr; 135cla, crb; 146cfl; Brad Ehrhorn 59bl; 105bcl; Peter and Suzie Erickson 64cla; European Southern Observatory 4; 5; 34cl, cr; 117cfr; 121tr; 129br; 134clb, crb; 144cfl; 147tr; 148tl; 149clb, crb; 152tl; 155tr; European Space Agency 20tr; 43car; 50bc; 51bc; 50c; 55br; Elliot Gellman 127clb; German Aerospace Centre (DLR) 48tl, cla, cfl, clb; Louis and Jennifer Goldring 102cfl; Piermario Gualdoni 11crb; 61clb; 76tl; 116tl; 119tr; 120tl; 122tl; 123cfr; 146tl; Mark Hanna 64cfr; Vanessa Harvey 98cfr; 136bl; Gunnar Hurtig 99br; Infrared Processing and Analysis Centre 77bl; 135tr; 140tl; George Jacoby 64cfr; Gene Katz 93br; Al Kelly 59br; Bill and Sean Kelly 126cfl; Kitt Peak Naval Observatory/NOAO/AURA/NSF 10ca, clb, cra; 11br; 26tr; 58tl; 59bl; 61tr; 62tl; 63br, cla, cra; 64bl, br. cfr; 67tr; 68tl; 73br, cfr, tl; 74bl, tl; 76bl; 77br; 78bl, tl; 79cfr; 80bl; 81tr; 82bl, tl; 83tl; 84cr, tl; 85br; 86bl, cfl, tl; 87tr; 88bl, cfl; 90bl, cra, tl; 92bl, tl; 93br, tr; 94cfr; 96tl; 97br, cfr; 98bl, cfr; 99br; 100tl; 101tr; 102cfl, tl; 103cfr; 107cra; 109br; 112bl, tl; 113tl; 114bl; 115cfr; 118bl, tl; 120cfl; 122bl; 123tr; 124bl, cra, tl; 126cfl; 127clb; 128tl; 130tl; 133tr; 136bl, tl; 137cfr; 139tr; 142bl, cra; 144tl; 145cla, tr; 146bl; 150tl; Peter Kukol 86bl; Wendee Levy 61tr; Steve Mandel 88cfl; Hillary Mathis 10cla; 63cra; 73cfr; 94cfr; 98cfr; 114bl; Doug Matthews 85br; Ross and Julia Meyers 118bl; George and Laura Mishler 112bl; NASA/ESA/AURA/Space Telescope Science Institute 2; 3; 11bc; 71crb; 74cl; 81cfr; 94tl; 99bl; 104tl; 127br; 132tl; 134tl; 149tr; 152clb; 157tr; 159tl; 160bl; NASA Jet Propulsion Laboratory 19tr; 20cl; 36-37; 38cfl; 39tl; 40bl; 42bc; 43bc; 46c, bc; 47cr, cbl; 48bc; 50bc; 51bc; 51cra, crb; 53crb;

54bl; NASA Johnson Spaceflight Center 21br; 22c; 30tl; 30-31b; 32cl; 35tr; NASA 21crb; 39ca; 43cra, cbl; 50c; 55br; National Optical Astronomy Observatory 53tr, 54tl; National Science Foundation 53tr, 54tl; National Space Science Data Center 38br; Jeff and Paul Neumann 54tl; Jeff Newton 120cfl; Dale Niksch 101tr; Northwestern University 38cfl, 39tl; Herm Perez 11cfl; 108tl; Planetary Visions 8 bl; 9 br; 18c; 19c; 20bl; 30cla, c, clb, 30bc; 31bc, tl; 32bc; 33bc; 34bc; 35bc; 38cla, c, bl; 40cla, cra, c; 41tl; 42cla; 43tl, cl; 46cla; 47tl; 50cla; 51tl; 53cra, cla, c; 54cla, c, cra; 55cra, cla, c, cfl; 60bl; 70tl, tl; 91br; 95cfr; 102bl; 106tl; 109cfr; 110tl; 120bl; 131tr; 138tl; 143cfr; 154clb; 158tl; 159crb; 162clb; 163crb, tr; Tim Puckett 20tr; Rich and Anne Quigley 73tl; T.A. Rector 142bl; Bob Rickert 88bl; Jim Riffle 132bl; 141tr; 154tl; Manny Sawit 53tr; Johannes Schedler 8cra; 11cfr; 79br; 87cfr; 89br; 113tr; 114tl; 116bl; 117br; 161br; Bill Schoening 11br; 109br; Chris and Dawn Schur 10br; tr; 46tl; 50tl; 64tl; 91tr; 96br; 111tr; Heidi Schweiker 77br; Stefan Seip 15cfr; 25tl; 38tl; 40tl; 75tr; 80tl; 83tr; 125br; 129cla, tr; 130bl; 137br; 142tl; 164; Jon Shallop 90tl; Nigel Sharp 63cra; 64bl; 76bl; 82bl, tl; 92tl, bl; 96tl; 97br; 102tl; 105cfr; 123tr; 136tl; 137cfr; Ken and Emilie Siarkiewicz 63br; 67tr; Space Science Institute 36; 37; 46bc; 51crb; Space Telescope Science Institute 21cbr; 42c, 42bl; 43cr, cbl; 47tr; 48cb; 53cfl; 55tr; Johannes Tan 73br; Thalia and Norman Terrell 145cla; University of Arizona 46c; 50bc; 51bc; University of Maryland 20cl; US Geological Survey 28; 29; 34tl; 54cfr; Daniel Verschatse 10cla; 133br; 140cfl; 148cfl; 156bl; 158clb; 160tl; Don Waid 66bl; Wei-Hao Wang 10crb; 56; 131br; 156tl; 161tr; Volker Wendel 11cal; 143tr; 151br; 155crb; 157br; 162tl; Doug Williams 96tl; 102tl; 105cfr; Hirokazu Yamamura 20br; Glen Youman 95br; 99tr; 126tl.

All other images © Dorling Kindersley.